MW01140698

Mexico's Economic Dilemma

Critical Currents in Latin American Perspective
Ronald H. Chilcote, Series Editor

Mexico's Economic Dilemma

The Developmental Failure of Neoliberalism

A Contemporary Case Study of the Globalization Process

JAMES M. CYPHER
AND
RAÚL DELGADO WISE

ROWMAN & LITTLEFIELD PUBLISHERS, INC.
Lanham • Boulder • New York • Toronto • Plymouth, UK

Published by Rowman & Littlefield Publishers, Inc.
A wholly owned subsidiary of The Rowman & Littlefield Publishing Group, Inc.
4501 Forbes Boulevard, Suite 200, Lanham, Maryland 20706
http://www.rowmanlittlefield.com

Estover Road, Plymouth PL6 7PY, United Kingdom

Copyright © 2010 by Rowman & Littlefield Publishers, Inc.

All rights reserved. No part of this book may be reproduced in any form or by any
electronic or mechanical means, including information storage and retrieval systems,
without written permission from the publisher, except by a reviewer who may quote
passages in a review.

British Library Cataloguing in Publication Information Available

Library of Congress Cataloging-in-Publication Data
Cypher, James M.
   Mexico's economic dilemma : the developmental failure of neoliberalism / James M.
Cypher and Raúl Delgado Wise.
      p. cm. — (Critical currents in Latin American perspective)
      Includes bibliographical references and index.
      ISBN 978-0-7425-5660-7 (cloth : alk. paper) — ISBN 978-0-7425-6848-8
(electronic)
      1. Mexico—Economic policy—21st century. 2. Mexico—Economic conditions—
21st century. 3. Mexico—Foreign economic relations—United States. 4. United States—
Foreign economic relations—Mexico. 5. Neoliberalism—Mexico. I. Delgado Wise,
Raúl, 1950– II. Title.
      HC135.C967 2010
      330.972—dc22
                                                                    2009051131

∞ ™ The paper used in this publication meets the minimum requirements of American
National Standard for Information Sciences—Permanence of Paper for Printed Library
Materials, ANSI/NISO Z39.48-1992.

Printed in the United States of America

Contents

Preface

This is a book about Mexico, the United States, and the recent economic policies and processes that have tied these two nations together in a relationship of asymmetric integration. Our main focus is on how and why Mexico has failed to achieve economic development in recent decades. We find that Mexico is "locked in" to a situation of adverse path dependence. The term "path dependence" has found common usage among orthodox economists in the past two decades: it is intended to describe the ways in which past activities, including the creation of institutions, serve to circumscribe and constrain the future course a nation may take in pursuing matters of economic policy. Much of the work of orthodox economics has been to understand the forces behind "virtuous circles" that scoot a nation's economy forward at a rapid pace.

The flip side of this analysis—pertaining to "vicious circles" and downward interactive spirals—has received much less attention. Although orthodox economists present path dependence as a relatively recent formulation, the point of departure for the construct could be traced back to the evolutionary economics of Thorstein Veblen, who frequently analyzed the rigidities of economic structures in terms of "cumulative causation." In either of its guises—the heterodox economics of Veblen or the better-known orthodox formulation—history matters, but it is not all that matters.

Moments of crisis are frequently the occasion for a national socioeconomic system to be put on a new path. This occurred in Mexico in the early 1980s when—for reasons detailed in this book—Mexico adopted a dramatically different set of institutions, while altering many preexisting institutional arrangements, including at the levels of ideology and policy. The outcome, as is well known, is that Mexico attempted to advance along a path guided by the neoliberal nostrums of the Chicago School of economics as propounded by Milton Friedman and his close associates. Mexico today remains enthralled with—and impaled upon—these ultra laissez-faire precepts. This could be seen on a daily basis as the ex-secretary of the treasury—a University of Chicago–trained economist—took the lead on policy matters through 2009.

But, at this moment, Mexico is struggling with its worst economic crisis since the 1920s. Whether the forces unleashed by this crisis will be sufficient to push Mexico off its current adverse path remains to be seen.

In this book we have sought to portray both the workings and the weaknesses of the neoliberal model adopted by Mexico in the 1980s. We also argue that if a new path can be taken, it should be one that recaptures some of the economic strengths Mexico exhibited in its most successful period—1940 to 1982. We would like, therefore, to take this opportunity to clarify any misperceptions that might otherwise arise regarding this perspective: we are not, in any way, suggesting that Mexico's dilemma can be solved by a simple return to the past or a retreat from the more recent processes of internationalization that frame the analysis of this book. Rather, if attainment of a new path is possible, it will be one that entails a repositioning of Mexico's economy and a reprioritization of the domestic economy in the context of the pursuit of a viable national project of accumulation. Reprioritization, however, does not mean that Mexico should ignore the range of advantages that may occur through a constructive engagement with international economic forces. Such a pattern of engagement, rather than the neoliberal posture of passivity in the face of these forces, has been demonstrated in the case of developing Asian nations to be one of the ways to attain and maintain virtuous circles engendering strong economic advancement under conditions of reasonably "shared" growth.

It is impossible to anticipate the many ways our analysis of Mexico might be misconstrued—in spite of every effort on our part to present complex aspects of the Mexican model in a clear manner. In this vein, our occasional references to the relative success of several Asian nations are not to be interpreted as a suggestion that Mexico could adopt an off-the-shelf model. Rather, there are many things Mexico could adapt from the Asian model, including its careful nurturing of the production base of the economy, its attention to the necessary fostering of technological learning and technological capabilities, and its emphasis on state *capacity* and *embeddedness*.

We have done everything in our power to uncover sources, materials, authors, and statistical materials that have a bearing on the themes raised in this book. Readers who do not work and live in Mexico may not be aware that the pursuit of the requisite information needed to support, assemble, and write this book has been an exceedingly demanding task. Mexico does not have the supporting infrastructure of libraries, journals, and reliable public information sources regularly found in the advanced industrial nations.

What this means, on a concrete level, varies in time and place. Let us give but one example: two fundamental chapters of this book deal with the maquiladora industry and what we term the disguised maquiladora firms that receive imported inputs in order to process, assemble, and export with the use of cheap Mexican labor. Until late 2006 the Mexican government and other sources carefully tracked many aspects of the maquila industry, while the disguised maquila operations received almost no attention. Then, to our surprise, the government announced that, officially, the maquiladoras were going to end. From the beginning of 2007, the maquiladoras would be folded into a new conceptual and statistical category—the IMMEX firms, as explained in the text—which would consist of the former maquila firms and the disguised maquilas. We took this new institutional structure as firm confirmation of one of the hypotheses we had formed in late 2005, and we looked forward with anticipation to a new set of statistical data and a new literature that would allow for greater understanding of the manufacturing export-led model dominating the Mexican economy. We are still waiting.

In spite of assurances that the IMMEX firms dominating the export sector would receive new quantitative attention and formation, the government, in effect, ended all statistical information on the maquilas and left analysts with what is now a two-year gap in the data. Hence, in the text, some data series have not been updated beyond 2006. The "little delay" with the reconstruction of the data in order to present information on the IMMEX firms is not an isolated occurrence. Hence, we are all but certain that, in a more perfect world, our research would have uncovered important results that would have improved or changed the presentation of this book.

This book is the result of more than four years of reflection and analysis. We began serious research on the subjects we analyze in this book in the fall of 2005. The idea was to present an interdisciplinary analysis bringing together economics, political economy, and migration studies. Since then we have cocreated the hypotheses, the concepts, and the analytical structures that constitute this book.

Chapter 1 presents a broad introduction to Mexico's socioeconomic structure. In this chapter we present the three underlying hypotheses we pursue. In addition we argue that the current, always fragile, export-led "model" has now been shown to be—through the impact of the crisis of 2008–2009—bankrupt.

Chapters 2 and 3 provide necessary historical background and context. In chapter 2 we focus on the rise of neoliberalism and the pivotal struggle for hegemonic dominance over national economic policy. We also provide a reassessment and reinterpretation of the much-maligned policy of import-substitution industrialization. In chapter 3 we trace how this new structure conditioned, and was conditioned by, the negotiation of the NAFTA. Here we also focus on the "selling of NAFTA" through hopelessly unrealistic trade models constructed by neoclassical economists who played a major role in the bogus scenarios of a new "win-win" relationship that would accelerate Mexico's economic development.

Chapters 4 and 5 offer detailed analyses of the maquila and disguised maquila processing and manufacturing operations that have been the spinal column of the new neoliberal model that crystallized in the late 1980s. In these chapters we examine a variety of fundamental themes, such as the hypothesis that the maquila industry is a generator of technological upgrading as it ascends through advancing "generations" of production. We also devote considerable attention to the auto and auto parts industry, which is the main focus of chapter 5. Here, and elsewhere, we explain the vitiating processes of disarticulation that have shredded the national production base of the Mexican economy.

Chapter 6 focuses specifically on what we term the *direct* export of labor—the massive migration of Mexicans to the United States. We see this migration as an effect of the neoliberal model, which is exclusionary in nature, spreading income opportunities to a small minority while leaving millions of Mexicans with no other option but to abandon their nation. On the United States side of the border, distinct processes are at work. Immigrant labor has been incorporated into the United States' transnational project to restructure U.S. production, now with the important participation of cheap Mexican immigrants.

Chapter 7 offers a brief final overview of the processes of the internationalization of capital and a critique of prevailing ideas regarding the manner in which "globalization" is understood to function. We also sketch two key initiatives necessary to overcome the current institutional "lock-in" effect and move beyond the policies than have maintained Mexico on a trajectory of adverse path dependence.

Zacatecas, Mexico
November 2009

Acknowledgments

Authors have their names placed on the covers of their books, and those who in great measure make such an event possible are often lost from view. But all work is collective.

Over the course of the past four years, numerous individuals have provided assistance during the various stages of preparation for this book. Many will not be mentioned because our fieldwork was often conditioned on the anonymity of firms, individuals, and agencies that were interviewed. Some will not be mentioned due to our own oversight—for this we apologize in advance. None, other than the authors, bear any responsibility whatever for the contents of this book.

We would first like to express our gratitude for the assistance we have received from our faculty colleagues in the doctoral program in development studies at the Universidad Autónoma de Zacatecas: Guillermo Foladori, Rodolfo García Zamora, Humberto Márquez Covarrubias, Miguel Moctezuma, Gerardo Otero, Oscar Pérez Venya, and Henry Veltmeyer. Oscar Pérez Venya was particularly helpful in terms of numerous suggestions as to how and where our fieldwork could be undertaken, in opening a path to several important institutions in Aguascalientes, and in locating crucial literature. We have been fortunate to work with the program's proficient secretarial staff: Concepción Olivia Martínez, Montserrat García, and Aranceli Herrera Flores. We have also obtained much assistance from Max Luna Estrada and Elizabeth Rodríguez, the information technology specialists in the program. In addition to solving many computer-related problems, Elizabeth was responsible for the construction of several of the figures and tables. Finally, Carina Alcenar provided assistance on chapter 6, including assembling the bibliography for that chapter. Leticia Damm, based in Monterrey, translated chapter 6.

James Martín Cypher conducted numerous interviews for this book beginning in 2007 and stretching over the course of 2008. The following individuals graciously interrupted their very busy and productive lives to offer their interpretation on many issues as well as provide us with research materials on many occasions: Celso Garrido, Enrique Dussel Peters, Clemente Ruiz Durán, Arturo Guillén, Marcela Hernández Romo, Arturo Lara Rivero, Daniel Lund, María de los Ángeles Pozas, Sergio Sosa Barajas, Gregorio Vidal, and the professional staff at CNIMME (Consejo Nacional de la Industria Maquiladora y Manufactura de Exportación).

We would also like to acknowledge the assistance of Alejandro Alvarez, Antonio Avalos, Paul Bowles, Juan Castaingts, Eugenia Correa, Alejandro Dávila Flores, Noela Invernizzi, Mauricio Maria y Campos, and Juan Carlos Moreno-Brid.

Special thanks are due to Kathryn Kopinak, Robert Prasch, and Jon Shefner, each of whom read a chapter of the manuscript and offered detailed and helpful comments. We incorporated most of their very perceptive suggestions.

We thank Kevin Gallagher, who extended an invitation to James Martín Cypher to present a research paper on foreign direct investment in Mexico, at the Latin American Studies Association meeting in Brazil in June 2008. The paper presented some of the research results to be found in chapter 5 of this book. Spirited commentary from the floor, particularly from Dr. Rhys Jenkins, was also important in the reformulation of several issues analyzed in chapters 4 and 5.

Much of the background research for chapter 5—including all of the field research—was supported by a grant received by James Martín Cypher from SEPLADAR—the Secretaria de Planeación y Desarrollo Regional del Gobierno del Estado de Zacatecas. SEPLADAR provided generous funding to support comprehensive field research in the north central region of Mexico. This research included the completion of a broad quantitative survey questionnaire and an extensive qualitative interview conducted with fifteen auto parts suppliers producing for the auto production/assembly plants in Mexico (and for direct export). These companies, as it turned out, were all transnational corporations. We were anxious to collect information on national suppliers—Mexican-owned firms—but none turned up in our sample. Some were medium-sized entities with few foreign operations. Others were owned by some of the largest corporations in the world—operating plants in several nations and/or several sites in Mexico. They were Canadian, Japanese, and United States–owned operations—overwhelmingly firms from the United States. Several were captive suppliers to the giant transnational auto producers/assemblers. We would like to directly thank these companies for their cooperation and insight. Unfortunately, this is not possible since our initial terms of agreement were to maintain the anonymity of these plants. We also interviewed the owners/managers of one industrial park. In all but a few of these extensive on-site plant visits Dr. Aldo Alejandro Pérez Escatel actively participated in the qualitative interviews—which involved a set of preestablished, open-ended questions. Dr. Pérez often interjected his own observations and questions—which frequently led to some very helpful exchanges revealing information that the research project would not have otherwise discovered.

We normally spent three hours in completing the quantitative questionnaire and the qualitative interview. More often than not, part of this time was spent within the factory, where we frequently were able to question the operatives and to observe production processes. Usually these tours included an impromptu lecture by the plant manager and/or a production-oriented member of management. One of the most interesting results of this project was that with the rarest of exceptions, the plant managers (without any prompting on our part) generally shared many of the very critical views we present regarding the weakness of national and regional economic policy and the need for a structural change in this policy. This was the last, and least probable, outcome we anticipated from the field research. This was all the more interesting because in no way, either in the questionnaire or in the preset qualitative questions, did we broach the question of economic policy or their opinions regarding the merits, if any, of an industrial policy. Nor, once this area had been opened up by the subjects under interview, did we express any of our views on the issue of the coherence on national and regional industrial policy—or on any other issue.

In general the critical responses we received from those who worked at the point of production in the auto parts plants were reproduced—at a more general and sophisticated level—by the state-level secretariats of economic development. Once again, this was a result we had not anticipated. In none of our interview questions did we attempt to steer the discussion in this direction or to maintain the topic once it had been broached. We conducted extensive interviews with the secretariats of the states of Aguascalientes, Coahuila, San Luis Potosí, and Zacatecas. In the latter case we conducted several interviews or meetings with the professional staff. We thank Jaime Javier Loredo for arranging the important interviews in San Luis Potosí and for his participation in those meetings.

Sedezac (the secretariat in the state of Zacatecas) was instrumental in opening doors and otherwise helping us gain access to the usually closed world of the manufacturing firms in Mexico. We would like to express special thanks to Sedezac and to its director, Nicolás Castañeda.

We owe a tremendous debt to the very able members of the professional staff and the chief economists at the secretariats in Aguascalientes, Coahuila, and San Luis Potosí. Their understanding of the developmental needs of Mexico and their professional competence lend credence to the idea that Mexico might engineer a turn away from the pervasive neoliberal stance that has systematically undermined the national supplier base. Certainly these meetings with the professional staff of the secretariats were the most important we conducted in terms of creating a much deeper understanding of the dilemmas of the national supplier firms. We were struck by the impressive strategies to gain more value through raising national content that these secretariats have frequently employed in their interaction with some of the most powerful corporations in the world. Their approach, unlike that of the policy makers at the national level, was far from passive. We did not anticipate how closely the thinking of the secretariats followed many of the general lines of analysis we have pursued in this book. The grant we received from SEPLADAR, facilitated by the Oficina de Coordinación de Investigación of the Universidad Autónoma de Zacatecas, not only generously funded the field research and our participation in the LASA meeting in Brazil, it further funded two trips to Mexico City, where the individual interviews mentioned above were conducted. Finally, in regard to SEPLADAR we also want to acknowledge receipt of funding for the translation of chapter 6.

Only good fortune could explain an invitation extended to James Martín Cypher to attend a lecture by, and a dinner for, the chief plant manager of the giant Nissan plant in Aguascalientes. This then facilitated passage to the plant itself, where an extensive interview, followed by other correspondence, allowed us to pose a series of questions to those who run the most productive Nissan plant in the world, including the corporation's Japanese plants. We thank the top managers for their openness and cooperative spirit.

We should add that openness and a spirit of cooperation were not elements we necessarily encountered in attempting to gain perspective from many of those who are active on a day-to-day basis in the manufacturing sector and at the policy-making level. Many of the transnational corporations went to great lengths in concocting pretexts to prevent us from scheduling interviews. Nor were we successful in our attempt to conduct an interview with either of the internationally competitive auto parts companies controlled by the Mexican conglomerates, or *grupos*.

Our research was greatly facilitated by our extensive use of library resources generously made available by the Latin American Studies Program at Simon Fraser University.

We especially wish to thank Jessica Gribble at Rowman & Littlefield, who (along with Ronald Chilcote) convinced us that Rowman & Littlefield would be the ideal publisher for our manuscript. In making the decision to offer us a contract, Ms. Gribble sent an initial set of sample chapters to two anonymous reviewers. We would like to thank them for their very substantive comments. When coordination of the project was turned over to a new editor, Susan McEachern, Editorial Director of International Relations, Geography and Area Studies, we again encountered highly professional, always punctual support and guidance. We also appreciate the help received from Carrie Broadwell-Tkach.

Last, we would like to acknowledge the essential support received from our families, who, with good grace, have enabled us to maintain our long focus on this project.

Chapter One

Mexico's Socioeconomic Structure and the Current Crisis

Mexico's economic dilemma consists of the fact that, on the one hand, the existing economic strategy is carrying the nation to higher and higher levels of disarticulation, stagnation, and migration. On the other hand, agents of change and ideas of change have been precluded from Mexico's policy discourse. The current situation has been described as follows by two prominent analysts: "Mexico has lost its way"; "It appears as a nation with weak institutions, uncertain of its international identity: a sleeping giant that from time to time becomes agitated without being able to move"; "A country, one could say, with too much of a past, and too little future" (Castañeda and Aguilar Camín 2009, 34–35). In short, Mexico's dilemma consists of a status quo that is intolerable. The nation exists under conditions determined by an institutional "lock-in" effect that serves to guarantee that fundamental structural change has increasingly been deemed unthinkable by the powers that be—and often by the underlying population.

Mexico's economic structure has, as its pivot point, the export of manufactured products—with auto and auto parts exports occupying pride of place. In the first half of 2009 Mexico's exports and imports fell by 30 percent. Even more remarkable, auto and auto parts exports fell by 40 percent. Not surprisingly, then, the gross domestic product (GDP) fell at an annual rate of more than 10 percent in the second quarter of 2009—with an expected total annual reduction of 6.6 percent according to the United Nations' Latin American Commission. Mexico's GDP at the close of 2009 was equal to that of 2005, but there were nearly five million more citizens. Net foreign direct investment (incoming direct investment minus outgoing direct investment)—a strategic economic indicator in the government's view—was only $3.8 billion US, a decline of 83 percent from 2008. To find statistics that would come close to

1

matching the economic disaster Mexico confronted in 2009 it would be necessary to go back to the Great Depression years of the early 1930s.

A very old and very tired cliché comes to mind in the current context: "Whenever Uncle Sam sneezes, Mexico gets pneumonia." Tired as it is, and as tired as we are of hearing it, it has never been truer in Mexico's long history than it is today. Mexico hitched its star to the United States in the course of the 1980s. The knot was tied in what was thought to be an irreversible fashion by the North American Free Trade Agreement (NAFTA), which came into effect at the beginning of 1994. Since the 1980s, when the Mexican government, led by the highly organized peak business associations run by the conglomerate-owning economic elite, bet its all on an export-led model, Mexico's economic success has been overwhelmingly dependent upon the growth in the consumer market in the United States—which has absorbed 85 to 90 percent of Mexico's exports in recent years.

Concentrated Economic and Political Power: Mexico's Conglomerates

The concept of the Mexican conglomerates is an all-important distinction necessary to facilitate an understanding of the structure of Mexico's society. One way to grasp the tremendous degree of concentration of wealth and income among the top strata of Mexican society is to analyze the Mexican stock market. According to the World Bank, this market facilitated the trading of shares of 170 large companies—with the ten largest nonfinancial, family-controlled companies accounting for 61 percent of the entire stock market capitalization (World Bank 2003, 1). These companies, and the next ten largest companies in Mexico, are all 100 percent family controlled according to a 2006 World Bank study (Guerrero, López-Calva, and Walton 2006, 9). In the ten largest companies, the top three shareholders owned a total of 64 percent of the capital of these companies (World Bank 2003, 1–2). The World Bank added the following summary: "In many firms, one class of shares gives full voting rights to the family controllers, while others have limited or no voting rights. Financial and industrial groups have been key in Mexican economic development. Business groups are characterized by vertical, horizontal, or conglomerate integration. Holding companies make most key decisions, including financing, dividend policy, fixed assets, and hiring of top managers" (World Bank 2003, 2).

Generally these vast conglomerates are known as the *national power groups* or simply *"los grupos."* This term would encompass more than the top twenty firms—perhaps as many as thirty or more, each of which would, in turn, own and/or control numerous other major firms. A "typical" *grupo* thus might own or control as many as ten or fifteen relatively large firms. The well-known ALFA group, based in Monterrey, offers a good example of the structure of the many large *grupos*. ALFA's sales in 2009, when the international market had been rapidly shrinking, were 52 percent international and 48 percent domestic. ALFA owns four large firms: (1) Alpeck, one of the largest polyester producers in the NAFTA countries, with eighteen plants located in three nations; (2) Nemak, one of a tiny number of Mexican-owned auto parts firms, consisting of twenty-nine production plants in thirteen nations (Ford owns 7 percent of this company); (3) Sigma, devoted to the production of frozen foods, operating thirty plants and 141 distribution centers in nine nations, annually processing eight hundred thousand tons of frozen foods; and (4) Alestra, a company that provides fiber-optics communications to 198 cities in Mexico (AT&T owns 49 percent of Alestra) (Hernández Morón 2009, 5A). In 2008 ALFA was the tenth-largest private firm operating in Mexico. Measured by sales, eight of the top twenty private-sector firms were Mexican *grupos* in 2008, the remainder being transnational firms and Mexican-owned nonconglomerate firms such as CEMEX.

More generally, "large firms" in Mexico—some 3,051 firms—constitute only 0.3 percent of all companies, but they own 74 percent of all business assets, pay 69 percent of all salaries and wages, employ 52.3 percent of the (formal) workforce, and produce 74 percent of all value added (Maria y Campos et. al. 2009, 88–89). Of these large firms, 403 account for 75 percent of all of Mexico's exports (González G. 2009, 24).

Mexico's top four hundred firms, with sales income equivalent to 41 percent of the annual gross domestic product, pay on average only a 1.7 percent tax "burden" on their income according to a study conducted by an agency of the Mexican treasury (Posada and Zuñiga 2009, 32). Meanwhile, common citizens pay a 16 percent value-added tax on all consumer purchases, excluding food and medicine.

Concentrated economic power has since the mid-1970s increasingly been transferred into the arena of public policy primarily through the agency of the large and well-organized peak business associations (Ross Schneider 2002).

As a result, Mexico's fate has been to spiral downward since December 2007, when the United States entered its worst economic downturn since the 1930s. As the sliding pace of the economic contraction turned into an avalanche in late 2008 and early 2009, Mexico's top economic advisor, Agustín Carstens, then the secretary of the treasury, announced that Mexico's economic duress amounted to no more than the equivalent of "a little sniffle."

While he seems to have adjusted his perspective—in August 2009 he announced that Mexico was suffering an unprecedented "financial shock"—denial has been the coin of the realm in the higher circles of the political elite throughout the current economic crisis. President Calderón (2006–2012) immediately sought to redirect public attention from Carstens's comment by asserting that the United States had "touched bottom." The implication, apparently, was that in a brief moment, the heady consumer-fueled growth of the U.S. economy that vacuumed up the production of Mexico's export-oriented manufacturing plants (overwhelmingly foreign-owned and dominated by U.S. firms) would resume.

Alan Riding once wrote a fascinating book about Mexico and the United States, brilliantly summing up the underlying relationship in the title, *Distant Neighbors* (Riding 1984). A central hypothesis of the book is stated in the foreword: "Probably, nowhere in the world do two neighbors understand each other so little" (Riding 1984, xi). One might think that Mexican policy makers would have struggled hard to overcome their conception deficit of the United States given that they have geared the entire success (and failure) of their economy—ideally designed to nurture more than 110 million citizens—to the expansion of the U.S. market, which has absorbed more than 80 percent of all manufacturing exports in most recent years. But this has not been the case. Thus, when President Calderón confidently stated (more than once) that the U.S. economy had "touched bottom," what he attempted to communicate—what the Mexican populace understood him to have communicated—was that Mexico would soon find its way back to the "good old days" when U.S. consumers loaded up on debt, pulled the equity out of their homes, and financed a boom in imported consumer durables that was as impressive as it was seemingly endless.

According to U.S. Federal Reserve data, consumer debt exploded from 1990 to 2000—rising by 94.4 percent, from $3.6 *trillion* to $7.0 trillion. This seemingly miraculous feat was then almost exactly repeated from 2000 to 2007, when total U.S. household debt leaped from $7.0 trillion to $13.8 trillion. Total household debt (mortgages, car loans, credit card debt, etc.) exploded from 62 percent of GDP in 1990 to 100 percent in 2007. All this was occurring even as average U.S. production workers' wages (covering 80 percent of the workforce) were falling! The stock market boom of the 1990s and the real estate boom of the subsequent decade (until late 2006), along with a policy of flooding the U.S. credit system with historically unparalleled amounts of liquidity, fueled an unprecedented spending orgy. While all this was taking place, more and more U.S.-based manufacturing plants shifted their operations (all or in part) inordinately to Mexico or other nations.

This process has continued. In mid-August 2009 President Calderón traveled to the north central city of San Luis Potosí to inaugurate a new General Motors auto plant—at the very moment that GM had become a bankrupt firm in the United States, sustained by unprecedented federal government assistance. The GM plant in Mexico, of course, had been planned and financed several years prior to GM's fall. Still, the shift to Mexico has continued: the Whirlpool Corporation announced in late August 2009 that it would move a refrigerator plant located in Evansville, Indiana, to an industrial park in Mexico, shifting 1,100 jobs in the process. Whirlpool, a company with annual sales in excess of $16 billion, stated that its most recent shift of production operations to Mexico (which would likely later involve transferring another three hundred jobs at a "product development center") resulted from its ongoing corporate strategy: "To reduce excess capacity and improve costs the decision was made to consolidate production within our existing *North American manufacturing facilities*. This will allow us to streamline our operations, improve our capacity utilization, reduce product overlap between plants, and meet future production requirements" (Jelter 2009, italics added).

This book is a study of what amounts to a new constellation of economic forces and a new economic geography succinctly summed up by the Whirlpool Corporation as "North American manufacturing facilities." U.S. workers have been caught in a whirlpool of economic forces tugging them down as Mexico has become a favorite location in the "race to the bottom" strategy unleashed by what is conventionally known as "globalization"—or the further internationalization of capital. At the same time, our research (detailed in chapter 6) shows that from 1994 through 2008, one of every six jobs created in the United States was filled by Mexican-origin workers. That is, 3.8 million employment positions were held by Mexicans in this period.

While capital will continue to move to Mexico (and elsewhere), seeking low (or cheap) wages and high productivity, it is currently doing so at a rate that is 40 percent lower than it was two years ago (in 2007).[1] Foreign direct investment will not revert to previously achieved levels, as Mexican policy makers imply. This, however, is only part of the misperception voiced and implied by President Calderón and his economic advisors; the underlying problem is that the U.S. economy will not "return to normal" as defined by the period from 1990 to 2007. There is no going back to an economy that achieved negative savings and a record-breaking ratio of consumption to GDP of 72 percent (as was achieved by 2007 in the United States). Mexico rode an unparalleled consumer boom pushing up the consumption-to-GDP ratio from 68 percent in the year prior to NAFTA's coming into effect (1993). This 5 percent rise in U.S. consumption as a share of GDP might seem insignificant until we recognize that in 2007 it amounted to 69 percent of Mexico's entire nominal GDP. As U.S. consumption rose both in numerical and relative amounts, Mexico (or, more accurately, U.S. and other foreign-owned firms operating in Mexico) was positioned to ride on the crest of this wave of expansion.

However, as James Galbraith has recently and perceptively written, there is "No Return to Normal" possible in the future of the U.S. economy (Galbraith 2009). U.S. consumers, as a group, are now forced to cut their discretionary consumption to the bone. The varieties of purchases of consumer durables, particularly auto and electronics related, can be deferred for months or years and drastically reduced overall. Here we find Mexico's current dilemma: (1) falling incoming foreign direct investment (now reduced to defensive strategies designed to cut production costs in a *shrinking* market—rather than the exploding market of the 1990–2007 period), and (2) stagnant or falling sales of consumer goods geared to be exported to the U.S. market. To return to Alan Riding, Mexican policy makers have not mastered the dynamics of the U.S. market because they, like their U.S. counterparts when considering Mexico, have but the flimsiest of ideas as to how the political economy of the U.S. is constructed (and reconstructed). Having gone "down," according to the neoclassical economic thought that guides the U.S.-trained economists who surround President Calderón, the U.S. economy will (automatically) return to an "equilibrium"—causing massive exports to once again move north across the Mexico-U.S. border. Such is the teaching of orthodox mainstream economics that has no real theory of economic crisis, let alone a historically conscious analysis of moments of structural change—such as the present one.

THE MEXICAN MODEL

In short, what has long been termed the new export-led model of development is kaput. The so-called Mexican model was never understood within the context of what economists term a "model," that is, a very rigorously presented set of assumptions, conditions, and mathematically determined relationships intended to show how Mexico could achieve long-term, steady-state economic growth. Rather, the "Mexican model" has been colloquially understood as a relatively loyal application of what generally became known as the "Washington Consensus" in the 1980s. Specifically, the Washington Consensus was brought to the foreground in Latin America as a result of the 1989 conference "Latin American Adjustment: How Much Has Happened?" under the auspices of the well-connected Washington-based think tank, the Institute for International Economics. At that conference and elsewhere, the chief economists of eight deeply indebted Latin American nations (including the all-important "MBA" trio—Mexico, Brazil, and Argentina) were encouraged to follow "that which Washington [read the U.S. government, the World Bank, and the IMF—hence the "Washington" Consensus] believes countries ought to do" (Ahumada 1996, 54–55). The goal was the seeking of "convergence" between economic policy making in Washington (under presidents Ronald Reagan and George H. W. Bush) and in the eight major nations of Latin America. What was the Washington Consensus? At that moment in time its chief advocate put forward ten points, quickly called the "Decalogue," throughout Latin America, thereby evoking the imagery and authority of the ten biblical commandments. Certainly, however presented and argued, the number-one tenet of the consensus was based on what was then the most widely accepted and least critically analyzed set of ideas in economics—the classical British economist David Ricardo's so-called law of comparative advantage, first presented in 1817.[2]

Applying, however loosely, Ricardo's analysis to Mexico suggested that Mexico should export products where it had a relative advantage (plentiful cheap labor), as long as that labor could find employment by way of the export of capital from nations such as the United States (which had an abundance). According to the back-of-the-envelope and seat-of-the-pants analyses that prevailed in the 1980s (particularly in the United States, but also in Mexico), if capital were free to flow across the border to Mexico (foreign direct investment), and if inputs (parts, components, and semifinished products) and final goods (exports and imports depending on the nation) were free to move from one nation to the other (no tariffs, quotas, or nontariff barriers), then Mexico would "specialize" in labor-intensive, low- and intermediate-skill level manufactured exports, while the United States would specialize in high-skill exports such as aeronautics, machine tools, medical equipment, high-end computer equipment, design and engineering, and so on. *Trade would balance, all analysts predicted.* As capital moved to Mexico, this would "free up" U.S. labor to climb the skill ladder—raising wages—which, in fact, were scheduled to rise in both nations, according to the advocates of the policy. Bringing "good economic policy" to Latin America—particularly Mexico—was all part of the "win-win" strategy that the Washington Consensus proffered. No nation in Latin America, probably no nation in the world, more fervently adopted the Washington Consensus. No other nation has held to the precepts of the consensus with more determination than Mexico—right up to today. In Mexico there is an old saying that clearly applies: "more Catholic than the Pope." Because the linchpin of the consensus was the uncritical acceptance of Ricardo's "law"—something that had been applied with a certain degree of success during the raw materials boom of the early- and mid-nineteenth century in Latin America, during what was known as the "liberal" or "free trade" era—the entire consensus package (and all other policies of a similar nature) quickly became known as "neoliberalism."

Our purpose, in this book, is to "unpack" exactly what all of this theorizing has actually meant in both the Mexican and U.S. contexts. A priori, at the time these issues were under great discussion and debate (1991), we argued that the end results of building policies on these theoretical abstractions would be a "lose-lose" situation for Mexican and U.S. workers and a "win-win" proposition for U.S. capital, in particular, and for some of the Mexican conglomerates, or "national power groups" (Cypher 1993b). Since then, the unfiltered evidence has not caused us to change our stance. Instead it has led us to a deeper and more systematic analysis of the new era known as "globalization."

As one Mexican economist has noted, "All neoliberal economists are neoclassicals, but not all neoclassicals are neoliberals." Neoliberalism can be summed up as an extreme perspective within the economics profession that proclaims a faith in the idea that economic institutions and individuals will achieve their maximum potential *only* under conditions where market forces are virtually unconstrained by any limits save those that establish and enforce property rights. Translating, this means a virtual absence of any social safety net, the private ownership of all resources and production facilities, the absence of regulations on corporations and labor markets, and, of course, the unconstrained movement of capital and all goods across borders. If all this seems familiarly close to what is understood as the Chicago School of economics (further analyzed in chapter 2) as propounded by Milton Friedman and associates, that is because we can trace the origins of neoliberalism to Friedman and his acolytes, who first instituted the economics of "freedom" by way of the Pinochet dictatorship in Chile after the September 11, 1973, coup. Neoclassical and neoliberal economists are essentially ahistorical in their analyses—which is a polite way of noting that they are historical illiterates. Of course there are brilliant neoclassical economic historians practicing their craft. But, sadly, their work is generally pushed to the margin—to be opportunistically utilized in the event that their findings can be massaged to support some aspect of neoliberal dogma. And this leads to the all-important distinction between the best of the neoclassical school of thought (which dominates the economics profession in the United States) and the neoliberals (who have dominated to the point of exclusion the public policy arena in Mexico since President Carlos Salinas, 1988–2004, took power). Grudgingly, creative neoclassicals (such as Joseph Stiglitz and Paul Krugman) have been awarded the Nobel Prize for their work, which demonstrates commonly encountered conditions wherein the free play of unregulated market forces yields suboptimal economic results. In short, most neoclassical economists recognize (and marshal the evidence to prove) that unregulated markets frequently "fail"—in the sense that they are suboptimal. This perspective is anathema in the higher circles of economic policy making in Mexico, where dogmatic faith in market fundamentalism is embraced in the best of times and even more so in the worst of times—such as today. Market fundamentalism, as applied in Mexico, suggests to Mexican policy makers that their role is to ensure that the public sector remains small and fiscally balanced, the money supply is under strict control, foreign currency reserves are large, and the exchange rate is relatively stable. *It is assumed that*, if these "fundamentals" are maintained, the economy will grow at or near its potential rate, productivity will be high, and all those really willing to work will find jobs.

Unfortunately, under this neoliberal formula Mexico's economy has performed weakly in the best of times—as detailed in chapter 2. More generally, as we show in this book, it has been marked by stagnation, astonishingly high levels of emigration, and an exploding "informal" economy where perhaps a majority of the economic population ekes out a precarious hand-to-mouth existence.

Our analysis of the Mexican "model" is likewise devoid of the abstractions commonly associated with the word "model" in conventional economics. We scrutinize the *political economy* of this model in a defined historical period, giving full weight to a range of (transdisciplinary) factors generally ignored by both neoclassical and neoliberal economic analyses. Most particularly, we do not shrink from an analysis of *power and social structure*. Power is that elusive but all-important variable that generally defies quantification but does yield its explanatory essence through a contextualized qualitative institutional analysis.

The theses advanced in this book are the following:

a. Rather than being a successful model based on the export of manufactured products, Mexico has created a new model based on the exportation of cheap labor in three areas: (1) the maquiladora industry, (2) the disguised maquila sector, and (3) the escalating emigration of millions of Mexican workers excluded from the labor market as a result of the internal "logic" of the new export-based model.
b. The new labor-export model constitutes a fundamental element in the process of industrial restructuring of the U.S. economy that began in the 1980s, continuing through 2009.

The following chapters are devoted to both the details and the implications of the above-mentioned processes for Mexico. We begin by analyzing Mexico before it fell into its current labor-export model. We then analyze why and how the nation was converted to serve the labor-export model, highlighting the ideological and economic agendas that gave rise to NAFTA.

We then focus on what that process, which locked in the manufacturing export-led model, has meant for Mexico's increasingly dependent production system. Here we present data and analyses that demonstrate the emergence of a disarticulated economy in Mexico, one where a significant division is to be found between the two maquilized sectors and the remainder of the economy.

- The maquilized sectors of the economy have since late 2006 been grouped under the acronym "IMMEX program" firms. That is, the maquila firms and those which we have termed the disguised maquila firms (who are highly dependent upon manufacture products exports but who are *not* operating within the technical confines of the maquila regime) are now both part of the "Manufacturing, Maquiladora and Export Services Industry Program," or IMMEX. These firms accounted for *76 percent of all of Mexico's manufacturing exports in 2008* (CNIMME 2009, 5:5d).[3] More broadly, they accounted for 60 percent of all exports in the same year, even in the face of record high prices for Mexico's oil exports.
- Approximately *90 percent* of the export production of the IMMEX firms (the maquilas and the disguised maquilas) was produced for export to the United States in 2007.
- More than *44 percent and as much as 60 percent of all formal manufacturing employment* in Mexico in 2008 was generated through internationalized processing activities via the cheap labor–export model by the IMMEX firms (Capdevielle 2005, 568; CNIMME 2009, 5:5d).[4]
- The IMMEX firms, the largest portion owned by U.S. capital transplants, succeeded in raising Mexico's share of total U.S. imports from 6.7 percent in 1993 to 10.3 percent in 2008—in spite of the recent surge in U.S. imports from China (De la Cruz, Koopman, Wang, and Wei 2009, 8).
- IMMEX firms produced a trade surplus of $46.2 billion US in 2006, surpassing the petroleum sector's surplus of $37.3 billion, even in the midst of the commodities boom. In 2000 the IMMEX surplus was more than three times greater than the petroleum surplus (CNIMME 2009, 6:5e; INEGI various years).

While all of this has bolstered the profit margins of the transplant firms, the net result for Mexico is an economy that lacks continuity, autonomy, and dynamism. It is one where the productive apparatus has been dismantled and reassembled to fit the structural requirements of the U.S. economy, leaving

Mexico in control of certain low-value-added resource-based activities and a range of other rentier pursuits in tourism, finance, and real estate. Instead of advancing its productive apparatus, Mexico is falling further behind (relatively) because in essence the labor export–led model is structurally designed to transfer Mexico's economic surplus away from its potential positive usage. The process of subordinated integration fails to advance the productive apparatus of the economy through investments in expanded research, development, and technological applications and through public sector infrastructural investments designed to rapidly improve Mexico's quality of education, public health, and autonomous industrial base. Symbiotically, the Mexican elite (in its bifurcated economic and political dimensions, as defined below) coexists with and facilitates the perceived structural dimensions of the restructuring process as delimited by U.S. economic interests. In this process, certain rentier benefits befall this elite, while it carefully maintains its option of engaging in devastating capital flight—or deploying the threat of capital flight—to preserve these benefits. In short, we analyze the *social structure of distorted dependent accumulation* built up in Mexico in the past thirty years. We offer a case study of Mexico's socioeconomic system that comfortably fits the term "transnational dependent capitalism"—based on the exploitation and exportation of cheap labor (see note 2). Transnational dependent capitalism entails the disarticulation of the Mexican economy within a transnational process of rearticulation between U.S.-sited advanced production and engineering processes exported to Mexico, which then link to Mexican assembly, and finally the re-export of final manufactures to the U.S. consumer market. Under this system Mexico is dotted with enclaves—primarily and increasingly in the north and north central states—undertaking asymmetric production processes wherein the low-value-added activities of the internationalized production chain occur in Mexico. And, in the final analysis, the significant profits arising from these activities (via transfer prices or other mechanisms) are repatriated to, primarily, the U.S.-based firms that are the dominant participants in this new economic model.

Thus, we present an analytical and critical account of transnational production that runs directly in opposition to the standard, purely abstract, ideologically driven "win-win" portrayals of "globalization." We take fully into our account, within this broad process of unequal development and unequal exchange, the role of Mexican migration into the United States. That is, we break with what is often the conventional account of migration—that it is a function of its own dynamic. Normally, migration studies are not contextualized within a broad political-economic framework. We, on the other hand, attempt to understand migration as a process that is derivative of a dynamic restructuring of present-day U.S. capitalism. Chapter 6 of this book, then, is devoted to the migration process and the role of and consequences for migrant Mexican labor in this process of restructuring.

Our efforts to deconstruct/reconstruct this new, complex, internationalized form of production have necessitated the formation of new analytical categories in order to capture, describe, and interpret the new, often transnational, realities of this process. We attempt to make visible a set of relationships embedded in current reality that have remained in gradations of obscurity in numerous previous research efforts on aspects of the cheap labor–export model. Above all, this is frequently the case due to the fact that analyses of the globalization of production are separated from migration studies.

ON ORIGIN AND METHOD

The origins of this book can be traced to the preparation of a conference paper delivered at Princeton University and subsequently published in a much foreshortened version in the *Annals of the American Academy of Political and Social Science* in March 2007. In preparing that study we drew upon our extensive background research on both the Mexican and U.S. economies and societies conducted over the past thirty-plus years. From those days until today, a major source of information has been the extensive body of research literature produced on both sides of the Mexico-U.S. border. To encounter a modest portion of that work—only those sources cited herein—readers are referred to the bibliography.

In addition, the book is based upon extensive primary or original field research, including numerous interviews with key policy makers, particularly at selected state-level secretariats of economic development. The fieldwork, carried out in the course of 2007 and 2008, also involved the implementation of a broad quantitative and qualitative survey instrument utilized to gain a current detailed understanding of the inner workings of several foreign-owned and (some) nationally owned manufacturing firms in the north central region of Mexico. Under the auspices of the government of the state of Zacatecas, through the office of the Secretaría de Planeación y Desarrollo, one of us secured generous funding from the 2007 program "Proyectos para el Desarrollo Regional, Innovación y Capital Humano" to pursue a study of the auto and auto parts industry in the north central region of Mexico. That study focused on the industrial/manufacturing economic development strategies of the adjoining states of Aguascalientes, Coahuila, San Luis Potosí, and Zacatecas. The field research also involved a number of interviews conducted with industry officials and academic specialists in Mexico City from late 2007 through midyear 2008. In the following chapters we generally do not make specific reference to this research. Rather, those research findings constituted vital background information that has allowed us to better ground, contextualize, and understand the nuances of Mexico's industrial economy in tacit ways that we could never achieve through our own readings of data and analyses. The field research created new degrees of depth and perception as well as important and detailed information—some basic and scarcely available that was particularly important in the formulation and writing of chapters 4 and 5 that focus on the export industrial base of Mexico.

We have found that official statistical categories, tied as they are to their origins (wherein their methods of gathering and grouping sets of data served the goals of analyzing a single national economy and its distinct and separate structure of production), are severely limited when it comes to analyzing internationalized forms of production. Because of this we have often attempted to systematize information in new categories and/or concepts that serve to illustrate processes fundamental to the new internationalized system of production and the new division of power between what Raúl Prebisch termed the "center" and the "periphery."

Beyond these basic sources and theoretical conceptualizations our method has also been to conduct a scrupulous daily reading of two or more Mexican newspapers as well as a national newspaper of record in the United States. We take seriously the historian's assessment that the newspaper account is a fundamental source, and it, along with related Internet material, forms a basis that contributes to the first draft of history.

WHAT NEXT?

If the cheap labor export–led model is now irretrievably broken, as we have come to conclude, the relevant question would seem to be, "What next?" What will be Mexico's next adopted model of development? There are two important partial answers to this all-important question. First, nothing can be changed—whether it is working or not—if key policy makers cannot recognize the nature of the problem. Second, nothing can change if there is no critical mass of opposition—sparked in all likelihood by social movements—to the status quo. Currently, the commitment to the status quo is jarringly high. As will be discussed in greater detail in chapter 3, the Business Coordinating Council is the most powerful of the peak business associations. Known as the CCE, this entity has exerted a strong and growing influence over the determination of the parameters of economic policy making since the late 1970s. In the midst of the alarming 2009 crisis it could find no problems whatsoever with the export-led model. This its leader, Armando

Paredes, stated unequivocally on August 25, 2009, as he proclaimed there
was no necessity to either change or adjust the model. According to Paredes,
"The problem is to be found in the fact that we have not advanced the [needed
structural] reforms" (Becerril 2009, 1). The term "needed structural reforms"
is key code terminology in Mexico; its specific content changes from time
to time. Basically this line of argumentation suggests that *if* the structural
changes instituted by the neoliberal shift since the 1980s went even further in
the direction of relying upon unregulated market forces, Mexico's economic
traumas would be obliterated. In some moments the specific thrust of those
who urge further structural reforms centers on the complete privatization of
the energy sector. At some moments momentum has been built up to privatize
the social security system. A perennial target is Mexico's relatively strong
labor law, which tends to level the playing field a bit between nearly all-pow-
erful employers and totally vulnerable workers.

Until late August 2009, the CCE and many in President Calderón's economic cabinet were urging the imposition of the 15 percent value-added tax
(IVA) on all food and medicine. This was to be *structural tax reform*, thought
to resolve the growing public sector deficit that had opened in the course of
2008–2009. Press accounts suggest that the number of poor in Mexico—always a somewhat contested number—has jumped by six million in the course
of 2009. What then would the tax on food and medicine do to the vast majority of Mexicans who live on a meager income? How, by further undercutting the domestic market, would a *sales* tax on food and medicine cause the
"model" to come back to life?[5] These are the questions that common citizens
ask themselves when they encounter, almost daily, the siren songs of the
economic and political elite who firmly believe that Mexico's dilemma can
be overcome by imposing even greater degrees of neoliberal adjustments on
Mexican society. And, as David Ibarra (secretary of the treasury from 1977
to 1982) has vigorously argued, Mexico's structural fiscal problems have
everything to do with Mexico's low (and frequently evaded) direct *income*
tax, further reduced from 1997 onward. This theme, however, is never raised
in policy-making circles for the simple reason that, according to Ibarra, "the
power groups do not want to pay taxes" (González Amador 2007, 23).

Nor are these blind steps toward deepening Mexico's immersion in the
neoliberal morass merely urged by those who occupy the pinnacles of power
in Mexico. "There is no better situation than an economic crisis" in which
to undertake structural reforms, stated Ellis J. Juan, the director for Mexico
of the Washington-based Interamerican Development Bank (Saldaña and
Becerril 2009, 8). Among the reforms urged by Mr. Juan we find mention
of fiscal reforms (putting the IVA on food and medicine), the privatization
of infrastructure (roads, water, etc.), the privatization of the public-sector

energy firms, and the elimination of the legacy of the Mexican Revolution embedded in the proworker labor law. When the concept of the Washington Consensus was formed, the powerful Interamerican Development Bank was, of course, a charter member. It is therefore of some importance that there seems to be deep unison between the agents of this consensus and the peak business organizations as to what Mexico should be engaging in to confront the current crisis.

But these are not the only voices clamoring for change. There is a chance, albeit very slight, that Mexico could begin to unwind the neoliberal era. The justifiably famed U.S. institutionalist economist Thorstein Veblen was fond of the saying that sometimes the left hand does not know what the right hand is doing. On August 19, 2009, the press outlined a new plan by the government to use the national development bank Nafinsa—famed for its ability to allocate capital and create new and very dynamic industrial firms in the 1940s, 1950s, and 1960s—to create much-needed bank credits for small and medium-sized businesses. Further violating the chief tenets of neoliberalism, President Calderón stated that the government should increase the portion of its purchases made in the national market, particularly the portion bought from small and medium-sized businesses (*El Financiero* 2009, 27). Even further, Calderón stated that he wanted much higher *domestic content*—35 percent instead of 20 percent previously—as a condition for making government purchases from national suppliers. Meanwhile, the once-powerful Camara National de la Industria de Transformación (the national manufacturers association, or Canacintra) has been able to gain a bit of traction for an argument it has relentlessly made over the past eight years. Canacintra has called for the overturn of the single-minded focus on the export-led model that has facilitated the growth of foreign-owned firms while decimating the ranks of the national manufacturers (Posada and Reyna Quiroz 2009, 27). But Canacintra is not a peak business association, and it does not represent the business elite.

In countless press reports Canacintra has gained headlines for speaking frankly about the need for a reinvigorated, modernized industrial policy. "Industrial policy" is a freighted term—nowhere more so than in Mexico. In essence, it can be stated that industrial policy (IP) entails processes and activities that have some common points of reference with state-led industrialization policies such as those that dominated Mexico's economic policy making in the 1940–1982 period. (We review the debate over state-led policies in chapter 2.) Industrial policy is intended to be much more analytically directed and agile than were the state-led policies, often termed import substitution industrialization, or ISI. IP is used to restructure an economy, which in Mexico's case would mean a primary focus on the domestic market

and a secondary focus on a dramatically reconstituted export sector designed
to steadily advance national content and higher skill levels in a diversified
range of exported products. IP is not restricted to industry—it can be used
to promote the agricultural or service sectors. IP can be oriented toward the
achievement of static efficiency, by overcoming market failures and capturing externality effects, for example. IP, particularly as it has been employed
successfully in Japan and throughout much of East Asia, is often used to
achieve the larger gains deriving from dynamic efficiency. To engage in IP a
nation must have high *state capacity*—sufficient to subordinate transnational
and national capital to a developmental project. Utilizing such capacity and
working in parallel cooperation with the private sector, IP is most commonly
associated with the creation/promotion of specific sectors and the sunset of
other sectors in order to overcome adverse *path dependency*. Nations that
employ IP are frequently concerned with accelerating technological progress
through state-run research centers and the inducement, through reciprocal
measures, of enhanced and targeted private-sector expenditures on technology to promote production upgrading to achieve higher levels of efficiency
and new forms of competitive advantage. Figure 1.1 illustrates the nature of
the *developmental state*, focusing on three key variables—*power, purpose,*
and *state capacity*.

The power variable focuses our attention on the issue of *compliance*—the
ability of the state to actually achieve coherent consent regarding the priori-
tization of the development project. But this power is conditioned by a deep
(embedded) alliance with the business elite to ensure that the nation will not
be stalemated by factional disputes over state-led initiatives. The *purpose*
variable emphasizes the fact that the developmental state is capable of pro-
jecting a viable *national project* of development, often through harnessing
a strong and broadly accepted conception of nationalism. This vision can
find policy expression through industrial policy (IP), including the adoption
of flexible and deep import substitution industrialization (ISI) or export-led
industrialization (ELI) strategies (or viable combinations of the two). Of
greater importance than the discussion over preferred strategies (ISI and/or
ELI) is the ability of the state to demonstrate *capacity*. Capacity breaks into
two components: first, *competence*, which includes the capability of coordinating processes among competing agencies (*interagency coherence*); and
second, *embeddedness*, which begins at the level of industry-state coordinating boards but then reaches down into the production and knowledge bases
where the society maintains and advances its production apparatus, bringing
into motion and furthering its technical abilities by way of a *national system
of innovation* (discussed in chapter 5), its managerial skills and capacities,
and its trained/skilled labor force.

Figure 1.1. Three Key Variables of the Developmental State

Developmental

State Formation	=	**Power**	+	**Purpose**	+	**Capacity**

Power →

cohesive capacity to:
- direct & prioritize a development project
- demand performance compliance (autonomy)
- maintain an alliance with business elite

Purpose →

(mobilization of a development vision)
→
ISI &/or ELI
(guided by IP)

Capacity →

(competence ↔ embeddedness)
→
civil service   industry-state boards
- merit-based   →
- rule-based   production/knowledge base
- interagency   →
  coherence   technical, managerial, labor

* Directing and prioritizing a development project = *coherence*

** Ability to demand and achieve performance compliance = *discipline capability*

Source: Adapted from Cypher and Dietz 2009, 225.

To make such a dramatic turn in policy Mexico would have to accept the fact that unregulated markets in developing nations generally tend to function inadequately in allocating financial capital to long-term industrial projects. In the past, to close this "market failure" gap somewhat, Mexico gave great latitude to Nafinsa—the national development bank (Arés 2007). The fact that Nafinsa is once again in the news as an important social actor is significant. Industrial policy also is generally associated with initiatives to promote the national industrial base by emphasizing local content—particularly in government purchases. That President Calderón has recently gone on record as favoring such a step could signal the beginnings of an important turn in policy. More generally, industrial policy must be understood in broad conceptual terms, as Dani Rodrik has argued:

> The right model for industrial policy is not that of an autonomous government applying [optimal] taxes or subsidies, but of strategic collaboration between the private sector and the government with the aim of uncovering where the most significant obstacles to restructuring lie and what type of interventions are most likely to remove them. Correspondingly, the analysis of industrial policy needs to focus not on the policy *outcomes*—which are inherently unknowable ex ante—but on getting the policy *process* right. We need to worry about how we design a setting in which private and public actors come together to solve problems in the productive sphere, each side learning about the opportunities and constraints faced by the other, and not about whether the right tool for industrial policy is, say, directed credit or R&D subsidies or whether it is the steel industry that ought to be promoted or the software industry. Hence the right way of thinking of industrial policy is as a discovery process—one where firms and the government learn about underlying costs and opportunities and engage in strategic coordination. The traditional arguments against industrial policy lose much of their force when we view industrial policy in these terms. (Rodrik 2004, 4)

In short, even this brief description of the essence of industrial policy demonstrates that Mexico would have to orchestrate a *paradigmatic shift* to achieve a *national project of accumulation* in order to exit from the cul-de-sac that we have termed "Mexico's dilemma." A structural delinking (partial or complete) from the United States' "national project of accumulation"—the cheap-labor export model analyzed in this book that currently defines Mexico's model—would be a prerequisite in the application of industrial policy. The nature and consequences of the absence of such a policy for national firms, and for endogenous development processes, will be examined in chapter 5.

Our field research at a number of the offices of the state-level secretariats of economic development (along with attendance at their national conference devoted to economic development issues, where many representatives of these secretariats delivered analyses of their developmental strategies) convinced us that a significant portion of the policy leaders at the state level are operating in accord with the general outlines of Canacintra's call to jettison neoliberalism and adopt some form of loosely articulated state-led industrialization strategies that would parallel in broad terms industrial policies successfully deployed in developing Asian nations since the 1950s and 1960s. We did not expect, by any means, to encounter such a vision—nor to hear it articulated so forcefully at the state level in a nation where centralization and conformity have long been the requisite behavioral rules to follow. To be sure, those state secretariats in the largely nonindustrial states did not advance arguments for a renewed Mexican industrial policy. Thus, the secretariats are not united, and they all approach the issue of a national industrial policy from their own microcosms. To the extent that it is possible to imagine a "bottom-up" process—so uncommon that it is all but unknown and unrecorded in Mexico—the secretariats could conceivably play an important role in altering policy-making dynamics. Our research revealed that the secretariats in the industrial states are aware of what the other secretariats have achieved and failed to achieve, and how they have gone about orchestrating their success. The secretariats that acknowledge that Mexico must create and adopt an endogenous strategy for development have achieved deep embeddedness with both national and transnational manufacturers in their regions. The most sophisticated (at least in the north central region) are well informed and well staffed. They exhibit a deep understanding of the growing difficulties encountered by national producers. It is therefore important to recognize the recent call by the technical secretary of the Mexican Association of the Secretariats of Development (AMSDE) for the adoption of a national industrial policy as a viable long-term alternative to the neoliberal model (Soria Hernández 2009, 8). This position was adopted after lengthy consultations among the secretariats and between them and Canacintra. The call made includes advocacy for the creation of the vital policy trinity of embedded state autonomy—the deep coordination of state developmental organizations with the private sector and the universities. The advocacy of a *paradigmatic shift* also comes from Mauricio de Maria y Campos, who was, until the close of President de la Madrid's term in 1988, the powerful subsecretary for industrial development of the secretariat of trade and industrial development, SECOFI (Maria y Campos et al. 2009).

Chapters 2 and 3 detail some of the dramatic turning points in the restructuring of economic policy during the 1980s and early 1990s that consolidated the rule of the Chicago boys and their ideology, resulting in the ouster of the crucial (but wavering) "developmentalist coalition" of top policy makers such as de Maria y Campos, who were replaced by an ideologically charged, opportunistic "free trade coalition"—significantly shaped by the agenda of interested U.S. corporations (Thacker 2000). When de Maria y Campos held a leadership role in government in the 1980s, he was one of the advocates of a concerted effort to adopt a new development model that would build on the gains achieved in the 1940–1982 period. This effort was led to some degree by his immediate superior, Hector Hernández Cervantes, the head of SECOFI. Their project started as a measured attempt to carry out a state-led revitalization of Mexico's economy—targeting strategic sectors for various forms of policy assistance. The policy shift included promoting export-led growth while rejecting a program of indiscriminate opening to imports and foreign capital (SECOFI 1988). But by December 1987, with the signing of the threshold Economic Solidarity Pact, policy makers at SECOFI—the main voice for the creation of industrial policy—were completely "ostracized" and "unable to generate coordinated action against [massive privatizations and trade and investment] liberalization" (Schamis 2002, 118).[6] Even before the orchestration of the Economic Solidarity Pact, which marked the total defeat of the "developmentalist coalition," the application for the entry of Mexico into the GATT (subsequently dissolved into the World Trade Organization) in 1985 and the serious economic crisis of 1985–1986 were defining moments in the breakup of the power of the developmentalist coalition (Cypher 1990, 177–95). The GATT decision, urged by SECOFI, opened Mexico to the free traders' agenda and doomed any hopes of a conditioned engagement with foreign direct investment and trade. The crisis of 1985–1986 "eliminated the last attempts to make a gradual transition toward a new growth model" (Garrido and Quintana 1988, 54). A new era of *savage reconversion* commenced—now opportunistically supported even by officials such as SECOFI's Hernández Cervantes.

Shortly thereafter, Maria y Campos's position was filled by Fernando Sánchez Ugarte, a recipient of an economics Ph.D. from the University of Chicago who served at high levels in the neoliberal governments from President Salinas's administration (1988–1994) until the beginning of 2008 (Babb 2001, 166). Unlike Hernández Cervantes and de Maria y Campos (during the brief period of SECOFI's advocacy of industrial policy), Sánchez Ugarte and his fellow "Chicago boys" believed (as did their intellectual godfather, Milton Friedman) that *the best economic policy was no policy whatsoever*: "The role of the government is to promote the creation of an economic environment that is conducive to the efficient operation of competitive markets, which will motivate private investment and the generation of productive employment" (Sánchez Ugarte, Fernández Pérez, and Pérez Motta 1994, 49). Returning to de Maria y Campos, he (like many other influential former members of the policy-making elite) has continued to participate in policy discussions as a member of the Consejo Mexicano de Asuntos Internacionales (Mexico's equivalent to the United States' powerful Council on Foreign Relations). His most recent intervention ("Industry's Moment for Directional Change Has Arrived"), appearing in the nation's top business newspaper, is important in that it reflects on the industrial advances made by nations such as Korea and China since 1988—all with the aid of state-led industrialization policies (de Maria y Campos 2009). Meanwhile, Mexico has deindustrialized because, argued Maria y Campos in a large study on the theme under his direction, Mexico in 1987 abandoned its industrial policy (de Maria y Campos et al. 2009). His work reflects the exasperation of more than a few critics of the status quo who were once relatively quiet former members of the political elite.

Could it be, then, like the volcanoes that have been known to erupt from the flattest of Mexican cornfields, that an alternative strategy will take vague form in the midst of the current crisis? We can make no predictions on this point. But we can introduce one last Mexican saying that we regularly encounter: "Better the devil that you *do* know, than the one you *do not* know." Having lost so much over the past thirty years, people may not be ready to opt for dramatic change in the economic model that carries new risks of failure. Yet a variety of social movements and forces contributed to the presidential elections of 1988 and 2006 wherein opposition candidates with a mandate to carry through on a *national project*, constituting a clear rupture with the reigning neoliberal model, clearly won sufficient votes to be declared victors—had there been unbiased elections (Barberán 1988).

However, there are no social movements at the moment that would prove to be the catalyst for fundamental change in economic policy. It is important to resist the idea that because neoliberalism has clearly been the underlying cause of the wrenching current crisis both in Mexico and the United States, there will be, ipso facto, a dramatic change in economic and social policy. Here and elsewhere, history is the laboratory of analysis. It is important, therefore, to recall another period that seemed to signal an abandonment of neoliberal policy: in the early 1980s Chile—after having embraced at breakneck speed as much of the neoliberal transition as could be imagined from 1973 onward—was forced to experience a devastating economic and social crisis. Policy makers took a few steps back in certain crucial areas, and they slowed the pace of advance of the neoliberal project. But they did not abandon it. Even when democratic government was restored in the late 1980s and up to the moment under several "socialist" governments, the neoliberal project has remained the bedrock of social and economic policy (Cypher 2004b).

Nonetheless, we believe that the current crisis *could* rapidly change the policy dynamics in Mexico. As a recent MUNDOS national poll illustrates, Mexico's socioeconomic dynamics are now extremely fluid, with all portions of the economic pyramid experiencing remarkable downward mobility in the past ten years. All of these changes presumably carry political consequences—and all changes noted can be confirmed through scrutiny of official data sources from the secretariat for social development (SEDESOL) or other entities that document the deterioration that has occurred in recent years among all social classes.

Table 1.1 focuses on a fivefold level of social stratification. At the top, in 2000, the upper class constituted 3 percent of the population (group A)—estimated to have fallen dramatically to 2 percent by 2010. The income scale within the upper class is extremely broad, ranging from the lower limit of $240,000 US per year to a few households with annual incomes above $1 billion. From within the upper class come the members of Mexico's bifurcated hierarchical elite. At the pinnacle of power sit the *business elite*. They have the power to largely determine the range of policy possibilities for the nation. As will be analyzed in subsequent chapters, the business elite exercises its power to set the range of the policy agenda through a small number of peak business organizations, such as the CCE mentioned above. The lower partner in the elite comprises the *policy makers*, first clustered around and in the office of the president, but also including the powerful cabinet secretariats, some members of the Senate, the House of Deputies, and selected state governors. The members of the upper class do not, in many ways, live in Mexico so much as they seem to float above it. They live surrounded by a retinue of servants—maids, drivers, gunmen, gardeners, and so on, who curry to their every whim. They have two or more fortified luxury residences and frequently travel abroad—where they ensconce massive financial assets. Further important details regarding the socioeconomic characteristics of the upper class (and all those below) are summarized in the fourth column of table 1.1. In the fifth column of the table are the summary findings of the national poll regarding matters pertaining to electoral politics.

Next in the class pyramid is the *upper middle class*, constituting a mere 7 percent of the population in 2000, yet falling significantly to an estimated 5 percent by 2010 (group B). The following group, *the middle class* (group C), included 25 percent of the population—it is divided into substrata C+, C, and C–. Like other groups higher in the socioeconomic pyramid, the middle class has experienced massive downward mobility—an estimated one of every five falling into the working class or even below in the first decade of the twenty-first century.

Table 1.1 Contemporary Dynamics of Mexico's Socioeconomic Stratification

Categories & Trend Changes Changes, 2000–2010	Census Period 2000	Estimated Census 2010	Wealth & Income (Average Characteristics)	Position Regarding Electoral Politics
A) Upper Class (losing about 1%)	3%	2%	Annual Income: >$240,000 US Ownership: two or more homes, apartments, or luxury sites Domestic Service: a retinue of servants Banking & Finance: one or more foreign bank accounts, savings and checking accounts in three or more banks, four to five credit card accounts	Identification with the ruling party Assumed participation in the governing elite No evidence of a commitment to fundamental change in status quo
B) Upper Middle Class (picking up some 1% from A, but dropping 3% overall)	7%	5%	Annual Income: ≥$72,000 US, ≤$240,000 US Ownership: large house or apartment, two autos (less than two years old) Domestic Service: one (or more) household servants Banking & Finance: savings and checking accounts in two or more banks, two to three credit card accounts	Conditioned identification with the governing party Participation in the reform tradition, mainly through PRI or PAN politics May vote with the left in Mexico City

(continued)

Table 1.1 Contemporary Dynamics of Mexico's Socioeconomic Stratification (*continued*)

Categories & Trend Changes, 2000–2010	Census Period 2000	Estimated Census 2010	Wealth & Income (Average Characteristics)	Position Regarding Electoral Politics
C) Middle Class (picking up 3% from B, but dropping 8% overall)	C+ 5% C 10% C− 10%	4% 8% 8%	Annual Income: ≥$15,000 US, ≤$72,000 US Ownership: own or rent modest house or apartment, own car Domestic Service: non-live-in maid, partial or full-time (C+ & some C strata) Banking and Finance: savings and checking accounts in two banks, two credit cards C and C− groups most vulnerable to current credit problems; incomes largely from salaries C and C− households divided between the *formal* and *informal* economies	C segments are the locus of political transitions since the mid-1980s They tend to abandon traditional political loyalties, voting for various political parties They embrace alternation in power and a split ballot Some traditional voting in these sectors Fluidity of the sectors tends to give similar characteristics to the middle class & marginal sectors
D) Working Class Sectors (picking up 8% from C, but losing 10% overall)	D+ 15% D 10% D− 10%	12% 11% 10%	Annual Income: ≥$1,800 US, ≤$15,000 US Ownership: own or rent small house or	Some traditional voting in these sectors Fluidity of the sectors tends to give similar

	%		
		characteristics to the middle class & marginal sectors	
	30%	apartment, some own a car Banking and Finance: some savings, checking, and credit account usage D+ component is upwardly mobile, partially unionized D & D– component is downwardly mobile house with few to no services	
E) Marginal Sectors (picking up 10% from D)	40%	Annual Income: <$1,800 US Ownership: rented house or apartment, or occupied house with few to no services Banking and Finance: marginal use of banks for check cashing, some debit card accounts The poor operate outside of the formal economy, on the margins of the consumer market Slight hope of social mobility	Marginal poor are clients of social programs designed for political support of governing party All major parties have continued client-style relations with the poor

Sources: Based on our analysis and the MUND Group, *Opinion and Policy Report Series* 9, no. 25 (Sept. 1, 2009): 1–3, based on a MUNDOS National Poll, conducted infield August 24–28, 2009, and Supplement A to the above report, "Market Research Categories in Mexico, 2009."

Some 35 percent of the population fell into the group D category "Working Class Sectors"—subgrouped into strata D+, D, and D–. Once again, the entropic forces of the economic model have pulled this down—the largest strata—in 2000. It is anticipated, based on current national polling data, that this class will see its ranks trimmed to 33 percent of the population by 2010.

Finally, group E, constituting 30 percent of the population in 2000, occupied the "Marginal Sectors"—dominated by those who exist in the "informal" sector. The informal sector—those who are not officially listed as operating registered businesses or employees not listed in the official accounting of the labor force as determined by social security or similar entities and working without officially sanctioned labor contracts—transcend the category "Marginal Sector." Some informal sector participants are to be found in category D, and sometimes even in substratum C–.

To summarize, the data projections suggest that in the ten-year period 2000–2010, Mexico has undergone a significant shift wherein stratum A has shed one-third of its members (from 3 to 2 percent), category B fell from 7 to 5 percent, and C fell from 25 to 20 percent, while D dropped slightly to 33 percent and E jumped from 30 to 40 percent. The pauperization of Mexico's populace, confirmed by other data, sets the stage for a possible rapid shift in the general political dynamics of the nation.[7] Yet the balance of forces *at the present moment* suggests some sort of limping continuity. If we are correct in that assessment and in the analysis offered in this book, Mexico's long agony under the unbearable burden of neoliberalism—even should some palliatives be introduced—currently shows no definitive signs of ending. No clear indicators exist to allow us to foresee a quick end to *Mexico's economic dilemma.*

Chapter Two

The Political Economy of Mexico's Export-Led Model

By any reasonable standard, particularly by relevant historical standards, Mexico's economy has failed since the neoliberal era began in earnest in 1988. Manifestations of the failed economic strategy abounded in early 2009. For example, Mexico's long and torturous relationship with the International Monetary Fund (IMF) reached new heights when in April the IMF extended a $47 billion line of credit—a record amount for Mexico. On the same day that the megaloan was announced, the National Statistical Agency (INEGI) declared that the manufacturing sector was declining at an all-time record annual rate of 16 percent. This, as the daily press announced, was worse than what had occurred in the bleakest months of the worst crisis Mexico weathered in the later half of the twentieth century—the 1994–1995 downturn. The IMF saluted Mexico for its "solid economic policies" and its "fiscal discipline" while forecasting that the downturn in GDP (−3.7 percent) would be nearly as bad as the crisis of 1983 (González Amador 2009, 1). By August 2009 the forecasted downturn for 2009 made by Mexico's Central Bank was −7.5 percent and the comparison had moved from the 1990s to the 1930s. Only months before, in late 2008, Mexico's Chicago School–trained secretary of the treasury scoffed at the idea that Mexico's economy was in trouble, dismissing the situation as being no more than a "little sniffle." Mexico, after all, had "armoring"—big foreign currency reserves and vague plans for (modest) countercyclical public spending infrastructure projects. Mexico's difficulties spread beyond the crashing economy. The president was at work trying to dispel charges (national and international) that he presided not merely over a failed economic model, but over a *failed state*.

It was once common to encounter a vision of Mexico that violently contrasted with a widespread current view that Mexico's economic policy has failed. Indeed, when Mexico's national economy grew at the then-spectacular

27

pace of 6.49 percent per year (inflation adjusted) from 1940 to 1982, it was common to view Mexico as an "economic miracle." Understanding why it was that Mexico achieved such rapid growth is no mystery—growth of the industrial sector, particularly manufacturing, pulled the rest of the economy along. Over the 1940–1982 period, the industrial sector grew at the annual rate of 8.03 percent (Becker 1995, 37). Clearly, the drive to industrialize Mexico was the underlying factor behind what many termed the "Mexican miracle." Per capita annual income growth during this period averaged an impressive 3.1 percent. Subsequently, annual per capita income growth then collapsed, falling to only 0.76 percent from 1983 through 2008 (Arroyo Picard 2007, 181; CEPAL 2008a, 120). Throughout the 1940–1982 period Mexico's strong economic growth was, in varying degrees, largely "shared"—peasants and workers sometimes even gained relative to other class strata. From 1983 through 2008, however, the meager benefits to be garnered were snatched by the highest economic strata (with some attention given to "targeted" public policies of income transfers to the most desperate). In the 1983–2008 period, foreign corporations and foreign investors had a proportionately greater claim on Mexico's wealth as the earlier nationalist stance evaporated. What little economic improvement could be found during this latter period arose through a process that economists frequently defined as "exclusive" or "polarizing," to be contrasted with the "inclusive" nature of economic growth during the 1940 to 1982 period. In a word, the new policy framework was termed "neo-liberalism" (discussed in the following section).

Clearly, it is simplistic and inaccurate to attempt to encapsulate the entirety of a nation with a one-word description, be it "failed" or "miracle." Equally clear is the fact that Mexico once had a highly functional, endogenous, *social structure of accumulation* that has been replaced by a *restructured/rearticulated/ subordinated* economy wherein the prime motor force of accumulation is exogenous—driven by the United States. This great transformation is the subject we explore in this book. It is a subject of great controversy. Our objective is to add some much-needed clarity regarding the major themes of the current era as they relate to the performance of the economy and to processes of migration. In pursuing these issues, we find our subject to be not only Mexico, but also the United States.

In striving to answer the question, "What has happened to Mexico?" we therefore break with a long-dominant position of analysts—the country study approach. The methodological base of much of the work of the United Nations' research center in Santiago—CEPAL—which incubated many of the classic ideas associated with Latin America's structural economic problems, was grounded in processes of complex international interdependence. We continue in this tradition, finding that to locate core causal factors in Mexico it is frequently necessary to pursue matters from within the social formation of the United States. Although now out of fashion, we find it is necessary to critically introduce elements of the "dependency framework" to interpret events since 1982. This framework of analysis—in its different theoretical perspectives—prioritizes *external factors* as conditioning the internal dynamic of capital accumulation. In this case the influence and power of the U.S. state and U.S. corporate interests are understood as being, *in some instances*, crucial and determinant in the policy decisions that have conditioned Mexico. Our view, as we hope to make clear and compelling, is that *autonomous* forces and factors in Mexico exert a great deal of power over most policy decisions and critical conjunctures. But in analyzing significant turning points it is also necessary to incorporate an analysis of U.S. policy objectives. In short, we frequently find a *codetermination process* at work, involving the power elites both of Mexico and of the United States.

MEXICO CAUGHT IN THE WEB OF NEOLIBERALISM— A BRIEF EXPLANATION

The term "neoliberal" began to be used throughout Latin America in the early 1970s to describe the extreme embrace of "free-market," Chicago School policies in Chile and Uruguay. The term literally suggests a "new liberalism," or a renewal of emphasis on the laissez-faire economic doctrines of Adam Smith. But neoliberalism, with its dogmatic antistatist thrust and its fundamentally libertarian posture, goes well beyond Smith's doctrines. It constitutes a distinct combination: first it draws from "Austrian School" advocates, particularly Friedrich von Hayek's *Road to Serfdom*, and the ideas of Hayek's mentor, Ludwig von Mises. Equally important, if not more so, is the ideologically charged "positive" economics of the Chicago School, featuring Frank H. Knight, George Stigler, Gary Becker, Arnold Harberger, and, above all, Milton Friedman. Their uncritical probusiness/antilabor zeal for a social Darwinist, law-of-the-jungle version of capitalism marked out a position far to the right of orthodox neoclassical economics.

In a study that emphasizes the Austrian roots of this archconservative approach, Kim Phillips-Fein emphasized the seminal role played by von Hayek and von Mises in the emergence of this Chicago School strain of thought (Phillips-Fein 2009). Behind von Hayek and von Mises in the 1940s and 1950s were arrayed a very discreet assemblage of anti–New Deal, large and medium-sized U.S. manufacturers whose deep pockets assured that Hayek's secretive Mont Pelerin Society would prosper. Milton Friedman was soon incorporated into this society.

The backers of the society, and of Hayek's work in general, would subsequently bankroll Friedman's efforts to create an accessible probusiness/anti-state manual (*Capitalism and Freedom*) designed to build general hostility to the ideas of the U.S. New Deal policies of the Roosevelt administration. The story of this effort has been detailed in Robert Van Horn and Philip Mirowski's *The Rise of the Chicago School of Economics and the Birth of Neoliberalism* (Van Horn and Mirowski 2009).

Although von Hayek, von Mises, and Friedman attempted to make great claims of scientific objectivity regarding their gauzy, ethereal, and ahistorical paeans to market forces, Friedman gave the game away in a letter to Hayek wherein he referred to "our faith" in what is essentially a mystical vision of a fictional set of "free-market" forces that will guide society to an optimum (Phillips-Fein 2009, 284). As Naomi Klein showed, this strange combination of probusiness tenets was finally raised to the status of an exclusive national economic policy via the military coup that installed a dictatorship in Chile in 1973. "Economic freedom" and "liberty," as propounded by the neoliberals, thus found its realization only by way of the violent suppression of all other ideas regarding economic policies. Arnold Harberger—éminence grise of the Chicago School—was, in this instance, a critical agent of change in Chile (Klein 2007).

From the 1970s onward, Mexico's embrace of these neoliberal ideas partially came through the Chicago School's influence on policy makers at the central bank and from there to elite university curriculums in economics, such as those of the Autonomous Technological Institute of Mexico, or ITAM (Babb 2001, 159–98). But equally important, if not more so, has been the ideological role of the powerful Monterrey industrial elite that initiated the creation of the peak business association, the CCE (the Business Coordinating Council) in 1975 (as discussed in a following section). The Monterrey group's antilabor organization, COPARMEX, founded in 1929, subscribed to an extreme version of laissez-faire that coincided with, and apparently anticipated, the rise of neoliberalism under Hayek's and Friedman's proselytizing. According to Marcela Hernández Romo, in the 1970s COPARMEX wanted the CCE to adopt a much more confrontationist stance than the peak business organization was willing to abide (Hernández Romo 2004, 89–122). The Monterrey group has proceeded to vigorously pursue for more than a hundred years an essentially neoliberal agenda: "At the ideological level, above all, they have advocated that the business leader be viewed *as the new State*, as the alternative and as the solution to the conflicts originated by the government. They have not sought to subsume themselves within the State, *they want to be the State*. They have attempted to establish a new scheme of relationships with society at large, the Church, and the government through the creation of a patrimonial corporatist State—a State orchestrated by a coalition of family-dominated businesses" (Hernández Romo 2004, 89, italics added).

The Monterrey group views itself as distinct from the business leaders whose origins are traceable to the tutelage of the state in the 1940–1982 period. They are, in their words, "a triumphant caste" similar in most ideological respects to the large- and medium-sized manufacturing capitalists who had backed Hayek and Friedman in the United States in the 1940s and 1950s. In our view, the diffusion of the ideological power and influence of the Monterrey group gave shape to Mexico's *endogenous* version of neoliberalism. This antistatist project gained new momentum from the interventions of economists trained at the University of Chicago.

In stating this, we are aware of the important *exogenous* forces unleashed in the era of World Bank "structural adjustment programs" that were crossconditioned via a series of important IMF loans Mexico received in the 1980s and later. This massive and cumulative lending operation was, of course, fully supported by the United States, which urged upon the World Bank and the IMF the imposition of a neoliberal agenda for Mexico (Woods 2005, 218–32). In all of this, the meeting of the priorities of transnational corporations, above all those based in the United States, received uppermost consideration in the complex policy shifts that occurred—whether initiated directly by the Mexican state, the World Bank, or the IMF. In this sense, once again, we find a *codetermination process* at work, involving both the power elites of Mexico and the United States.

THE BREAKDOWN OF IMPORT SUBSTITUTION INDUSTRIALIZATION

The closing years of President López Portillo's term (1976–1982) were marked by plummeting oil prices and escalating interest rates as global monetarism emanated from the U.S. Federal Reserve system. Mexico's rapid economic growth in the 1976–1980 period was driven by an unprecedented buildup in oil exports. External dependence has always come at a high price in Latin America—a lesson Mexico has had to relearn more than once in its long history. Using its oil wealth as collateral, Mexico borrowed heavily from international banks who engaged in "loan pushing" during the oil boom. As the boom came to a close in 1981 the Mexican economy spiraled out of control, as foreign debt service could only be met by further borrowing. Unable to extend the fragile financial structure any longer, the banks and the peso collapsed in 1982. Mexico's economic elite and political class responded by engaging in massive capital flight. In reaction, López Portillo enraged the financial sector (and the *grupos* or conglomerates that owned the banks) by nationalizing the banking system. Creating a rapprochement was the uncomfortable task of López Portillo's successor, President de la Madrid Hurtado (1982–1988).

While the bank nationalization of 1982 was certainly a catalyst sparking determined elite opposition to the state's influence in the economy, the economic elite had long felt its influence was ebbing: total state expenditures (state income plus borrowing) rose from 9.2 percent of GDP in 1950 to 12.5 percent in 1960, then to 21.1 percent in 1970, and finally to 48.7 percent in 1982 (Cypher 1990, 142). In addition to the size of the state sector, the business elite had become alienated over a governmental policy shift favoring further land reform. Furthermore, greater (though modest) power was conceded to unions under President Echeverría (1970–1976). Echeverría was viewed as a serious opponent of the economic elite because of his new policy of *shared growth*, which shifted moderate amounts of income to workers and peasants. He was viewed, particularly by the archconservative "northern faction" of Monterrey-based industrialists and financiers (Mexico's largest and strongest block of private business interests), as having broken an implicit *political pact* with business (Cypher 1990, 99–100; Valdés Ugalde 1997, 173–94).[1]

De la Madrid confronted an impossible situation: his first year in power was defined by a GDP decline of 4.2 percent—the worst economic performance since the days of the revolution. Mexico was forced to borrow extensively from the IMF, the World Bank, and the U.S. government, which, under President Reagan, had recently embraced Chicago School neoliberalism. De la Madrid was caught in a pincer movement with the international financial institutions and the U.S. government on one side and the large private-sector interests on the other. Through their peak business organizations such as the Business Coordinating Council (the CCE), the business elite began pushing as hard as possible for a reduction in the state sector and a total rejection of the state-led economic policy that had defined Mexico since the days of President Cárdenas (1934–1940). The peak business organizations largely spoke with one voice in their advocacy of a radical program to privatize the vast state-owned manufacturing, industrial, and service sector firms that then defined much of the structure of the economy. This coincided perfectly with the IMF's programs of austerity and opening of the economy to foreign trade and investment, the World Bank's structural adjustment project to shrink the state, and the U.S. government's project to force free-market policies on Mexico as the price of any assistance.

Lurking behind all these combined forces was a strong perception, first encouraged by economists, and later endlessly echoed as "common sense" by government officials and especially business interests, that import substitution industrialization was "exhausted." This perception eventually became a mantra—a version of Margaret Thatcher's "there is no alternative"—TINA—form of dogma. Import substitution industrialization (ISI) seems not to have been well understood by the economists who sought to attack the underlying policy that had both led and guided Mexico's spectacular economic growth from the 1940s until the petroboom of the late 1970s.

The central problem in this discussion was that *Mexico's version* of ISI was opportunistically taken as the *definitive version* of ISI. Mexico, in fact, practiced what might be understood as *light or shallow* ISI policies that often consisted of the credit subsidies, tax exemptions, and the creation of tariffs and barriers shielding domestic producers from matching the evolution of international production capabilities. In a pioneering study on this theme, Fernando Fajnzylber made reference to "incomplete" and "frivolous" ISI attempts in Latin America in contrast to what may be termed *deep* ISI policies, in effect industrial policies, as practiced in Asia (Fajnzylber 1983). In the Mexican case, short-term incubation of infant industries was frequently transformed into a practice of long-term sheltering of firms and industries that maintained retrograde production practices and failed to reinvest their sizable profits in advanced technological capacities. Mexico lacked the *state capacity* to break this deadlock situation because, in a circular fashion, Mexico lacked a developmental state (as described in chapter 1 and Figure 1.1). As Alice Amsden has shown in comparative detail, Asian nations, following the broad outlines of ISI policies, and for the same reasons, were able to build their own national manufacturing champions. There, ISI policies emphasized selective, conditioned, and minimal reliance on foreign direct investment (FDI). Long-term investment in scientific research and engineering capabilities eventually yielded increasing returns in many areas as the Asian nations encouraged dynamic practices in product *upgrading*, thereby moving these economies away from labor-intensive production and simple products built with borrowed technology to practices that entailed technological learning and then technological *creation* (Amsden 2001). Not only did Mexico fail to develop a critical, creative, and dynamic application of ISI policies, it (both then and now) ignored the centrality of technological and scientific advancement—instead passively relying on transnational firms to introduce technology by way of FDI.

The attack on ISI was led by many analysts and interests but was buttressed by a widely cited study published by Julio Boltvinik and Enrique Hernández Laos (Boltvinik and Hernández Laos 1981, 456–534). These authors projected an exceedingly narrow, literal, and erroneous conceptualization of ISI: for them ISI was "exhausted" because by the late 1970s Mexico had already built sufficient capacity to provide through national production most all of the consumer goods needed by the economy. Further, great strides had been made in the national production of "intermediate goods" (inputs into the production process such as cement). However, largely untouched by ISI interventions was the import-dependent "capital goods" sector (machinery and equipment). It was argued that Mexico lacked the deep technological skills necessary to create nationally made substitutes for foreign-made capital goods. Thus, it was commonly argued, ISI was "exhausted" because most consumer and intermediate goods were already nationally produced and creating a viable capital goods industry was viewed as out of the question.

But what was ISI about? There was no shortage of answers to this question in Mexico. Yet in the rush to condemn the role of the state and the legacy of state-led development, scant attention was given to many of Mexico's best-informed voices regarding the economic programs of the state sector. In synthesis form here are the major contributions of the ISI strategy in stimulating economic development in the era of rapid growth:

1. ISI created new, necessary institutions that would never have been built by "free-market" forces because of the risk involved and/or due to prohibitive capital costs.
2. State-led development strategies maintained national sovereignty over resources such as oil, but were limited in developing scientific and technological innovation capacities.
3. Government-owned firms (or mixed public/private firms) permitted the expansion of sectors inadequately developed by private initiative.
4. Government firms, such as state-owned hospitals, fulfilled necessary social functions.
5. Government firms could help maintain an adequate level of employment (they could be consciously structured to adopt labor-intensive production methods).
6. State-owned businesses of high capital intensity could stimulate private investments in supporting activities, thereby propelling forward the entire economy.
7. State investments frequently functioned to introduce new process technologies and/or fundamental new products that raised the technological capacities of the economy at large (Cypher 1990, 141).

Any interested observer can study the tremendous success that developing nations have achieved through *systematic or deep* ISI—particularly in Asia (Amsden 2001; Chang 2003; Wade 1990). Asian nations used a distinct and highly successful stage approach to ISI that Mexico could have easily followed in the 1960s and 1970s. Starting with the substitution of simple consumer goods, Asian nations—particularly Korea and Taiwan—built proficiency and mass production capabilities by selling into their own market using infant industry forms of promotion. Once accomplishing that goal, these nations attempted to raise the proficiency of their domestic producers by selling their new, simple manufactures abroad. In doing so they raised their level of efficiency to world standards and achieved outsized economies of scale by having access to an extremely large market. With new know-how and foreign exchange earnings the Asian nations were ready to incubate a successor stage of capital and technology-intensive advanced consumer goods to be sold in their own market—while freezing out imports. Once again, having achieved minimal proficiency and experience in these areas, the new industries were led to compete in the international markets, thereby gaining access to economies of scale and new technological learning capacities. From here the industrial promotion cycle was extended to a *selected* array of capital goods. The process of first building capacity in the domestic market and later dramatically heightening this capacity in the international market was once again undertaken. Old industries and lemons were "sunset"—the state was both a *creator* of new capacities and an agent ready to jettison activities that had outlived their usefulness. In reference to figure 1.1 (chapter 1), the policies followed were evidence of the three necessary components of a developmental state—power plus purpose plus capacity. In short, as Robert Wade demonstrated, the Asians were intent on "*governing the market.*" As such, they were never passive, as has too often been the case in Mexico, regarding foreign investment. Only investors willing to put capital into projects that fit with the overall ISI strategy were welcomed. And some sort of technology sharing or reverse engineering was seen as a requisite by-product of accepting any foreign participation in the development schema (Cypher and Dietz 2009, 323–32).

Clearly, in the late 1970s, ISI was not exhausted in Mexico. Mexico's incipient version of ISI, however, was in need of fundamental change. By Asia's standards, ISI had hardly been tried. Thus, ISI is not an erroneous doctrine "proven false" by time—as can be readily understood by a simple study of Asia's success.

These points were well understood by a small cadre of professionals who sought to realign Mexico's ISI strategy during President de la Madrid's term. A dwindling cadre of "developmental nationalists" sought, under the PRO-NAFICE 1984–1988 program (the National Program to Develop Industry and Foreign Trade) to revitalize and redirect the ISI policies (de Maria y Campos et al. 2009, 37–41). PRONAFICE consisted of a rear-guard attempt to engage in a limited industrial policy designed to target and promote ten strategic

sectors of the economy. The general idea of PRONAFICE was to (1) consolidate the production chains of products designed for the internal market, (2)
selectively support the production of machinery and equipment—or capital
goods—that were overwhelmingly imported, (3) develop export capacity in
crucial sectors such as autos, and (4) support the general expansion of export
capacity (de Maria y Campos et al. 2009, 38). In short, PRONAFICE was an
ambitious program designed to restructure the Mexican economy through the
deepening of the then-existing shallow ISI programs. The 1980s, however,
were an extremely difficult period, as noted earlier. Oil price declines, bouts
of inflation, and the pressures of a profound foreign debt crisis all combined
to undermine the funding and long-term focus needed to realize the aspirations of PRONAFICE. The introduction of PRONAFICE came at a moment
of high tension between the business elite and the "developmentalist coalition" policy makers who sought to continue and deepen the era of state-led
industrialization. These tensions served to drive the peak business associations into a determined opposition to the broader aspirations of PRONAFICE
(Cypher 1990, 178–86). As a result, only five of the ten strategic programs
ever received funding—and for most of these the support was woefully insufficient. (One of the exceptions was the maquiladora industry, which commenced a growth spurt in the 1980s, as discussed in chapter 4).

During the ISI era, as Mario Cimoli and Jorge Katz have shown, nations
such as Mexico established incentives that allowed for a limited interactive
process of technological learning between local economies and the branch
plants of transnational firms (Cimoli and Katz 2001). During the neoliberal
era they documented an "unlearning" process whereby international firms
operated in their own closed technological enclaves while host "free-market" governments remained unwilling to impose demands, regulations, or
restrictions. Such governments, Mexico's above all, presumed that some
"invisible hand" would automatically spread learning effects into the national
economy.

It is worth recalling that in the crucial pivotal years of the early 1980s,
when Mexico eventually set a new course destined to arrive at its current state
of perdition, voices of opposition held some sway. Vladimir Brailovsky's
study, *Industrialization and Oil in Mexico*, advocated an expansion in ISI
strategies while claiming that Mexico's developmental barriers were *exogenous*, not *endogenous* (Brailovsky 1980). He, and others, pointed to the
rapid, large, and indiscriminate reductions in tariffs during the petroboom
era that had swamped many domestic producers with a level of international
competition they were unprepared to meet. Between 1977 and 1981 imports
grew at an annual rate of 28 percent—in clear violation of the national plan
that had stipulated a 14 percent rate of growth (Sosa Barajas 2005, 81–82).

Already under the allegedly "statist" presidency of López Portillo—in several of the agencies of the federal government where national policy was created and implemented—neoclassical economists dogmatically committed to a "free-market" strategy and the end of ISI interventions were powerfully entrenched. In this instance and others, they were able to wield decisive influence over trade and tariff policy—indiscriminately opening the floodgates to foreign imports without having created a competitiveness strategy for Mexican-owned firms.

THE AUTO SECTOR

The dispute over policy created a zigzag pattern in many important areas during the last years of the ISI era. For example, in 1977 the government passed a decree mandating that Mexico-based automobile producers collectively generate a positive trade balance (Mexico would export more cars than it would import) by 1982.[2] The decree served to turn around the situation in the auto industry, inducing a new pattern of production in the foreign-owned auto plants that drew in sizable foreign investments to meet the standards of the decree. However, there was no decree regarding auto parts. For the auto sector as a whole (autos plus auto parts) the trade deficit in 1980–1981 was four times greater than the average trade deficit for the sector in 1971–1979 (Sosa Barajas 2005, 126). Far from being an example of the failure of the ISI strategy, the decree itself had served its purpose. The problem was in the *unsystematic* nature of the decree—something easily remedied had policy makers sought to constructively engage the ISI strategy rather than sink it. In the late 1970s a study of the input-output relationships of the auto and auto parts sector clearly showed that further expansion would yield increasing returns through forward and backward dynamic linkage effects that induced investments, thereby creating employment, learning, and technological transfers. Growth in the sector would proceed at a rate higher than the general growth of the economy—meaning that it had "leading sector" potential, pulling along much of the national economy. As Sosa Barajas emphasized, the decree of 1977 was a "missing link" in Mexico's ISI strategy. At last, the approach was to follow along the path the Asian economies had traveled. The new strategy focused on *combining* support and incentives for the development of the *internal and external market*. Clearly, however, the flaw—easily correctable—was the exclusion in the decree of the auto parts industry.

With the peak business organizations on the attack as never before, and with wider splits opening between de la Madrid's nationalist economic advisors and a new cadre of U.S.-trained neoclassical economists who viewed

Mexico's interventionist past through the prism of meticulously constructed and totally irrelevant economic models of perfectly competitive advanced economies, President de la Madrid backed away from the development objectives embedded in the 1977 auto decree. In 1983 the Decree for the Development and Modernization of the Auto Industry was promulgated. Its purpose was to *drop* the required degree of national content from 60 percent to 36 percent by 1994 (Sosa Barajas 2005, 131). At the same time, in 1984, the effective tariff level for the auto parts industry was dropped from 28 percent to only 4 percent in 1987. Whatever hope there might have been for using the auto industry as a "leading sector" was gone. The most promising candidate for "national champion" stature had been decimated.

The gutting of the nationalists' strategy could not be solely attributed to the influx of neoclassical "whiz kids" who surrounded de la Madrid. Due weight must be given to the urgings of the IMF and the World Bank, both of which argued that Mexico's lengthy attempt to build up a national auto sector was "inefficient." In spite of the faith of these international financial institutions in "free-market" forces, the deregulation of the auto industry—as part of the new export-oriented strategy now imposed on the Mexican economy— yielded negative results: the import coefficient in the auto parts sector soared from 46 percent in 1983 to 71 percent in 1991.

Nevertheless, at this point public policy changed once again: A series of partial state interventions continued—in spite of the neoliberal ideology of Mexico's recent governments. By the early 1990s, the results in the auto sector were so disastrous that ISI strategies were again implemented in 1994. As a result the auto parts sector's trade deficit was reduced, eventually allowing the auto sector (auto exports plus auto parts exports minus imports) to operate with a very large trade surplus ($16.3 billion US in 2008). The inadequately funded National Development Plan 1995–2000 of President Zedillo (1994–2000)—a defensive nationalist initiative induced by the crisis of 1994–1995—allowed for some new caps on imported vehicles, thereby permitting a deepening of the industrial base in auto assembly and production. In 2004 all government support for the auto sector that had been permitted under the NAFTA accord was suspended. Nonetheless, as will be discussed in chapter 5, even under the neoliberal presidency of Vicente Fox, new follow-on state promotional policies were put in place in 2003.

POTENTIAL SUCCESS IN CAPITAL GOODS

Although subsequent commentary regarding the López Portillo petroboom era generally portrays government policy as cavalier and shortsighted, this was far from the whole story. The petroboom held within it genuine possibilities for the recasting of ISI strategies. There was a natural fit that Mexico's "developmentalist coalition" struggled to bring to life. Specifically, Mexico rapidly became a major participant in oil exports, thereby necessitating a demand for oil tankers that was initially met almost completely by imported ships. Of fifty-eight industrial sectors, shipping had the highest import coefficient in the early 1970s. Mexico under previous ISI policies, however, had already built a vast and relatively sophisticated (even innovative) steel industry. López Portillo's government, between 1977 and 1982, began a new initiative: "the fabrication of large ships of great complexity in national industrial shipyards characterized by a high level of technology" marked "the beginning of a new era" (Sosa Barajas 2005, 153). Indeed, Mexico quickly began to build what are known as "Panamax" ships, tanker ships of up to 80,000 tons of displacement that were the largest to fit through the Panama Canal. One of the three new or greatly expanded state-owned shipyards, AUVER, located in Veracruz, was charged with the task of processing thirty-five thousand tons of steel per year. This planned capacity exceeded by 3.5 times the total amount of steel processed at full capacity in all other national shipyards combined. From 1971 to 1975 the output of the national shipyards grew at an annual rate of 2.9 percent. With the new ISI project, between 1976 and 1982, production jumped to an annual rate of 17.9 percent (Sosa Barajas 2005, 154). Potentially the new strategy had the capacity to "pull" the entire artisan fishing industry into modernity. Given its access to two oceans, Mexico's new ISI strategy held out the possibility of creating a dynamic competitive advantage in a high-value-added industry (commercial fishing). This might easily have led to downstream activities such as fish processing and exporting. The sudden end of the petroboom, however, and the new affinity for neoclassical "free-market" policies meant that none of the broad potential from this project was to be realized.

NAFINSA: LAST EFFORTS TO REORIENT ISI

The history of Mexico's ISI era is inextricably tied to Nacional Financiera (Nafinsa), the largest government "development bank." In 1940, Nafinsa was directed by the Mexican government to pursue the following objectives: (1) promote industrialization, (2) promote the production of intermediate and capital goods, (3) invest in infrastructure, (4) help stimulate and develop indigenous entrepreneurial talent, (5) build confidence within the Mexican private sector, and (6) reduce the role of foreign direct investment in industry. Nafinsa went through two major stages: aggressive promotion of industrialization from 1940 to 1947 and then promotion of infrastructure and heavy industry from 1947 to the early 1960s. In making its investments, Nafinsa emphasized potential linkage effects. An emphasis on linkages is well known today, but in the early 1940s Nafinsa engaged in innovative policy making. In a classic study of Nafinsa, Calvin Blair emphasized the "systematic" nature of Nafinsa's investments:

> Nafinsa established in 1941 a department of promotion and began to make systematic studies of industrial development projects. With a predilection for manufacturing, it promoted enterprise in practically every sector of the Mexican economy over the course of the next several years. The roster of firms aided by loan, guarantee, or purchase of stocks and bonds reads like a "who's who" of Mexican business. (Blair 1964, 213)

In addition to promoting parastate firms, Nafinsa engaged extensively in lending long-term capital to the private sector and in forming partnership investments with both the Mexican private sector and international firms. Nafinsa was the state's anchor in a new economic model "based in the collaboration between the State and the private sector" (Arés 2007, 212). The Mexican state, primarily through Nafinsa, was the origin of 56 percent of all the fixed capital formation from 1950 to 1970 (Arés 2007, 213). By 1961, Nafinsa's investments were supporting 533 industrial firms, and its long-term investments were twice as large as the sum of such loans deriving from the entire private banking system. Nafinsa's role was a major pillar in what was then known as the "Mexican miracle." Nafinsa continued to be a prominent development agency through the 1980s, but its golden age was in the 1940s and 1950s, when the private sector's reluctance to commit funds to industry was particularly acute. By the early 1990s, all but thirteen of the hundreds of state-owned firms that Nafinsa had helped to create had been privatized, merged, or liquidated as successive neoliberal governments promoted privatization waves.

Given its tremendous influence in Mexico's growth strategy during the ISI period, it is hardly surprising that Nafinsa's highly regarded professionals opposed the new development model propounded by (1) de la Madrid's neoclassical economic advisors, (2) the new peak business organization, the CCE, (3) the IMF, (4) the World Bank, and (5) the United States under presidents Reagan and George H. W. Bush. Once nearly on a par with Mexico's central bank and the treasury secretariat, Nafinsa fell from the peak of Mexico's political-economic structure under President Echeverría (1970–1976). Yet in 1982 Nafinsa still provided 37.5 percent of all the credit available to the manufacturing sector. By 1991 this had fallen to only 10.3 percent (Becker 1995, 39).

Highly skilled at maneuvering within the structures of policy making, Nafinsa's specialists engaged in a rear-guard attempt to counter the momentum toward the construction of the neoliberal model in the 1982–1994 period. Nafinsa did not dispute the need for new export capabilities, which would demand a radical restructuring of the ISI model. Rather than scrapping that model, Nafinsa sought to build on the success Mexico had achieved—now by way of an active *industrial policy*. Industrial policy seeks (as we have noted) to provide, through state-driven activities, a *national project of accumulation*. In Mexico's case the economists at Nafinsa sought sector policies that would incubate key manufacturing activities such as autos and electronics that were understood to hold great competitive potential in the international arena (Casar Peres 1989). Yet, unlike the neoclassical economists and their neoliberal allies, Nafinsa maintained that Mexico should not abruptly and indiscriminately drop its tariffs and other forms of leveling the playing field between a backward and disarticulated national economy and those of the advanced industrial nations. Indeed, Nafinsa emphasized the fact that *no* advanced industrial nation had ever achieved its industrial status by following simple laissez-faire policies (Becker 1995).

State intervention, argued Nafinsa's economists, was a sine qua non of national economic development. This meant that Mexico would have to discriminate between forms and types of foreign direct investment and condition its role of host to foreign capital by way of adroit bargaining strategies (Pérez Aceves and Echavarría Valenzuela 1988, 43–45). Further, foreign direct investment (FDI) should be selectively permitted to the degree that technological learning and sharing could be achieved. Finally, and most importantly, FDI should be conducive to the development of a national industrial base of supplier companies that would acquire know-how through their interactions with the transnational corporations that were the repositories and creators of a great portion of technological capabilities.

Nafinsa opposed direct subsidies and tax reductions while favoring the incubation of crucial sectors through (1) the receipt of preferred access to credit, (2) an enhanced infrastructure, and (3) directed education and training programs. Targeted tax incentives and special credits were proposed to induce technological modernization and the adoption of cutting-edge technical changes (Becker 1995, 114–15). Guillermo Becker was prescient in highlighting the critical lack of advancement in research and development, particularly in the private sector. He advocated an array of interventions:

1. Strengthen a joint program of research and development between the universities and large industry, "establishing goals and specific programs of collaboration" (Becker 1995, 109).

2. Increase both short- and long-term financial and fiscal support for firms that make investments in scientific research and development of technology.
3. Search out methods, through a technically oriented program, to acquire and transfer cutting-edge industrial technologies.
4. "Establish a six-year investment target for the nation in scientific research and technological development that—at minimum—doubles the present level of such spending in relation to the GDP, pursuing private sector objectives that are periodically monitored" (Becker 1995, 111).

Above all, Becker argued that it was "indispensable" to establish a permanent program designed to create and integrate the production chains of national suppliers. Such a strategy would form the base of the national technology program. It would be necessary for the state to prioritize certain sectors of the manufacturing base and immediately pursue such a program (Becker 1995, 120). Failing this, the Nafinsa economists stressed, the policy of increasing low-value-added exports would simply result in Mexico's importation of capital goods and materials, leaving the country with a host of structural inadequacies: a generally stagnant industrial base, declining employment, deindustrialization, a backward educational system, weak performance in the area of endogenous technology, design, and innovation, a miserable level of technical training, a lack of integration with the supplier chains, and a general failure to modernize small and medium-sized firms (Becker 1995, 89).

THE RISE OF THE NEOCLASSICAL TECHNICIANS AND THE NEOLIBERAL IDEOLOGY

As we have shown, there is no real basis for the idea that ISI had been exhausted and that there was no alternative for Mexico other than to embrace an ultra laissez-faire national economic policy. Rather than adapting to new national *industrial and technological policies*, a series of events occurred that would shift the policy locus from reliance on endogenous economic forces to exogenous forces—forces that Mexico could scarcely influence in any way. The great transformation in policy, taking place in fits and starts during the six-year term of President de la Madrid, was subsequently consolidated during the whirlwind term of President Carlos Salinas (1988–1994). The structural changes completed in his term have yet to be altered in any meaningful way: the policies pursued under presidents Zedillo (1994–2000), Fox (2000–2006), and Calderon (2006–2012) have been noted for their continuity or "stability."

The crisis of 1982–1984 began a crucial process of restructuring the relationship between the state and the powerful peak business organizations, particularly the CCE. "After taking office at the end of 1982, President de la Madrid targeted the CCE in his efforts to win back *"confianza* and private-sector support" (Ross Schneider 2002, 98). A complex change began wherein the CCE and other peak organizations became crucial participants in what had been heretofore a largely closed policy-making process. Of course, the peak organizations had long been "consulted," and their views on national economic policy were given serious consideration. Yet state economic policy makers had long acted with a high degree of autonomy that they were now forced to forfeit. Business became much more embedded in the policy-making process, frequently setting the parameters. Co-consultation became the order of the day as the de la Madrid term neared its end: "Meetings between top government officials and the CCE became frequent. . . . From May 1986 to May 1987, the CCE had eighteen 'extraordinary' assemblies (in addition to its ordinary meetings), most of them with secretaries and sub-secretaries of economic ministries. Over the same period, CCE delegations met with President de la Madrid nine times and more than forty times with economic ministers" (Ross Schneider 2002, 98).

Apparently, the earliest initiatives for a new *free trade, export-led* strategy came from the Chicago School economists at Banco de México—the central bank (Thacker 1999, 59). By 1985 the IMF and the World Bank were active cosponsors of this project (Thacker 1999, 59). "When President Miguel de la Madrid fell in line with the [Bank of Mexico's] position in July 1985 . . . , the relative power of the free trade sponsorship acquired enough political momentum to lead Mexico toward trade opening" (Thacker 1999, 59).

Signaling the shift, Mexico joined the GATT in 1986—an event that most observers regard as a watershed. Obviously, membership in GATT meant that Mexico's tariff structure would be greatly revised and reduced. More significant was the symbolic threshold now crossed—until this watershed had been reached, Mexico had resisted membership in most international organizations, such as OPEC, where its independent, nationalist stance might be compromised. Soon Mexico would seek incorporation into the OECD—often known as the "Rich Man's Club"—since external affiliations appeared to confer a certain status the political elite now avidly sought.

Such changes, however, did not come easily as significant portions of the policy-making elite were deeply vested in the past—none more so than de la Madrid: ". . . the economists and other officials in the de la Madrid cabinet were by no means unanimously convinced of the desirability of a broader liberalizing program. De la Madrid [was] . . . a 'liberal developmentalist' of the sort that abounded in Mexico . . . during the 1950s. [They] firmly believed in the necessity of state intervention to promote development, including such measures as import substitution" (Babb 2001, 179–80). It is no minor designation to assign to de la Madrid the label "developmentalist." We agree with Babb on this crucial point, and we find unconvincing a broad literature that seeks to define de la Madrid as a neoliberal.

It is beyond doubt that the initial steps down the path to a full embrace of neoliberalism began during de la Madrid's term. But this momentous transition occurred because of the internal split within the ranks of the policy-making elite, and because of the mounting pressures on the state to move toward the neoliberal posture. These pressures came not only from within the several key secretariats of the state apparatus, but also and especially from the organized business elite—particularly from the Business Coordinating Council (CCE). Likewise, great weight must be placed on the neoliberal agendas pursued by the IMF and the World Bank as they successfully sought to make Mexico their greatest experiment in the application of a set of ideas later known as the "Washington Consensus."

Burrowing from within, in the relentless and undoubting style for which the Chicago School economists have become renowned, was Francisco Gil Díaz. Gil Díaz held an economics Ph.D. from the University of Chicago. He maintained a close relationship with the father of Chile's "Chicago boys"— Arnold Harberger. He and his central bank colleagues and allies within the secretariat of the treasury eventually won the debate over the direction of future economic policy. This victorious faction also drew strength from its active cooperation with World Bank policy initiatives. In 1984 the World Bank engineered a "trade policy loan"—the first ever granted to any nation—in order to implement massive trade "liberalization" (Babb 2001, 181). According to London's *Financial Times*, "Mexico went much further in reducing its trade barriers than the bank required" (Babb 2001, 181).

Mexico's policy makers were pressured to engineer concession after concession in the larger context of an economy that was clearly in a state of decomposition: In 1985 a letter from Mexico's central bank to the IMF struck an agreement to completely revise Mexican trade policy. In 1986 the United States pressured Mexico to accede to the IMF's free-market austerity model as the price to be paid for U.S. intercession in Mexico's negotiations with international banks to alter the burden of the foreign debt (Babb 2001, 181).

In an earlier time, growth had been driven by a rapid buildup of government investment that pulled along the rest of the national economy. From 1960 to 1980 public-sector gross capital formation (investment) grew at the spectacular annual rate of 10.6 percent (Sánchez Ugarte, Fernández Pérez, and Pérez Motta 1994, 19). With the state taking such a dramatic lead for such a long time period, it is hardly surprising that private-sector investment growth was also extremely high—averaging 7.1 percent. This illustrates the benefit of the "crowding in" effect—exactly the opposite result from the Chicago School's insistence that government spending "crowds out" the private sector. Indeed, it was the very purpose of the ISI strategy to "hothouse" private-sector investment by way of massive public-sector investments in crucial sectors that would generate a positive "externality" of inducing private-sector investment.

But now, in the siege atmosphere that set over Mexico for some time beginning in 1981, public-sector investment collapsed—falling at an astonishing annual rate of 7.8 percent for the period 1980–1985. Shrinking the state and starving it absolutely of any surplus that might be used to expand the capital base of the public sector was the *central idea* behind the new neoliberal strategy imposed upon Mexico. With but the scantiest of (distorted) "evidence," the ideologues pursuing the Washington Consensus model claimed that the state was the locus of all the inefficiencies within the economy. Meanwhile, the Asian states, particularly Korea and Taiwan, continued to pursue their version of ISI—further ramping up their economies in the course of the 1980s. In Mexico, as one would anticipate, the collapse in public-sector investment pulled down private-sector investment, which fell at an average annual rate of 2.2 percent. No economy could withstand such a downdraft wherein overall investment (public plus private) fell at an average annual rate of 4.5 percent in the 1980–1985 period (Sánchez Ugarte, Fernández Pérez, and Pérez Motta 1994, 19).

While the macroeconomy seesawed with two brutal downturns being experienced in 1982–1983 and 1986, the entire *sexenio* of de la Madrid was marked by a slight decline—GDP fell at an average annual rate of 0.1 percent (Cypher 1990, 158). This meant that *per capita income* fell at an average annual rate of 2.6 percent—or more than 16 percent through de la Madrid's term. For workers and the many millions whose income was determined by the minimum wage, matters were much worse. Manufacturing wages, adjusted for inflation, fell roughly *38 percent* from 1982 to 1988, more than double the rate of the general fall in the standard of living (Gambrill 2008, 65).

The neoliberals claimed that by shrinking the state, the private sector would flourish and investment—led by foreign capital—would soar, raising productivity and income as imported technologies were transferred into the production base. Mexico's experience has been distinct. From the onset of the neoliberal era, investment in manufacturing was weak, when not negative: from 1984 through 1993 such investment fell at an average annual rate of 3.4 percent, after which it grew at a near-stagnation rate of 1.8 percent annually from 1994 through 2000. But then, from 2000 through 2006, manufacturing investment again fell at an annual rate of 3.9 percent (de Maria y Campos et al. 2009, 69).

During the 1980s Mexico's economy was not merely sinking, it was being *structurally transformed*. The template for the new model was clearly based on the IMF's and World Bank's conception of *export-led development*. Export-led defined the new model. But *development*, in any meaningful sense, had all but ended for Mexico's majority. As we noted at the outset of this chapter, the growth of average annual income per capita was only 0.7 percent from 1983 through 2008. *None* of this meager growth went to the working class—in fact, real (inflation-adjusted) wages for manufacturing workers in 2002 were roughly 14 percent below their 1983 level (Gambrill 2008, 65).

Exports as a share of GDP had been very low in the 1960–1980 period— only 4.8 percent on average (Sánchez Ugarte, Fernández Pérez, and Pérez Motta 1994, 17). In short order this ratio would climb to nearly one-third of GDP: from 1985 through 1993 the export of Mexico's manufactured products "grew at a faster rate than any other country in the world" (Sánchez Ugarte, Fernández Pérez, and Pérez Motta 1994, 121). These exports were focused primarily on the U.S. market, where Mexico's market share of U.S. imports more than doubled from 1985 through 1993 (Sánchez Ugarte, Fernández Pérez, and Pérez Motta 1994, 145). The largest force in this rapid transition was the maquiladora industry—the vast assemblage of largely foreign-owned (particularly U.S.-owned) assembly plants that import virtually all of their inputs (minus labor) and, at that time, exported all their production. This industry's crucial importance in Mexico's new economic model will be discussed in detail in chapter 4.

Although in its general formation neoliberalism eschews any role for the state in the economy aside from that of a minimal "watchman," proponents of the export-led model argued that it was possible to grant an exception: The state could and should be a *promoter* of exports. This exception, however, is very curious. The Chicago School economists who ran the new economic policies in the industrial sector under President Salinas maintained that the role of the government should be strictly limited to "creating an environment for the efficient operation of the markets" while maintaining macroeconomic stability (Sánchez Ugarte, Fernández Pérez, and Pérez Motta 1994, 50, 119). In practice, Mexico's policies went far beyond any reasonable interpretation of these strictures, actively seeking to boost manufacturing exports through dramatic revisions in Mexico's foreign investment law and through targeted credits and subsidies to firms that were candidates for the new export-led model (Cypher 1991). Thus, while the new neoliberal dogma maintained that the state was the source of all economic inefficiency and that the resolution of the problem of the state was simply to shrink it to its minimal watchman level, in practice the Mexican state was both reduced and *redeployed*. Had there been any rigorous theoretical and empirical basis for the antistate perspective, it would have been impossible to confer upon the state such a central role in the new model.

As we have mentioned, the state, throughout the *light* ISI era, *initially* performed with a degree of adequacy in driving and guiding the economy. Yet weak and mistaken policies had a cumulative effect over time. Mexico breezed through what is known as "easy ISI"—the incubation of simple consumer goods industries—and then foundered, while the Asian nations seized on technology-centered strategies of upgrading, exporting, and diversifying never seriously attempted in Mexico. Had the state in the early 1980s been redeployed to construct a new *national project* built around the internal market, in the first instance, Mexico should have been able to recapture the dynamism it exhibited in the 1940–1982 period. To have done so, however, it would have had to build a dramatically different policy structure. Even later this could have been possible, it seems, had it not been for the fact that the presidential election of 1988 was effectively annulled by the Institutional Revolutionary Party (PRI), which stole the election from the nationalist victor, Cuauhtémoc Cárdenas (Krause 1998, 25).

Looking back on the restructuring engineered by the neoliberal faction within the de la Madrid administration, and especially the Salinas administration, Celso Garrido and Ricardo Padilla argue that the "negative externality" of the new model was the "segmented economy that 'externalizes' outside of the country all the dynamic factors of economic activity" (Garrido and Padilla 2007, 86). Further, they maintain that the "redirecting" of the economy toward the external market (through programs of privatization of state-run firms and deregulation—such as the abandonment of a cohesive tariff policy, which facilitated a tidal wave of imports—with the projected objective of attaining higher levels of efficiency) "never occurred, at least in the manufacturing sector" (Garrido and Padilla 2007, 95). In fact, the result was growth in the exports of manufactures *at the cost of shrinking of the domestic market for manufactures*. In this context, the nation *deindustrialized*, with the manufacturing share of the GDP dropping from 23 percent in 1998 to 17 percent in 2003. Manufacturing employment accounted for 12.8 percent of the labor force in 1982, falling to 11.8 percent by 2006 (de Maria y Campos et al. 2009, 65). Declines in this crucial sector have continued—employment fell by 12.6 percent from 2000 to 2008 (Secretaría del Trabajo y Previsión Social 2009). Their solution to the current impasse was to "rearticulate the external sector with the internal market" (Garrido and Padilla 2007, 86): ". . . under the new economic organization we have two economies: that of the external sector with a consistent expansive tendency and that of the consistently stagnate internal market" (Garrido and Padilla 2007, 99). In short, Mexico has to come to terms with a devastating industrial dualism that has arisen as a result of the embrace of the neoliberal export-led model.

FOREIGN DIRECT INVESTMENT:
A CORE COMPONENT OF THE NEOLIBERAL MODEL

The "externalized," manufacturing-led model was driven to some considerable degree by foreign direct investment, particularly from the United States. Mexico's two revisions in the law governing foreign direct investment (FDI) in the late 1980s and early 1990s opened up the Mexican economy as never before, leading to a surge in foreign investment that was impressive. During de la Madrid's *sexenio* (1982–1988), cumulative FDI slightly more than doubled. This pattern of cumulative increases in excess of 100 percent was repeated during both President Salinas's term (1988–1994) and that of President Zedillo (1994–2000). Then, President Fox's administration (2000–2006) witnessed a cumulative burst of 131 percent in FDI. After 2002, however, FDI ceased to grow in a largely linear fashion, with 2003, 2005, 2006, and 2008 showing relatively weak results (Secretaría de Economía 2009; Sánchez Ugarte, Fernández Pérez, and Pérez Motta 1994, 155; Guillén Romo 2004, 197).

The passage of the North American Free Trade Agreement (NAFTA) in late 1993 coincided with the second revision of the foreign investment law. The NAFTA agreement would appear to be a major reason for the abrupt increase in U.S. FDI from 1993 onward. Annual increases in U.S. FDI in Mexico averaged slightly more than $2 billion per year from 1990 through 1993. Then, from 1994 through 2000, they averaged $6.45 billion (Guillén Romo 2004, 197).

While the Mexican government has long portrayed the growing levels of FDI as important (if not fundamental) to Mexico's success, taken in broader context it becomes clear that only a small amount of Mexico's overall economic performance can be explained by levels of FDI. FDI, even when it finds its way into *productive* investments rather than largely superfluous expenditures on luxury shopping centers, hotels, ostentatious office buildings, or something similar, can either be *greenfield* investment (creating new plants or equipment) or a *buyout* of an existing firm. The data available do not allow for this distinction, but buyouts have been quite significant, judging from accounts of international acquisitions reported in the business press: Mexico was considered one of the top receivers of FDI in 2001, yet 71 percent of such investment was devoted to the purchase of already-existing Mexican companies (Gazcón 2002, 15). In any event, *under the most optimistic assumptions that ignore nonproductive investments and acquisitions*, FDI expressed as a share of total annual investments (or gross fixed capital formation) was only 10 percent in 2000 and 8.9 percent in 2006—two representative recent years (CEPAL 2008b, tables 2.1.1.41, 2.1.1.67).[3] If we generously assume a 10 percent addition to capital formation from FDI, and if we also wave away the problem of unproductive investments and related issues, using straightforward growth model calculations, one can estimate how important FDI is to growth. It can be shown that in 2006, when Mexico had a very successful year with GDP growing at a 4.8 percent inflation-adjusted rate, had there been *no* FDI, the growth rate would have fallen to approximately 4.1 percent (Cypher and Dietz 2009, 462). Put another way, even though FDI grew by 27 percent in inflation-adjusted terms from 2006 to 2007, the Mexican economy slowed down—growth that year was a modest 3.2 percent. Thus, even when Mexico achieved a high rate of growth of FDI, considered to be a great catalyst for the economy according to the neoliberal model propounded by the Mexican government along with the IMF and the World Bank, Mexico's growth rate *declined* by an impressive 33 percent. Clearly then, the importance of FDI in determining Mexico's economic performance is modest. And even when FDI is growing strongly from year to year, the economy can experience a significant *slowdown* in its rate of growth.

GROWTH: A LONGER VIEW

Proponents of Mexico's neoliberal export-led project have experienced two brief periods of euphoria when it appeared that Mexico might be undergoing a successful process of restructuring. As we have mentioned, the all-important de la Madrid years (1982–1988) were brutal, particularly for the working class. Then, according to noted historian Enrique Krauze, came "the man who would be king"—Carlos Salinas (Krauze 1998, 771–78). For a brief moment many observers, both in Mexico and abroad, announced that the new "Mexican miracle" had arrived: real economic growth averaged a healthy 4.25 annual rate from 1989 through 1992 (Nadal 2003, 57). The following year, 1993, the economy slowed to a rate of 1.9 percent. The crucial election year of 1994 seemed to find the neoliberal model in strong condition, with growth rising to 4.5 percent. A closer look, however, showed that the economy was terribly off balance. Mexico had a record trade deficit of 7.1 percent of its GDP in 1994. The Salinas administration was orchestrating an economic bubble—foreign borrowing was boosting the short-term growth possibilities of the economy. An economy with this sort of trade deficit was totally out of consideration in the context of the new neoliberal model. After all, the ISI era had been dismissively critiqued by virtually all observers because Mexico failed to build up its export capabilities in many areas. Now, with the pivot of growth being the export of manufactured products, what had happened?

Answering this question is one of the major objectives of this book. Before going into the detailed discussion undertaken in following chapters, we will review but a few of the major elements to be considered in evaluating the new export-led model. As mentioned, Mexico was quick to boast of the fact that between 1985 and 1993 the export of manufactured goods grew faster than in any other country in the world. A rapid structural transformation took place in the export sector during those years, with manufactured exports rocketing from 37.6 percent of all exports in 1985 to an astonishing 81.8 percent in 1993 (Sánchez Ugarte, Fernández Pérez, and Pérez Motta 1994, 145). In those heady days, the promise of vast new export opportunities under NAFTA had seduced most observers into the belief that Mexico had finally overcome the problems that had led to the collapse of the petroboom of the 1970s and the long stagnation of the de la Madrid era.

Had Mexico refound its formula for success, as Salinas and his advisors, particularly the arrogant secretary of the treasury, Pedro Aspe, who frequently spoke and wrote of the "Mexican way," proclaimed (Aspe 1993)? The Mexican economy fell apart in 1981, when the trade deficit was a record 6.1 percent of GDP. Now the trade deficit shot up to 4.6 percent of GDP in 1991, then to 6.7 percent in the following year, and to 5.8 percent in 1993. The Mexican economy was defying economic gravity year after year—an all-but-unheard-of stunt that Salinas's advisors interpreted as a vote of *confidence* in the new export-led model. Then came 1994, when, as mentioned, the trade deficit reached its outer limit—7.1 percent of GDP. At that time the IMF used a sort of crude shorthand to identify economies that were operating outside of safe conditions. A 3 percent deficit was considered a sign of great instability—at 5 percent the red lights were blinking nonstop, according to the rough formulations. By the known standards of international economics, it was as if Mexico were hurtling at the rate of 150 miles per hour the wrong way down a one-way street. A crash was foredoomed.

Once the devastating crisis of 1994–1995 came to an end in early 1996, the economy expanded at a rapid pace—growth averaged 5.4 percent for the five-year period of 1996–2000. During that time, as had been the case under Salinas, a boastful swagger became the hallmark of Mexico's political class. NAFTA, observers were told, was working. Mexico had refound the magic elixir of growth. President Zedillo (1994–2000) dismissed any and all critics of the new neoliberal model as "global phobic." Zedillo ushered in the end of the PRI's long one-party rule: his successor, President Fox (2000–2006), confidently predicted that he would lead the economy into six years of 7 percent real annual economic growth.

But the growth during the last five years of Zedillo's term was partly due to the catastrophic decline in GDP during 1995—the GDP adjusted for inflation did not reach its 1994 level again until late in 1997. The growth that then occurred was almost completely induced by the "new-economy" information technology (IT) boom in the United States. Once the NASDAQ index of IT stocks collapsed in early 2000—signaling the end of the speculative dot-com bubble—the Mexican economy began to unwind. President Fox's rhetoric notwithstanding, the Mexican economy was stuck in a trough of stagnation for three long years: over the course of 2001, 2002, and 2003, the Mexican economy expanded by only 1.5 percent. Per capita income declined, as the maquilization scheme fell apart. One of the leading sectors of Zedillo's maquila strategy, textiles and apparel, was decimated by new competition from China. There was a massive exodus of "footloose" foreign firms in labor-intensive processes, leaving Mexico bereft of a growth strategy.

Deep troubles in the U.S. auto industry led to another wave of U.S. capital shifting into Mexico in the 2004–2007 period. This helped to assuage the wounds opened by the decimation of the textile, apparel, and shoe industries, among others. The return to the bubble economy in the United States from late 2003 through late 2007 allowed for surging manufacturing exports. But equally important this time around were remittances from the millions of Mexican migrants to the United States who had been forced to flee their own country as a result of the neoliberal model—particularly its NAFTA component. And while Mexico was not as dependent as almost all Latin American nations on commodity exports, the boom in oil and gas and a wide array of minerals further boosted Mexico's export earnings while pulling in a new wave of resource-seeking FDI. In the run-up to the presidential election of 2006, as is always the case, the federal government, the state governments, and the municipalities spent lavishly. The demand for construction workers and building materials boomed, pushing Mexico's growth to greater levels as the multiplier effects of such programs reached across the broadest strata of society. The remittances brought new levels of spending to those most in need. All in all, 2006 was a strong year, with growth hitting 4.8 percent. The afterglow of the election and the continual runaway boom in the United States through most of 2007 kept the economy expanding at a respectable level.

None of this, though, eliminated Mexico's growing employment deficit—the need to find jobs for more than a million new entrants into the labor market every year. To cut into the employment deficit, the economy would have to expand at a 5 to 6 percent level for years. No one perceived this as remotely possible by 2007. In 2008 the economy once again returned to near stagnation—growth of only 1.8 percent.

The year 2009, as mentioned, took Mexico deeper into its "stop" phase in the "stop-and-go" dependent model that has dominated the economy since 1989. The old cliché, "Poor Mexico, so far from God, so close to the United States," had rarely been more apt. With Mexico in an absolute free fall, the Chicago School economists guiding Calderon were silent. Business interests cried out for Keynesian-style interventions and massive spending on much-needed infrastructure construction. Mexico had reached a crossroad, and there were no coherent voices urging a credible solution. Mexico had hitched its wagon to the U.S. economy. The United States was bordering on a depression. Mexico would now reap the harvest that neoliberalism had sown for more than a quarter of a century.

Chapter Three

NAFTA: U.S. Restructuring, Mexico's Realignment

For Mexico, no economic event in the past quarter century can remotely compare to the battle over the passage of the North American Free Trade Agreement (NAFTA) and the still-reverberating impacts of this watershed policy change. In the matters we examine in this book, NAFTA is not all-determinant. But it does, more often than not, provide the crucial *structural context* that serves to frame and inform much of our analysis. Put another way, NAFTA, in its preparatory, implementation, and consolidation stages, demanded and induced *structural change* in Mexico. How, why, and to what effect these preparatory, implementation, and consolidation stages were realized is the subject of this chapter.

THE U.S. CONTEXT

Before moving directly into this tangled web of causality relating to the NAFTA in Mexico, it is fundamental to stress the *asymmetrical* nature of the agreement. That is, while Mexico underwent structural changes as a consequence of the NAFTA, the impact on the United States was of a distinctly smaller magnitude. This is not to argue that NAFTA, and what it represented both symbolically and actually, was a minor undertaking for the United States. Rather, for the United States, NAFTA was an important part of a much larger undertaking. Precipitating NAFTA, in the U.S. case, was the gradual creation of the so-called triad system of global economic blocks. The spokespersons and scribes of the great economic powers spoke and wrote eloquently of a brave new era of seamless "globalization" wherein states and nations would relinquish much of their historical role. However, in the 1980s, there was a concerted effort to build up the European Union (EU) and deepen its ties with parts of the "developing world" that had legacy linkages originating in European colonialism. Japan was doing much the same in Asia.

Reacting to all of this—and particularly to its obsessive fixation on the idea of "Japan as number 1" sometime in the near future—the United States sought to build its own defensive/offensive block: first NAFTA, then a Latin American free-trade association. In essence, the great powers were at work building a global system that was, in many respects, the obverse of a "horizontal" globalized economic system as pundits propounded with the "world is flat" hypothesis. While the rhetoric of free trade echoed endlessly, powerful nations were consumed in a battle for exclusive or privileged position in matters of finance, trade, and production.

The key to understanding what was (and is) new and essential in the current era is the latter term—production. Until very recently, international economics had been defined by matters of trade and finance. Production was geographically anchored. Nations either had a national industrial base or generally sought to build one. Formal economics, particularly as practiced by specialists in international economics, proceeded as if production were some sort of "given" backdrop consideration. For example, whenever nations imported too much and exported too little, the national industrial base would shrink as foreign-made goods (presumably cheaper and/or better) were substituted for domestically made goods. Nations could not remain in a trade deficit position for long: a scarcity of foreign currencies would occur, went the argument, due to the fact that the nation was not exporting enough to "earn" the foreign currencies needed to fund the imports. As a consequence of its "scarcity" the "price" of the foreign currency would be bid up, meaning that exchange value of the national currency of the deficit nation would be pushed down. As a result, the exports of the deficit nation would be cheaper, and imports more expensive. This would expand exports, while imports would be curtailed. The former deficit nation would "automatically" move into a position of trade balance.

The production system behind this simple model was a mere yo-yo. In the assumed theoretical world, it went up, down, and all around. In reality, where *time* is a crucial variable, the trade deficit country would experience the destruction of its import-competing firms. Bankruptcy would result in the scattering in every direction of precious collective skills honed over decades or longer. Even *if* the relative repricing of currencies eventually led to a situation wherein it became lucrative to export, the nation's industrial base could be decimated by the past surge in imports. While the trade deficit nation went through a process of *deindustrialization*, the state of the art (technological dynamism) in manufacturing would continually advance. Thus, recovery would entail a double task: re-create production systems that were highly interdependent and tactic, and recuperate from a technological lag that had been introduced during the deindustrialization stage. According to conventional neoclassical economics, producers in a nation were expected to achieve such a monumental feat without any particular guidance or *national promotion* from the state sector. To do otherwise was to embrace "trade policies" and violate the free-market strictures that guided international economic analysis.

Deindustrialization, caused by import surges and by the new mobility of capital, occurred in the United States through the course of the 1970s, if not before. International economists confidently waited—based on the neoclassical analysis sketched above—for the U.S. trade deficit to go away while deflecting and dismissing those "uninformed" commentators who saw something fundamental and irreversible taking shape. According to these commentators (who were often tied in some manner to the "Rust Belt" states around the Great Lakes hardest hit by new competition from emerging nations and Japan), the United States was caught in a downward spiral of deindustrialization. Such tendencies continued and broadened in the course of the 1980s. Only recessions reduced the purchasing power to import. Each recovery and expansion brought a new wave of imports, new rounds of offshoring of the national production base, and a growing sense among many policy makers and corporations that the United States was losing out in the new era of "competitiveness." These new trends and issues—all in some way linked to the new mobility of capital—framed and conditioned the national response of United States policy makers and U.S. corporations. These forces eventually sought promotion of the NAFTA as one major means of addressing the need to restructure the U.S. economy in the new era.

THE CREATION OF NAFTA

The NAFTA accord had a long legacy: significant, at least in retrospect, was the creation of the Bilateral Commission on the Future of United States-Mexican Relations in 1986—an organization that brought together policy academics on both sides of the border and eventually produced an influential five-volume exploration of all aspects of integrating the two nations under the concept of interdependence. In November 1987 the Reagan administration (1981–1989) signed the U.S.-Mexico Bilateral Framework on Trade and Investment with Mexico, designed in part to recognize "the importance of promoting a more open and predictable environment for international trade and investment" (Glade and Luiselli 1989, 135). In April 1988 the Omnibus Trade and Competitiveness Act of 1988, one of the most sweeping pieces of trade legislation in U.S. history, was passed. This act included text relating to the U.S.-Mexico Bilateral Agreement of 1987, urging the president "to continue to pursue . . . an expansion of mutually beneficial trade and investment" (Glade and Luiselli 1989, 134). In November 1988 President-Elect Bush met with President-Elect Salinas in the United States, where Bush officially advanced the idea for the first time of a bilateral trade and investment agreement. Salinas then responded, "I am not in favor of such a proposal" (Cameron and Tomlin 2000, 59). Nonetheless, in October 1989 Mexico and the United States signed an "understanding" regarding trade and investment facilitation talks, which included an action plan wherein a period of negotiations was specified, from October 1989 through October 1991. Clearly, the eventual consolidation of NAFTA was not about "trade": on numerous occasions the Mexican government made it perfectly clear that enhancing foreign direct investment (FDI) and portfolio investment, not trade, was the motivator for Mexico in entering into what would become the NAFTA negotiations (Cameron and Tomlin 2000, 1, 40).[1]

By late 1993 the NAFTA deal was all but tied—the only variable left consisted of a few members of the U.S. Congress who, for various reasons, were not ready to vote in favor. The Clinton administration used every tool, fair and foul, to deliver the vote. In his brilliant and all-but-overlooked account, *The Selling of "Free Trade,"* John MacArthur recounts how the promise of a duck-hunting trip with Clinton was enough to buy one congressman's (Bill Brewster's) vote (MacArthur 2000, 263). Brewster's constituents were, at the time, 100:1 *against* NAFTA. With President Clinton engaged in twenty-one distinct acts of documented "vote buying," the House of Representatives passed NAFTA by a margin of sixteen votes on November 17, 1993 (MacArthur 2000, 264, 274). With the U.S. Senate's pro-NAFTA vote a foregone conclusion and with the (at that time) rubber-stamp legislative process in Mexico operating as expected, the NAFTA came into existence on January 1, 1994.

By December 1993, as the Mexican government hurried to craft a new law on foreign investment (opening up virtually all of the economy with the exception of the energy sector), it appeared that the essentially neoliberal regional project had gained unstoppable momentum. Outspoken opponents of the NAFTA commenced to grid themselves for a new reality that many had thought avoidable until the ultimate congressional vote. Imagine, then, the incredulity experienced by these opponents in Mexico as they reached for their daily newspaper on January 2, 1994. We understand that such incredulity was shared by President Salinas when his advisors caught up with him while he enjoyed a beach vacation. A group known as the "Zapatistas" had taken over some towns in the state of Chiapas—the southernmost state in Mexico. In the country where *no pasa nada* (nothing happens), something totally unexpected had happened. The Zapatistas stated that their armed uprising—such as it was—pivoted on the January 1 implementation of NAFTA. In time, the Zapatista uprising faded. But the sense that something final and inevitable had occurred—a sense that hung over all commentary from November 17, 1993, to January 1, 1994—was forever gone. NAFTA led to flash-point disputes before its passage, and it has continued ever so. In the U.S. presidential election of 2008, NAFTA returned as a major theme, particularly in the Rust Belt states. The two leading candidates from the Democratic Party, Barack Obama and Hillary Clinton, were forced to make vaguely anti-NAFTA commentaries while evasively promising to address some of the most egregious effects of NAFTA if elected.

The wild speculation regarding a "new economy" that filled much of the ether during the United States' most lengthy expansion from 1993 to April 2000 served to deflect critical analysis of the impacts of NAFTA. At the same time, the Clinton administration relentlessly pursued a sleight-of-hand argument that seemingly was never challenged by the broad consensus of orthodox neoclassical economists—some of whom played their chosen role in bolstering the argument. Time and again, the Clinton administration released stories to the press wherein it showed that NAFTA was creating jobs for the U.S. workforce. These studies, however, counted only the shift in jobs from domestic production to export production. They never counted the jobs lost through displacement due to surging imports from Mexico. We, and a quite small number of others, engaged the Clinton administration, using detailed statistical evidence to show the relatively large number of U.S. manufacturing jobs lost to NAFTA (Cypher 2001). Yet, given the general prosperity of the new economy years, interest in the theme of the adverse impact of NAFTA on U.S. workers evaporated. Economists who had provided elaborate "computable equilibrium models" showing beyond the shadow of a doubt that NAFTA was a "win-win" deal (discussed below), never returned to see what had actually transpired. Orthodox neoclassical economists, confident in their theoretical prognostications, never checked on their predicted results. NAFTA, indeed, was over. . . . Or was it?

With (1) the collapse of the new economy beginning in early 2000, (2) the recession that broke out in early 2001, (3) the slow "jobless recovery" that lasted into 2003, (4) the false boom of the housing bubble economy (2003 through November 2007), (5) the continued waves of deindustrialization washing away millions of manufacturing jobs in the first decade of the twenty-first century, and finally (6) the accelerating economic downturn beginning in December 2007 leading to the virtual collapse of the major pillars of the financial system by late 2008, a general malaise regarding globalization issues led to widespread doubt and even hostility toward NAFTA among the underlying population. "Free-trade" ideologues within the economics profession and a retinue of congressmen, lobbyists, and corporate chieftains, of course, continued to seek further NAFTA-style agreements. To the degree that this coterie could operate with autonomy, it is conceivable that forces that combined to generate the NAFTA might maintain a slight forward momentum. But the sense that these forces had mounted a juggernaut, palpable in the "win-win" days of the early 1990s, was gone. For example, a U.S. national public opinion poll in June 2008 showed that 56 percent of the respondents sought renegotiation of NAFTA, while only 16 percent opposed renegotiation (Rasmussen Reports 2008). More telling was the response of those who had been directly affected by free-trade agreements in general—by an overwhelming 73 percent response, this group found that the effect had been negative. Only 23 percent of those polled thought that free-trade agreements in general resulted in net job creation in the United States. Clearly, NAFTA was only one of many factors that had led to the decoupling of wage income from productivity, as shown in figure 3.1. Deep and unprecedented real-wage stagnation was unquestionably a concomitant of the new era of globalization, wherein the NAFTA had played a critical role. Productivity had nearly doubled from 1972 through 2008 (increasing 95 percent) while real inflation-adjusted hourly wages had fallen by 8 percent.

NAFTA created an impressive surge—a doubling and more—of outbound U.S. foreign direct investment into Mexico, particularly in manufacturing. The reality of NAFTA helped create a new bargaining climate between U.S. manufacturing firms and their labor force. In effect, U.S.-based corporations had a new and very viable option to reinvestment in the United States—and many took advantage of it either directly (by moving their operations abroad) or indirectly. Kate Bronfenbrenner's research on union election campaigns showed that union election win rates were only 24 percent in campaigns wherein workers were threatened with a plant shutdown followed by the offshoring of production (Bronfenbrenner 2000, 27). Mexico was the country most often cited by employers as the probable offshore site. While unionization levels for nongovernment workers had been falling for years prior to NAFTA's passage, they have continued to fall at an impressive rate throughout the NAFTA era. In 1978, 43 percent of male blue-collar workers were unionized, while in 2005 the number had fallen to 19 percent (Economic Policy Institute 2008, 5). Overall, the unionization rate fell by approximately 22 percent between 1993 and 2007. By keeping unions out and on the defensive, the positive wage spillover effects that unions normally confer on nonunion workers are circumvented. Figure 3.1—capturing forces far greater than NAFTA—demonstrates the results for employers and employees to be expected in the era of the internationalization of capital. In the early non-"glo-

Figure 3.1.　Real Wages and Productivity for U.S. Production Workers, 1972–2008

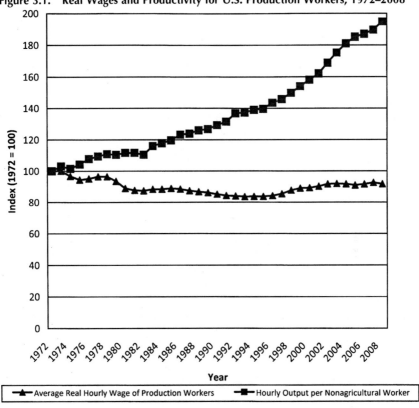

Source: "Hours and Earrnings," table B-47; "Productivity and Related Data," table B-49, *Economic Report of the President, 2009.*

balized" postwar era until the early 1970s, rising wages had closely tracked rising productivity. Since that time, workers' productivity gains—as a result of the weak bargaining position imposed on labor by the new mobility of capital—have gone to bolster corporate profits.

Labor markets are to some degree segmented. Thus several million Mexican workers who poured into the United States as a result of NAFTA—as discussed in chapter 6—often did not directly compete with U.S. workers in the manufacturing sector. Nonetheless, there is ample evidence that another factor contributing to the conditions found in figure 3.1 arises from the "race-to-the-bottom" forces operating in the U.S. labor market, where millions of Mexican workers, employed in the formerly high-wage unionized manufacturing sector (or elsewhere) have brought a distinctly lower "target wage" into the U.S. sphere of production. With this new imported leverage, U.S.

employers were better positioned to hold wages down or push them down further—for all production workers—even as productivity soared.

ECONOMISTS IN THE SERVICE OF NAFTA'S PROMOTERS

The public relations campaign to promote NAFTA was adequately discussed in the popular press. Missing from the discussion, then and now, was the crucial role of orthodox, or mainstream, economics in the selling of NAFTA—not only in the United States, but also in Mexico. In Mexico, for example, the powerful head of the secretariat of commerce and industrial development (SECOFI), Jaime Serra Puche, repeatedly argued that there was no possible debate over the effects of NAFTA. Serra Puche was a dedicated advocate of the ultra laissez-faire Chicago School approach, as demonstrated in the introduction he wrote to an important book, *Industrial Policy under Conditions of an Open Economy*, authored by three Chicago School economists he employed (Sánchez Ugarte, Fernández Pérez, and Pérez Motta 1994, 7–10). In the tense run-up to the U.S. congressional vote on NAFTA, Serra Puche proclaimed that twenty-three economic studies had been conducted on the effects of NAFTA and that "all 23 have shown that employment in all three countries (Canada, Mexico and the United States) would rise" (González Pérez, 1993, 3). Meanwhile in the United States, pro-NAFTA legislators such as Representative Phil Crane relied on the most widely cited studies to claim that "NAFTA is not a partisan issue" because it had been determined by these orthodox economists to be "a job creator here [in the United States] by every major study" (Wagenheim 1993, 1). Confronting reluctance in the United States to go forward with the NAFTA agreement, President Clinton tacked on side agreements—sold to the U.S. public as safeguards governing labor conditions and environmental impacts. Serra Puche, after meeting with Clinton's special trade representative (Clinton's interlocutor), returned to Mexico and "happily assured Mexican businesspeople that the side agreements were meaningless" (Faux 2006, 13).

The selling of NAFTA in the United States constituted a twofold process—the *organization* of the power bloc of interests in support, and the *disorganization* of the opponents (and potential opponents). In *disorganizing* the opponents the role of economic science was particularly crucial. Top international economic policy makers in the United States, such as the U.S. special trade representative, the U.S. International Trade Commission, the secretaries of commerce, labor, and the treasury, and peak *parallel* institutions such as the (liberal) Brookings Institution and the (right-wing) Heritage Foundation portrayed one cluster of "research" that supported NAFTA as scientific, authoritative, and inclusive. In the same instance, all other research was portrayed as nonrigorous, eclectic, and (above all) protectionist. The linchpin consolidating the neoliberal project was the construction of a *paradigmatic* intellectual construct whereby it was asserted and vociferously repeated that NAFTA was, of necessity, a "win-win" proposition for the United States and Mexico. A major part of the effort to sell the U.S. public on the NAFTA project had to do with a reshaping of Mexico's image. A series of purportedly "academic" and therefore "disinterested" studies flowed from the Brookings Institution (in this instance, closely tied to the World Bank), the Organization for Economic Cooperation and Development (OECD), and the Interamerican Development Bank designed to demonstrate that Mexico had learned its lesson—it would willingly disengage from the "developmentalist coalition" and follow the new neoliberal script (Lustig, Bosworth, and Lawrence 1992; Lustig 1992; OECD 1992; IDB 1992). What exactly made Mexico a viable candidate for a new economic partnership varied somewhat with each rendering. Still, the most often cited elements were:

1. Resumption of economic growth (due to the embrace of ultra laissez-faire policies)
2. Increase in foreign investment (due to the curbing of ISI and industrial policies)
3. Reduction in foreign debt
4. Elimination of the public-sector deficit
5. Privatization of state-owned industries
6. Increase in manufacturing exports

The real story, of course, was more complex and less clear. For example, Mexico had spectacularly failed to cover its surging imports with its rising manufacturing exports, opening up then a record trade deficit of nearly 7 percent of GDP in 1992. Well-known Mexican commentator Jorge Castañeda charged that the trade deficit—largely explained by runaway U.S. exports into Mexico—was a *conscious* maneuver on the part of ever-agile President Carlos Salinas to sell the NAFTA in the United States (Castañeda 1993, 41). After all, if the United States had an overwhelming trade surplus with Mexico, what could be the harm of opening up the Mexican demand for job-creating U.S. products even further?

In a public relations onslaught with few precedents, the United States government portrayed the epic struggle over NAFTA as one wherein a disinterested but powerful observer (the United States) merely wanted Mexico to receive its just rewards for exemplary behavior. In this touching account, President Salinas had engineered a successful program of economic modernization. Given this, it would be exceedingly shortsighted for the United States to forgo ratification of NAFTA, thereby imposing a policy defeat on a struggling nation in the midst of a dramatic turnaround. Further, Mexico stood out as the leading example to all struggling nations showing what could be achieved through discipline, hard work, and good economic policy—all of which ultimately was attributable to the primacy of both the market and the private sector.

Thus was constructed a towering myth of Mexico's "successful restructuring." Looking behind the curtain, Salinas's record was unimpressive. Growth was at half the level achieved in the 1940–1982 period. Rather than being an example of reliance on market forces, Mexico's privatizations had been scandalously corrupt—although, perhaps, the matter was not well understood in the United States at the time (MacLeod 2005; Teichman 1995). Mexico's growth, such as it was, had a great deal to do with forms of external assistance rather than private initiative driven by competitive market forces. The modest growth achieved was closely tied to massive, unprecedented support by the international financial institutions (the Interamerican Development Bank, the International Monetary Fund, and, above all, the World Bank). From 1988 through much of the 1990s, Mexico received more assistance from the World Bank than any other nation. The multilateral flows had the intended effect of bolstering financial flows and FDI into Mexico. In the case of the United States, bilateral flows were important—in 1992 the U.S. export-import bank (Eximbank) had an impressive $7.5 billion worth of export credits outstanding to Mexico, entailing fully 50 percent of its exposure to all of Latin America. As Mexican economists increasingly began to charge, the anemic growth was "exclusive" because wages fell across the board as the economy expanded. For example, in 1992 the poorest 29 percent of the labor force had wage income, adjusted for inflation, that was 64 percent below levels achieved in 1976 (Corro 1993, 26).

Mexico at that time had a curious way of tracking its foreign investments, lumping in financial flows with investments in plant and equipment. This was done in order to show big numbers to a willingly credulous U.S. policy-making elite bent, for reasons ideological and pragmatic, on responding to a massive lobbying effort by U.S. transnational corporations seeking to guarantee their global reach into Mexico. It is well worth recalling that the lobbying efforts and general selling efforts mounted in the United States by both the U.S. transnationals and the Mexican government were without precedent in the history of the United States (Cypher 1993a). Indeed, observers stated that Mexico's lobbying effort in the United States was, at that point in time, the most elaborate and costly ever mounted by a foreign government (Vita 1993, B1). Thus, behind the smoke and mirrors, the increase in private-sector investment in the Salinas period was suspect. Aside from growing investments in the maquiladora, electronics, and auto sectors (to be discussed in the following chapters), money seemed to be flowing largely into speculative activities driven by the surge of income received by the most affluent. For example, in Mexico City alone there was an estimated increase of more than $3.5 billion in commercial building construction from 1989 through 1992. More than $1 billion was sunk into 150 new shopping centers, $2 billion went into office buildings (many used to house the offices of stock brokerage firms trading shares in Mexico's wildly growing stock market), and one-half billion dollars was poured into new luxury hotels (*El Financiero* 1992, 3). In 1993, more than 56 percent of Mexico's accumulated FDI (as then defined) was sunk into the stock market. (As the fatal moment for the final vote on NAFTA neared, according to the authoritative Banco de México, 77 percent of the foreign investment flowing into Mexico was to purchase government debt, corporate debt, and stock market shares in the first quarter of 1993.)

The above details, of course, are far from a definitive list of the many largely ignored factors that could have served to demythologize the idea of President Salinas as a magical leader who, with well-trained Chicago-boy economists, was "remaking" (in reality "unmaking") Mexico. We, like other critical observers of the Salinas *sexenio*, took pains to point out the above relationships (to little avail) prior to the passage of NAFTA and long before Salinas's financial house of cards collapsed in late 1994. An ironclad myth of a "remade" Mexico had been constructed.

Astonishingly, this myth would be resurrected under President Zedillo during the growth spurt from 1996 to 2000. One good indicator of the weakness of the underlying economy at this point in time (and up to the moment) was the stagnation in manufacturing employment due to the dwindling internal market that depended upon the earnings of working-class and lower-middle-class Mexicans. But employment of production workers in the maquiladora export sector rose by 120 percent from 1994 to 2000 (Cypher 2004a, 362). Nonetheless, by offering wages that were only 60 percent of those in non-maquila manufacturing in 2000, the rapid employment growth in the maquila sector was insufficient to raise the overall wage bill (maquila plus non-maquila) received by manufacturing production workers.[2] Including production workers, technicians, managers, and professionals, 4.2 million labored in the manufacturing sector at its peak in October 2000, falling to 3.1 million in April 2009 (Secretaría de Trabajo y Previsión Social 2009). In nine years, 26 percent of manufacturing employment disappeared. The national industrial base, in spite of an on-and-off speculative financial boom, was shrinking.

It is in this broader context that the NAFTA economic modeling exercises of the orthodox economists, overwhelmingly conducted in the United States, must be understood. The great expectations of NAFTA's positive impacts on Mexico that were projected by orthodox economists through their modeling were explicitly or implicitly premised on the false assumption that Mexico's economic system had been successfully restructured. Thus, the "selling of Mexico"—an integral part of the larger process of the selling of NAFTA—consisted of a policy offensive to solidify the Salinas administration's neoliberal project while portraying it as the completion of the only rational course of action. A false past-future nexus was thus created, producing the underlying justification for the NAFTA project. Had the recent past been correctly revealed as a failure, the likelihood of future success with the incorporation of NAFTA would have been diminished. The process that linked the fictionalized past to the projected future pivoted, in many respects, on the exercises conducted by economists in the 1991–1992 period that were designed to predict the economic effects of NAFTA. Certain of these models—only those generating positive results for the United States and Mexico—were repeatedly portrayed as the *authoritative* studies by a variety of U.S. government entities and key policy-making organizations mentioned above. In addition, the powerful Washington-based Institute of International Economics should be mentioned. The list goes well beyond these participants to include the Mexican federal government agencies, the all-important U.S. transnational corporations, and their representative advocacy organizations such as the peak business association, the Business Roundtable, the quasi-governmental Advisory Committee for Trade Policy and Negotiations (dominated by the largest U.S. transnational corporations and established specifically to give them direct advisory authority over U.S. government entities), and the U.S. Alliance for NAFTA (known as USA*NAFTA).

USA*NAFTA was actually a lobbying front for the Business Roundtable (MacArthur 2000, 168). The Business Roundtable was created in the 1970s through the initiative of the leaders of the largest U.S. corporations, such as DuPont. Only 500 chief executive officers (CEOs) are allowed to be members—but they control trillions of dollars of corporate assets and tens of millions of workers' lives. "The guiding idea behind the Business Roundtable was that politicians might shrug off a company's middle management and paid lobbyists, no matter how large and powerful the company was, but they would listen to the CEO" (Phillips-Fein 2009, 190). According to MacArthur, the Business Roundtable consists of "a group of people so self-confident and secure in their access to political power that . . . they actually strive to keep their names out of the [news]paper. In their rarified stratum, satisfaction comes from getting their job done . . ." (MacArthur 2000, 168). USA*NAFTA's massive crusade to force passage of NAFTA, carefully chronicled in John MacArthur's *The Selling of "Free Trade,"* was facilitated by mailings to untold numbers of organizations and individuals involved in the issue, always with official stationery that carried their slogan, "North American Free Trade Agreement—Exports. Better Jobs. Better Wages." James Robinson, CEO of American Express, pushed members of the round-table into a vigorous effort to put the negotiations of NAFTA into a fast-track form in early 1991 by evoking the United States offensive in Iraq—the battle on the home front was the equivalent of "Desert Storm," he argued (MacArthur 2000, 216). As USA*NAFTA extended its efforts, it brought together a coalition of 1,000 members combining the top tier corporations of the Business Roundtable with other organizations such as the National Association of Manufacturers.

The most powerful weapons in their war strategy were the quantitative economic models showing the outsized mutual benefits certain to come from NAFTA. They widely and repeatedly publicized these models, and their efforts resulted in a largely successful effort to *intellectually hegemonize* the "win-win" outcome of the models. In this atmosphere, critics could not penetrate the precognitive fog orchestrated by the corporate onslaught.

COMPUTABLE GENERAL EQUILIBRIUM MODELS— WALRAS'S LEGACY

At the time we argued, and in retrospect it is clearly true, that elite policy making is not all-determinate but rather vulnerable, as is the important ideological function of orthodox economic modeling. Yet timing is of the essence. Accountability—for bogus arguments and/or slipshod economics—is not a generally accepted standard among those who set the rules or hegemonize a profession. No reputations among the self-anointed "scientific" and "rigorous" name-brand economists ever seemed to suffer from getting NAFTA wrong—spectacularly wrong. It was possible, as we argued at the time, to demonstrate that the predicted results of this orthodox modeling did not arise through scientific analysis, but rather as a result of methodologically inappropriate *aprioristic* assumptions (Cypher 1993a).

Without needlessly belaboring the matter, it is important to understand the broad nature of the models used to sell NAFTA. The "win-win" models were based upon a variant of a perfectly competitive general equilibrium model of a Walrasian nature. Léon Walras, a somewhat obscure nineteenth-century French economist, had some fanciful ideas that came to dominate much of theoretical economics at the close of the twentieth century. Walras assumed that economic systems were fluid, mechanistic, and harmonious. In such a system—stripped of history, institutions, and power—markets would assure that just the right amount of each and every product, in each and every market, would be produced and exchanged through flawlessly competitive markets. When trying to model the anticipated results of greatly enhanced *trade* (by assumption, *investment shifting* to Mexico was not part of the exercise), a technical variant of the Walrasian case, known as a computable general equilibrium (CGE) model, was used. The CGE model allowed the modeler to back out minor elements of Walras's restrictive theory. This permitted the modelers to simultaneously admit that the economy of a *developed* nation (the United States) was distinct from a *developing* economy (Mexico) while maintaining virtually all of the Walrasian assumptions regarding the workings of competitive markets. Mexico's oligarchic structure, entailing controlled markets manipulated by the national power groups (or conglomerates), uncompetitive capital markets, peasant agriculture, the informal economy of street vendors, and so on, was unaccounted for by these modelers who *assumed* these inconvenient structural features *simply did not exist*. Had they not, they would have had no basis to build their models.[3]

In the briefest form, these Walrasian-CGE style models assumed that all markets "clear"—which meant that in the labor market there could be no unemployment. Mexico's real rate of unemployment, could it be measured with any accuracy, would be alarmingly high. In essence, the unemployed become invisible to the statistical eye—migrating, performing juggling tricks at intersections in the cities, selling trivial products on the streets, or simply sitting at home or in a park. (Hence the terms "disguised" unemployment or the "informal" sector.) The list of other assumed conditions is relatively long—and each and every one must hold for the results to be valid. Among the other assumptions it is necessary that there be no market failures or externalities—meaning that market prices lead participants to buy and sell exactly the right (socially optimal) quantity of a product. If the social optimum varies from the market result, the market fails. If smog in Mexico City reduces the work efficiency of labor force participants (and it does), and if the buyers of gasoline are not somehow charged a fee that takes into account this external effect (and they are not), and if the victims of the smog are not somehow materially compensated for their suffering (and they are not), then the market for gasoline is not functioning as assumed in a Walrasian model. Ubiquitous externalities and market failures are part of the warp and weft of any developing nation, of course. But the list goes on—all firms are assumed to face competitive markets for their factor inputs. In reality, many companies have tremendous leverage over their workers, and they buy inputs from giant Mexican conglomerates and/or transnational corporations that frequently exercise immense power in pricing their products. And still the list goes on—banking and finance are assumed to be seamlessly competitive, all participants in all markets are rational, they have "perfect knowledge" of all economic alternatives and future effects, all consumers are rational maximizers, and so on.

In short, the make-believe Walrasian-CGE construct is at best silly and irrelevant. Only vast ignorance of the reasoning behind these models, never clarified but rather deliberately obscured by orthodox economists, could allow such a travesty as the purported economic case for NAFTA to have been made. But it was—and with great effect, as the public was incessantly bombarded with the general results of these models, which predicted greater growth in both nations, more employment, rising wages, and balanced trade. One of the most important assumptions that Walras ever made was that *economics was reducible to exchange*: matters of production and technology were not relevant to the CGE modelers (Hunt 1979, 266).

In other words—following the general theory of comparative advantage—Mexico's assumed-to-be fully employed, fully utilized production system was to *shift* toward the production of labor-intensive activities (because labor was cheaper) as a result of NAFTA. Meanwhile, (by assumption), the U.S. economy was also fully employed and fully utilized. Hence, production would shift toward capital-intensive and knowledge-intensive activities (because capital and knowledge were cheaper in the United States). But no one would be lost or injured in the shuffle (resources are fungible in competitive markets, by assumption). The importance of these assumptions is that the analysis then led away from production to *exchange*, or *trade*. As a "free-trade" deal, NAFTA was portrayed merely as *a shuffling of inputs toward greater relative specializations*—Mexico would do more of what it could do cheaper and sell its surplus to the United States. The United States would do what it could do cheaper and sell it to Mexico. Both nations' consumers would be better off because their existing standard of living would be enhanced. This result *could not* be achieved without specialization and trade because each nation (by assumption) had intrinsically different possible combinations of inputs (labor, land, and resources, accumulated stocks of machinery and equipment), which uniquely allowed for *complementary* specializations in each nation.

But, of course, NAFTA was not really a trade deal—it was a project to open Mexico to U.S. foreign direct investment. (In the early 1990s average tariffs on products shipped from Mexico to the United States were only 3 percent.) The models assumed there would be no shift in capital from the U.S. to Mexico. (Some models allowed for capital flows into Mexico but asserted that no capital would flow *out* of the United States. This assumption prevailed in spite of the fact that Mexico at that time was receiving roughly two-thirds of its FDI from the United States.) Only *exchange*, not production, would be important. Today many, perhaps most, economists share Walras's conceit that exchange *is* economics, thereby ignoring all-important production-related issues.

CGE models generally incorporate the multiple and very restrictive and unrealistic assumptions of neoclassical competitive general equilibrium theory with very selective use of innovations arising from the "new international trade theory." Coming into prominence in the 1980s, new international trade theory forms the theoretical basis for "win-win" scenarios in international trade. This stands in stark contrast to earlier factor price theories of trade, which demonstrate that a high-wage nation's labor force (the United States) would be adversely impacted by enhanced trade with low-wage nations.

The starting point for the argument that the hypothesized gains from trade are of a magnitude two to three times greater that that to be anticipated by earlier neoclassical trade models is the assumption that both trading nations encounter *increasing returns to scale* (systems of production become more efficient as output volume rises). Furthermore, these *increasing returns* are shared equally across all regions, industries, and nations. Remarkably, all nations are assumed to be competitive in trade, independent of their current costs and the state of their industrial base prior to trade. In addition to the *increasing returns* assumption, there exists, by assumption, *national product differentiation.* Differentiated products are products that somehow carry distinguishing characteristics. Under this assumption, Mexican auto-parts producers cannot attract capital investments away from the United States because, by assumption, U.S. auto parts are "differentiated." This assumption eliminates adverse dynamic effects of trade—particularly the elimination of a high-cost industrial structure (the United States) that is shifted to the low-cost nation (Mexico). In the old trade models, factor prices tended to equalize—predicting a big drop in wages for U.S. workers.

The new international economics (NIE) argued that this equalization process would not occur because the marginal product of labor (determining its price) rises as increasing returns occur. But also, in part, wages in the high-wage nation remain high because product differentiation leads consumers to "prefer" some U.S.-made products—even when prices might be higher. The results of all of these assumptions (increasing returns and product differentiation) function to ensure the generation of a "win-win" scenario.

In several of the models utilized, consumers are assumed to behave in a curious manner: by assumption, their expenditure share of imports versus exports is maintained constant—there can be no increased consumption of imports as a share of income by either modeled trading nation. This assumption of unitary elasticity of demand eliminates the possibility of shifting industries from one nation to another. James Stanford summed up the "Alice in Wonderland" character of the CGE models based in the NIE assumptions:

Predictions of the model depend on its assumed theoretical structure, but there is no way of empirically testing within the CGE model whether that assumed structure accurately describes the real economy or not. . . . CGE models are circular: if theory holds that free trade is mutually beneficial, then a quantitative simulation model based on that theoretical structure will automatically show that free trade is mutually beneficial. . . . [T]he apparent consensus of CGE modelers that a NAFTA will be mutually beneficial reflects more a consensus of prior theoretical views than a consensus of quantitative evidence. (Stanford 1993)

In spite of Stanford's brilliant critique, the CGE models formed the core of both the U.S. and Mexican governments' case for NAFTA. In February 1992 the U.S. International Trade Commission (ITC) hosted a conference promoting the work of the CGE modelers (USITC 1992). Acting as an uncritical promoter of these models that had generated the desired results, the ITC effusively stated that "CGE models are firmly grounded in economic theory," with "rigorous underpinnings" that showed that "all three countries are expected to gain" from NAFTA (USITC 1992, v). The U.S. special trade representative stated that the conference would demonstrate the administration's "serious commitment . . . to consider all *qualified* research results pertaining to *valid* arguments raised by *all* parties involved in . . . the debate" (USITC 1992, A-3, italics added). Similarly orchestrated events were set up by the Brookings Institution in early 1992, followed by yet another by the U.S. International Trade Commission in January 1993, again showing that NAFTA was, according to the economics professionals, without possible grounds for doubt, a "win-win" situation for the United States and Mexico (Cypher 1993a, 157–58). At this point it was left to President Clinton and his vote-buying techniques to carry the project to its triumphal end.

THE MEXICAN CONTEXT: A MORPHOLOGY OF NATIONAL CAPITAL AND FOREIGN DIRECT INVESTMENT

Ten years later, unsurprisingly, both the World Bank and the U.S. government reached the conclusion that only roughly 25 percent of the increase in Mexico's exports, subsequent to the passage of NAFTA, was due to the reduction in tariffs, trade barriers, and the guarantee of access to markets in each nation (Lederman et al. 2004). In other words, 75 percent of the increases in Mexico's exports were due to factors that were left out of account by the CGE estimates. Most of this, of course, could be explained by the surge in foreign direct investment, which Mexico received primarily from the United States. The remainder was to be explained by the restructuring that occurred within the Mexican national power groups (or conglomerates), as discussed below. In short, in only ten years the World Bank and the ITC had pivoted away from their "scientific" opinion that *exchange* effects would explain the results from NAFTA—capital would not move. Now they were forced to admit that investment shifts were at the core of the NAFTA project—something that could have been learned simply through close observation of the business interests that ultimately propelled and steered the NAFTA project while using the willing expertise of the economics profession to release clouds of obfuscation. In looking back at the NAFTA debate and the real effect that NAFTA had on Mexico, it is not possible to isolate the impact of NAFTA from other events that have influenced the course of events in Mexico.

Our goal is to offer a qualitative assessment of Mexico's socioeconomic performance during the period of *export-led growth*, recognizing that NAFTA has been a significant part of that larger project. From a historical perspective, it is clear that NAFTA was part of a long and complex process of opening Mexico's economy, a process in which institutions, accords, laws, understandings, and social relations built or formed during the epoch of President Cárdenas (1934–1940) were destroyed. Obviously, however, no matter how radical might be the change imposed, elements of the past cannot simply be erased.

When the crisis of late 1994 began, continuing with devastating force through 1995, it became obvious that the neoliberal model was failing. Instead of being a silver bullet, the NAFTA did not allow Mexico to sidestep its then worst economic depression since the 1930s. But in spite of all the devastation that followed from the Salinas administration's hothouse methods of advancing the neoliberal project, which ended in the wreck of 1994–1995, a sustained recuperation from 1996 to 2000 allowed for sufficient space to reconstruct a level of confidence in the new model. This permitted Mexico's political class to return to its agenda, amplifying structural changes while consolidating further the neoliberal model. But with the onset of a subsequent serious economic downturn (brought on by a recession in the United States in early 2001), the beginning of the end of the neoliberal model was in sight. Early in 2001 the majority of Mexicans surveyed indicated that NAFTA had not benefited Mexico (Moreno 2002, 169). This signified a momentous change from the generalized euphoria among most Mexicans in the early 1990s when Salinas confidently repeated that Mexico was on the threshold of entry into the first world. Mexico must "accelerate the internal economic transformation [and] increase our participation in the global market [because]" (said Salinas in his second presidential report) "we want Mexico to be part of the first world, not the third" (Puga 2004, 73). While many, encouraged by the political class, believed that shortly there would be steady signs of income convergence between Mexico and the developed nations, the development gap has widened. In 1980 Mexico's per capita GDP was 47 percent of the average OECD level, but by 2005 it had fallen much further behind, registering only 34 percent of the OECD level (Moreno-Brid and Ros 2009, 223). This calculation actually underrepresents the degree to which a median household lagged behind in Mexico since the distribution of income was even more unequal in the neoliberal era than it had been during the ISI era. The Gini coefficient of income inequality stood at an impressively high level of 0.57 in the early 1960s, then (during much of the ISI period) fell rapidly to its lowest point of 0.429 in 1981, after which it rose in the neoliberal era to 0.481 by 2000 (Boltvinik 2003, 394; Székely 2005).

Carlos Moreno-Brid and Jaime Ros succinctly state the anticipated benefits that Mexican policy makers believed would arise from NAFTA:

> The Mexican government saw NAFTA as an instrument to achieve three immediate goals. First, the agreement was thought to have the potential to boost Mexico's trade with and foreign direct investment (FDI) flows from the United States. . . . Second, it was assumed that NAFTA would induce local and foreign firms to invest in the production of tradable goods in Mexico in order to exploit the country's potential as an export platform to the United States. The third and decisively political and economic objective . . . was to guarantee the lock-in of Mexico's economic reform process. The belief was that ensuring the durability of market reforms and having privileged access to the North American market . . . would rapidly raise productivity, employment, and living standards. (Moreno-Brid and Ross 2009, 165)

All but the crucial last sentence turned out to be a correct estimate of the impact of NAFTA.

The Mexican government, of necessity, performed a requisite state function in representing Mexico in the negotiation of NAFTA. But an important question is subsumed in the above citation. Was it the Mexican government, acting with autonomy, that constructed the NAFTA accord? Researchers who specialize in the complex relationships between the state and the representatives of large private-sector actors maintain that NAFTA was a threshold event changing the time-honored relationship between state and capital. That is, in the setting of the general parameters of economic policy making, Mexico's business elite as represented by the Mexican Businessmen's Council (CMHN), the Business Coordinating Council (CCE), and other peak organizations, had for decades followed the lead of the president's top policy makers.[4] Between 1985 and 1994, however, a new structural relationship of "co-responsibility" had been established—with the construction of NAFTA marking a pivotal moment.

Cristina Puga has scrutinized the relationships between the peak business organizations and the state as well as the divisions among the owners of firms in several scholarly books and articles. Based on this work, she has concluded that the crisis of the early 1980s (along with the formation and consolidation of the CCE in the 1970s) led to the emergence of a new attitude on the part of the owners and managers of the largest "economic groups" (or conglomerates) regarding both policy making and the nature of the economic crisis of the 1980s (Puga 2004, 61). This reformulation of the status quo amounted to a "qualitative change between big business and the government" (Puga 2004, 61). As the outlines of the new model (neoliberalism plus export-led growth) emerged, the business leaders were "duty bound to develop new forms of communication with the government and to become directly involved in the design and institutionalization of the new model" (Puga 2004, 61). Events of this period, and particularly the long negotiation of NAFTA, "offered them a setting wherein they could both consolidate new forms of intervention and organize a system of collaboration that would permit them to overcome internal divisions and stimulate the participation and co-responsibility of the combined elements of big business" (Puga 2004, 61).

Puga maintains that the new model has been "promoted by the employers" who have "sustained the advance" of a "business operation . . . arranged with the state to formulate the main elements of economic policy" (Puga 2004, 7). The new relationship between state and capital, best symbolized by the NAFTA, was also the result of a new generation of business leaders who not only realigned the traditional subordinate posture of the business organizations in relation to the state, but also plunged into forms of political organization and direct action, culminating in their taking control of the state with the presidential election of 2000, which brought the Acción Nacional Party (the PAN) to power. The NAFTA negotiations "*began a singular collaboration with the government that was then converted into a new paradigm*" (Puga 2004, 9, italics added). Summing up her distinct and well-documented hypothesis, Puga stated:

> The analytical contribution of this work is to conceive the participation of the Mexican employers as a form of *economic coordination* that has collaborated in the institutionalization of new norms to guide the market and to formalize the export model of the Mexican economy; as such, [thereby] offering a distinct vision that goes beyond previous explanations . . . in order to understand the actions of business as a functional element in the maintenance of the social order and in the organization of the economy at a twofold level—national and international. (Puga 2004, 13)

Comparative confirmation of Puga's hypothesis has been carefully constructed by Vivek Chibber, whose *Locked in Place: State Building and Late*

Industrialization in India makes a convincing case for the idea that in India and Korea the "developmental state" eventually came to be partially dismantled due to endogenous forces (Chibber 2003, 245). In effect, the very success of state-led industrialization creates vast complexes of organized firms with deep technological capability. Such firms no longer are dependent to such a degree as before on the ability of the state to channel capital to them, as they acquire their own financial intermediaries or other means of finance. They also diversify and acquire supplier firms or in other ways ensure the availability of inputs. Independent in terms of technological proficiency, finance, and a web of supplier firms, large industrial firms no longer are mere creations of the state as before. They no longer are willing to be *disciplined* by the state—although they are anxious to maintain subsidies and other favors granted by the state. In effect, large firms push back and strive to open greater space within the economy for private-sector activity.[5] This led, at least in the Korean case, to a more laissez-faire environment. In the Indian case, firms desired more power/autonomy within the national economy but continued to seek the maintenance of the state-private industry alliance in regard to foreign competition. *The hypothesis, then, is that the state's very success in the creation of a cohesive new industrial core leads to the eventual decline in the role of the state in the economy as its support and interventions are no longer a requisite for rapid, sustained economic advance.* The relevant question, however, is the degree to which such a transition is in fact effective in terms of sustained growth. One might attempt to apply Chibber's analysis to the case of Mexico, for example, with the early 1980s as the moment of rupture between the state and industrial leaders. But Mexico's economic performance from 1981 to 2009 has been, at best, mediocre, and perhaps more accurately, dismal (as noted in chapter 1). Caution must also be employed in drawing too closely any international parallels because (as will be documented in the next two chapters) Mexico has never acquired the financial and technological depth—nor a proficient web of supplier firms—that would have been requisite to juxtapose "push back" from the private sector to a viable project of economic growth.

PRIVATIZATION: A NEW BEGINNING
FOR THE BUSINESS OLIGARCHS[6]

While it is generally assumed that the more vigorous approach that Salinas adopted regarding the theme of privatization was a reflection of a new turn by the state toward a more defined neoliberal trajectory, Puga maintained that the most pragmatic of the business leaders commenced a campaign at the onset of Salinas's term to exert more pressure in order to obtain private gains from the privatizations and to extract concessions from the privatization process (Puga 2004, 77). One of the major conclusions of Elvira Concheiro Bórquez's *El Gran Acuerdo: Gobierno y empresarios en la modernización salinista* (*The Great Agreement: Government and Business in Salinas's Modernization*) was that

> With the process of the privatization of important firms the largest capitalists were able to make profitable deals, but most important was that this established a new function for the business leaders wherein the limits of that which is strictly economic was erased. The process of the sale of the parastate firms—and this is perhaps the most important—*was a transference of power*. The Mexican State, having considerably reduced its economic power, brought itself closer to the neoliberal ideal of a "State without property," not only by revitalizing important industrial and financial corporations but also by having opened the doors of political power, which is to say that now private influence reached into areas heretofore closed to the economic groups. (Concheiro Bórquez 1996, 91)

For the great national economic power groups, the privatization process amounted to a process that, to use David Harvey's terminology, amounted to *accumulation by dispossession* (Harvey 2007, 34–35). It was all the more sweet because the state overwhelmingly reserved this national treasure for Mexican capital. Ninety-three percent of all the firms sold remained in the possession of Mexican businesses, although 20.5 percent of the value of the sold firms later was transferred to foreign firms that were already partners of the *grupos* (Concheiro Bórquez 1996, 83). "If we pay attention to what were then the plans of the government and to the favorable economic conditions [of the privatizations], business leaders were behind the projections of Salinas' advisors, showing interest only in those firms up for sale that they considered a guaranteed source of profit" (Concheiro Bórquez 1996, 83).

Particularly active in the formation of the privatization project was the CCE, which "consolidated its position as an intermediary in the formation of economic policy through an intense dialogue with government functionaries and the President of the Republic" (Puga 2004, 77). As mentioned in the previous chapter, the CCE held a truly impressive number of off-the-record meetings—a total of sixty-seven—with the highest policy-making levels of the government during the formative years 1986–1987. From this time forward the pace of privatizations, in terms of the amounts involved and the structural importance of the state-owned firms, accelerated. In May 1986 a period of *massive destruction* of state capital began with the privatization of the state-owned steel fabricator in Monterrey. In early 1988 the privatizations reached what Casar and Peres termed "priority" areas for the state—by the end of 1988 the sell-off reached into the realm of what had been defined as "strategic" areas of state-owned firms (Casar and Peres 1988, 176; Guadarrama and Cruz 1988, 24). Observers of the privatization process argue that it was a historical watershed of such grand magnitude that it can only be compared to epoch-making events such as the nineteenth-century realignment of economic power subsequent to the takeover and sale of the communal lands of the indigenous population and of the vast church holdings of that era, which created a new class of landed oligarchs (Concheiro Bórquez 1996, 92). Focusing in particular on the reprivatization of the financial sector during Salinas's term, the argument is that "only through an act of this magnitude could the current government regain the *confidence* of the private sector" (Concheiro Bórquez 1996, 92). The privatizations were never intended as a mere auction of public assets—sales were arranged behind closed doors, allowing the government great discretion in bestowing its favoritism on the *grupos*, thereby significantly increasing the gap between the largest conglom- erates and the medium and small firms (Puga 2004, 81). More important to the large business interests than the opportunity to obtain momentous profits, the privatizations are to be understood as part of a larger process: "In 1990 Rolando Vega, president of the CCE stated that 'there has not merely been a closing of the gap' with the government, but also [that] the private sector 'has been given a significance in the productive sector which constitutes a radical change'" (Puga 2004, 81).

FROM PRIVATIZATION TO GLOBALIZATION: COECE

By 1990 the Salinas administration began setting its sights less on the consoli- dation of the neoliberal model and more on a *new accommodation between capital and the state*, now prioritizing the idea that Mexico's fate must be tied to the dynamic forces of the global economy (Puga 2004, 73). Although Mexico had joined GATT in 1986 and had been able to greatly expand its ex- ports, Salinas was frustrated by numerous forms of informal trade barriers that served to reduce the expected benefits of the new focus on international eco- nomic linkages. Equally bothersome was the prevalence of dumping by U.S. corporations in Mexico. The peak business association, the CCE, had pushed for entry into the GATT. Opportunistically, the giant Mexican conglomerates sought realignment of their production for the global market, given that the internal Mexican market had effectively fallen off a cliff sometime in 1981. Structural conditions were leading Salinas to opt for NAFTA—which he did in early 1990. This decision, apparently, had a lot to do with the intervention of another of the powerful peak business organizations, CEMAI (the Business Council for International Affairs).[7] CEMAI's president at that time was the brother of the head of the CMHN (Mexican Businessmen's Council—see note 4 regarding this association). He and the proximate president of the CCE (who had been in 1989 an advisor to Salinas on economic issues) began to push for a NAFTA agreement, with the backing of the leaders of the automobile and petrochemical sectors. The Mexican government officially notified the nation that it had commenced negotiations for NAFTA at a meeting of CEMAI in March 1990 (Puga 2004, 118). A new alliance was now consolidated between the exporting firms, the large conglomerates, the peak business organizations, and the government—all components were instrumental in a campaign to convince the public of the desirability of NAFTA.

The most important element in this new alliance was the role of COECE (the Business Coordinator of International Trade), created in September 1990. COECE was, in fact, an arm of the CCE and its official representative in the negotiations over NAFTA. (The CMHN had also played an important role in its creation.) With COECE as the principal voice of business in the negotiation of NAFTA, the dominance of the largest Mexican conglomerates (or *grupos*) was established. In the same moment, the government set up a thirty-member special advisory council on international trade, allocating eleven of the powerful positions to members of the CCE and leaders of the *grupos*.

When the Mexican government announced plans in March 1990 to pursue NAFTA, the CCE quickly created COECE. COECE and the government, in turn, created decentralized advisory committees of about five officials and eight to ten representatives from businesses to accompany negotiations. These committees were first organized in twenty sectoral groups and later reorganized, as the negotiations progressed, into eighteen thematic groups. From 1990 to 1992, groups of business representatives and government officials held 1,333 meetings, roughly a dozen a week. At the outset, various sectoral and advisory groups worked to collect and analyze background data. Later, representatives from the advisory groups closely followed the negotiations, and government officials maintained constant contact with them. Business representatives were not allowed at the bargaining table with the United States and Canada but were figuratively and sometimes literally in the "*cuarto de junta*" (room next door). (Ross Schneider 2002, 100–101)

COECE constituted the fourth party throughout the negotiations among the United States, Mexico, and Canada. Mexican state representatives were always accompanied by COECE's top negotiators, whose approval had to be attained at every step in the negotiations. COECE did not merely frame the negotiating parameters for the Mexican state, it also played an active role in selling NAFTA to the Mexican populace and to the U.S. Congress. COECE contested many of the initiatives advocated by the U.S. negotiators, but it was so anxious to obtain new injections of FDI that it was willing to retreat on almost every major point save the denationalization of oil, gas, and electricity production.

COECE, for its part, and the Mexican government, for its part, quickly set up lobbying offices in Washington, D.C., to push for *fast-track* negotiations that would deprive the U.S. government of the option of altering any aspects of the secret deal that would be pounded out over a three-year period by U.S. and Mexican negotiators. Mexico's expenditures on lobbying for NAFTA from that moment forward were without precedent. While these forces essentially used the same methodologies to sell NAFTA in the United States as they did in Mexico, their efforts were largely focused on the United States. Officials in the Mexican government's lobbying office in Washington, D.C., met with 320 members of the U.S. Congress. The indefatigable head of the office, Herman von Bertrab, orated on behalf of the NAFTA project on 360 separate occasions (Puga 2004, 127).

COECE was not simply another addition to the peak business organizations. More important, COECE constituted a *qualitative* change in the relationship between the Mexican conglomerates and the state. Now the economic oligarchs would "convert themselves into active participants in the elaboration of public policies" (Puga 2004, 134). The relationship was such that many observers falsely understood COECE to be an official organization of the Mexican government. This confusion was understandable given the deep interpenetration between the state and the private sector: in preparation for the negotiation of NAFTA, the business leaders of COECE conducted approximately 400 conferences with the secretariat of trade and industrial development (SECOFI) and other cabinet-level entities (Puga 2004, 139). The very able leader of COECE, Juan Gallardo, whose impressive pro-NAFTA "road show" we attended in Los Angeles in 1991, stated that the objectives of COECE were to (1) form a common front of business interests, (2) provide a group of experts to guide the negotiations of NAFTA, and (3) serve the national business interests and provide the linkage between the private sectors in the negotiating nations. According to Jorge Márin, the representative to COECE from the textile and apparel sector (and later the president of CCE), COECE "was the crucial element of success in the negotiation" (Puga 2004, 141).

For Mexico's conglomerates, the initial objective of the agreement had been a new framework that would attract U.S. foreign investment—trade issues had not been a central concern. During the long period of the negotiations, the Mexican government was immersed in a complex process of institutional restructuring—changing regulations, laws, and even the constitution in order to consolidate the new export model. All of this was designed to provide the national conglomerates and transnational corporations the certitude that Mexico's economic structure would be irreversibly reconstituted.

In this context Mexico began to implement an industrial policy to fortify the export leaders, particularly to develop even further the maquiladora sector. Once passage had been achieved and presidential power had passed to Ernesto Zedillo (1994–2000), his administration—putatively tied to a laissez-faire stance—deepened and strengthened, with the approval of the peak business associations, this industrial policy. (Such efforts, however, were very limited in scope and fell far short of a *national industrial policy*.)

However, the crisis of 1994–1995 had dramatically impacted the Mexican conglomerates, limiting and in some instances destroying their plans for successful restructuring to meet the requirements of the new export model. The effect of the crisis was to bifurcate the Mexican business elite:

> In spite of the support received, the largest private Mexican groups did not have the (technological, productive, financial, and organizational) capacities to confront the competition and this was clearly manifest with the onset of the crisis in December 1994. . . .
>
> The consequence of this crisis gave rise to an unequal and contradictory process for the largest Mexican groups. For those that organized around the so-called financial groups this signified a) the loss of property and managerial control, and with it the erosion of their *dominating power* in the Mexican financial system; b) the recomposition of the economic power of these groups around the Spanish and U.S. banks; c) *the weakening of the industrial conglomerates connected to the process of the privatization of the banks*.
>
> For those groups not tied to the property and control of the banks the consequences had the following result: a) an accelerated process of transnationalization of . . . the Mexican groups by way of strategic alliances and foreign direct investment . . . b) a larger participation by the transnational corporations through FDI, mergers and strategic alliances. (Morera Camacho 2005, 36, italics added)

In short, the export model that the Mexican groups and the Mexican government had sought with single-minded tenacity had been realized. But, in a manner never anticipated, the resulting construct largely worked against their interests. And, due to the blunders, miscalculations, and sheer ineptitude of these dominant economic actors, they managed to seize defeat from the jaws of what might have been a qualified victory. Instead of being masters in their own domain while engineering a dramatic volte-face from state-led industrialization to a successful export-led model, Mexico had constructed what we have termed a cheap labor–export model. The impact of these momentous changes is explored in the remaining chapters.

Chapter Four

The Maquiladora Sector: Building Block of Mexico's Export-Led Model

When, in the early 1980s, Mexico's policy makers were under pressure to abandon their largely successful strategies of state-led industrialization and pursue the will-o'-the-wisp export-led model, the most expeditious and opportunistic step they took was to link this new strategy to the maquiladora sector.[1]

The maquiladora program is officially known as the U.S. Customs 806/807 program and also the Border Industrialization Program (BIP). It began in 1965 when the Bracero Program of temporary admittance of Mexican farm workers into the United States—commencing in 1942 during the labor shortages of World War II—was terminated. The maquila program, like the Bracero Program, was an official agreement between the Mexican and U.S. governments. The incentive for Mexico was to provide jobs in a largely forgotten northern border region that had for centuries been a land of neglect and poverty. The maquila program was a slight gesture, an effortless feint, creating the appearance of national integrity. In reality, through the 1960s and 1970s, Mexico's center of power (firmly based in Mexico City—with an important satellite in Monterrey) paid little, if any, attention to the BIP. It would be easy to conclude that the border was an embarrassment—almost another country—that was, at best, to be overlooked.

For the United States the BIP initiative was a small-bore program. As conceived and implemented, U.S.-based manufacturing companies were given an incentive to set up labor-intensive, Mexican-sited assembly plants along the extensive border from Tijuana to Matamoros. U.S.-made parts and components could move, duty free, into and out of Mexico. In 1966, for the first time, a new category appeared in the official statistics recording Mexico's balance of payments—*servicios por transformación* (the value added for "transforming," or manufacturing, products at the border). The entire program then registered a mere $3.2 million dollars—0.143 percent of the value of Mexico's export

79

earnings (INEGI 1985, 718). Ten years later the maquila sector accounted for only 4.4 percent of Mexico's export earnings. As the sun set on President Echeverria's term in 1976 and power passed to President Lopez Portillo, an astute observer of Mexico's political economy would have been unlikely to focus any attention on the sluggish trajectory of the maquila program.

Even in the pivotal year 1983, the maquilas generated merely 2.9 percent of total export earnings. In that year there were only six hundred maquilas—94 percent of them clustered in the four border states, particularly in the cities of Tijuana and Ciudad Juárez (Nacional Financiera 1995, 365). Three years later the maquila boom was apparent—there were 1,125 border plants. By 1994 more than two thousand plants were assembling components imported from the United States in order to export to the United States a wide variety of consumer goods and parts. Mexico's export-led strategy, now in full swing, had brought the maquila sector to center stage. Employment leaped from 151,000 in 1983 to 581,000 in 1994. At that point, 82 percent of the employed were classified as *obreros*, or workers—the ranks of the technicians and administrators were, and have remained, thin. The scramble to Mexico's border was led by a desire, primarily, to cut labor costs.[2]

This lure has not abated: the San Diego–based firm Made In Mexico, Inc., a maquila management services company, boldly stated on its website in 2009 that (with its assistance and guidance) its clients could cut labor costs by up to 75 percent if they transferred operations to Mexico (Made In Mexico 2009).

The maquila sector constitutes a starting point in a detailed analysis of the export-led model because it has by definition been associated with manufacturing exports. In many formulations it has been linked to the concept of cheap, unprotected, and essentially nonrepresented although "officially" unionized laborers, who generated 55 percent of Mexico's manufactured exports in 2004 (Bancomext 2005). Essentially, the maquila industry imports its inputs—components, parts, design, engineering, and so on (overwhelmingly from the United States). These various inputs combine with cheap production labor (pay *per day* in 2008 ranged from $4 US to $10 US, plus benefits) and a slight element of technical labor, to assemble the finished products and primarily reexport these products into the U.S. economy.

Employment in the maquila sector rose by 123 percent from 1994 to 2000—or to 1.3 million workers (INEGI 2009a). The Consejo Nacional de la Industria Maquiladora y Manufacturera de Exportación, or CNIMME—the powerful employers association of the maquila industry—estimates that for every direct job in the maquila sector three other jobs are created via the job multiplier effect (CNIMME 2008, 4). Thus, in the period of rapid growth of the maquilas—1994–2000—the industry was considered a growth pole both in terms of exports and in terms of the 2.157 million direct and indirect jobs created in these years. In other words, with the creation of an average of 308,000 new jobs per year in the first seven years of NAFTA, the maquila sector was the single largest source of job creation. Of the net addition to the employed during this period—approximately 3.31 million jobs—the maquila sector, via direct and induced employment (via the job multiplier effect), created an impressive 65 percent of national employment.[3]

After early 2001, however, employment fell and then stagnated. In 2006, the last year the government recorded employment data for the maquila sector, direct employment had been reduced to 1.17 million. In figure 4.1, it can be seen that the maquila sector's role in the national economy reached an upper limit and since 2000 has failed to play the role of a growth pole within the economy. In fact, value added now constitutes a declining share of the total value of the gross production (sales) in the maquila sector. Thus, in spite of the overall growth in maquila employment in the NAFTA era, and in spite of the rise in the total value of Mexico's maquila exports, Mexico now

Figure 4.1.   Maquila Surplus (Exp–Imp) as a Percentage of GDP

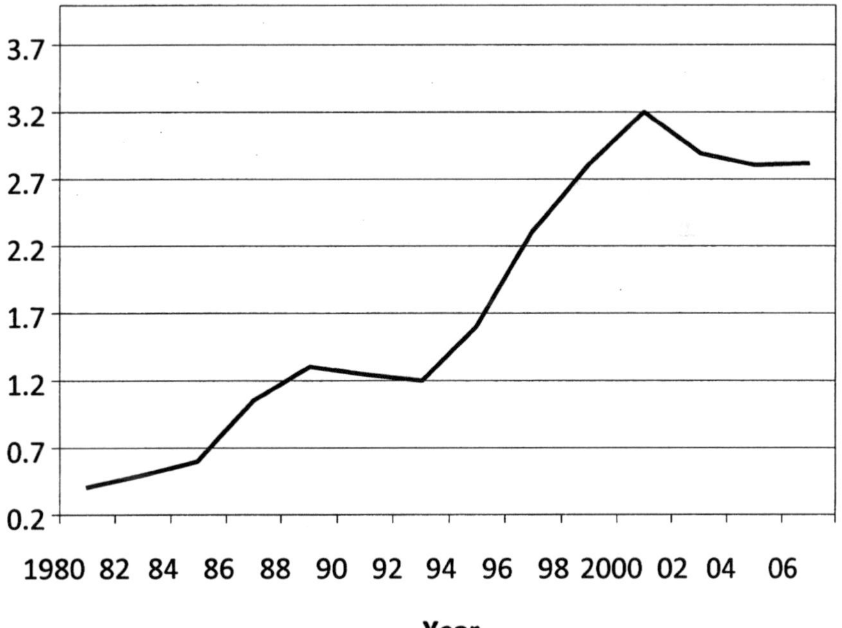

Year

Source: INEGI (Instituto Nacional de Estadisticas) 2006, *Estadisticas Económicas,* Sector Maquiladora; Rocha 2006, *Review of the Economic Situation in Mexico,* 386.

retains a smaller and smaller relative share of the economic benefits from
these activities, even as the costs in terms of aggregate physical effort rise:
the value-added ratio dropped from 18.2 percent in 1988 to only 8.2 percent
in 2003—a decline of 55 percent (Capdevielle 2005, 571).

In terms of opportunity costs, Mexico gives up more, relatively, every
year—which is to say that if Mexico had a viable developmental strategy, it
could either extract a larger share of the benefits of the maquila industry or
engage in a national process of upgrading, which would eventually lead to a
viable national development project based in other forms of manufacturing
activities. Also of note is the essentially static level of national integration
into the maquila sector as indicated by the coefficient of integration (national
inputs/gross production). Only 3 percent of total production value arises from
national component/manufacturing inputs (Capdevielle 2005, 570). Of that
amount, roughly 60 percent of the national inputs in 2003 derived from the
service sector in terms of cleaning, accounting, packaging and shipping, and
similar activities. Counting indirect activities such as packing, electricity,
transportation, and so on, national content as a share of the value of total production of the maquila sector was 8 percent in 1988 and 9.8 percent in 2003
(Capdevielle 2007, 81). As Capdevielle argued, there was no apparent trend.

In spite of the quantitative data that have repeatedly demonstrated the
weaknesses of the maquila industry, a significant cadre of Mexican researchers continues, up to the moment, to furnish qualitative studies of so-called
second- and third-generation maquila firms that, according to this body of
research, hold the potential for the many externalities posited by the new
growth theory (Cypher 2004a; Dutrénit and Vera-Cruz 2005; Lara, Arellano,
and García 2005; Villavicencio and Casalet 2005).[4] However, none of these
studies has ever presented convincing quantitative data suggesting that *in the
aggregate* the maquila sector is anything more than a cheap-labor assembly
operation with virtually no backward or forward linkages to Mexico's production system.[5] Nor, in spite of many efforts to do so, have these studies
ever established a significant dynamic trend sufficiently large to change the
fundamental structural nature of the maquila industry.

When the maquila sector was growing (in employment terms) between
1994 and 2000, direct jobs created paid 52 percent less than non-maquila
manufacturing, while living costs for the maquila workers clustered along
the U.S.-Mexican border were considerably higher than in other interior
states (Cypher 2004a, 362). In short, and in spite of the rosy predictions of an
indefatigable cadre of Mexican researchers, the maquila project was never a
national development strategy and is even less so today. Above all, it should
be emphasized that by its nature the maquila industry does not represent the
exportation of Mexican manufactured products; rather, it represents merely

the export of Mexican labor power *embodied* in the final assembled and exported products.[6]

The maquila boom reached its peak in early 2001, when more than 3,800 firms were operating throughout Mexico, most still clustered in the border states. At that point (as mentioned previously) 1,339,000 Mexican workers were employed in the plants. In 2001, 48.6 percent of the value of all Mexican exports came from the maquila sector. From 1983 onward the maquila sector was the propelling force in the new economic model, transforming the Mexican economy to a degree rarely witnessed in any economy. An introverted economy that regarded the export sector as an arena to realize economic rents in petroleum, mining, and agriculture quickly became an extroverted economy that centered its energies on increasingly complex and sophisticated manufactured products that achieved their competitive advantage through the embodiment of cheap Mexican labor.

But the long, steady growth in employment ended in 2000–2001. Two important, nearly simultaneous, events cast an enduring shadow over an industry that had carried the hopes for a revitalized, restructured Mexico. The first and most enduring was the U.S. economic slowdown—soon to be a recession—that began in 2000. With more than 80 percent of all manufactured exports flowing into the U.S. market, Mexican-based producers were suddenly faced with overcapacity and overinvestment while additional new plants, under construction, soon came into production. After the recession ended in 2001, the "jobless recovery" began in the United States—undercutting for years the growth in mass purchasing power. The recession in the United States officially lasted eight months, but the economy shed jobs for thirty-two months (Miller 2009, 15). It was not until March 2005 that a process of employment expansion resumed. Under these circumstances, the autos, electronic devices, information-technology products, and numerous other items that had previously flowed from Mexico into U.S. households were frequently deferred.

Until the impact of this situation percolated through both government policy-making circles and the Mexican business elite, a set of long-held assumptions had reigned: Mexico was gifted by circumstance—it adjoined the largest mass market in the world. With its ability to cut costs, Mexico occupied a secure niche, furnishing an important part of the insatiable mass U.S. market for manufactured consumer goods. But Mexico was now caught in a "scissors crisis." Its final market (the United States) showed signs of stagnation at the very moment that China was accepted into the World Trade Organization (WTO). Having the imprimatur of the WTO was important to potential corporate investors. Now, foreign direct investment (FDI) poured, at an even greater rate, into China—frequently at the expense of Mexico.

This was readily noted throughout the country in the apparel industry, but China impacted many other labor-intensive industries in the maquila sector. As startlingly cheap as Mexican labor was, the global markets were, in effect, reacting to the fact that it was "too expensive." Mexico's race to the bottom strategy had met its match.

When the official statistics tracking the maquila sector ended at the beginning of 2007, only 1,170,962 employees were scattered among 2,810 plants (INEGI 2009a).[7] That is, employment had shrunk by 12.5 percent, and the number of maquila plants had been cut down by 24 percent from its recent peak. With roughly one of every four maquila plants sitting idle—often as weed-encrusted tombstones lining the entry or exit of major cities throughout Mexico, a new social consensus, shared by all social strata from shoe shiners to executives, slowly sank in: Mexico had to abandon the dream that the maquilas would, to any appreciable degree, form an answer to a question that had long haunted Mexico—"Where will jobs be created?" By late 2009, after a decade wherein the maquilas had essentially failed to create any jobs whatsoever, the dream that the maquilas offered "starter" jobs (that would form the low rungs on a ladder that Mexico could climb to reach economic development) had been shattered.

It is worth recalling that during the years when many Mexicans had clung to this mirage (1982–2000), direct jobs increased by a factor of eleven. Furthermore, as mentioned, each maquila job carried a jobs multiplier effect (however limited) that further nurtured the illusions of the proponents of the maquila industry as a "job creator" for Mexico.

It also should be noted that in spite of the serious recent job losses from 2000 onward (before the devastating current downturn that began in September 2008), the value added produced by the maquiladora industry—essentially the total wage bill paid by the maquilas—rose by 15.3 percent (in inflation-adjusted terms) from 2000 through December 2006 (INEGI 2009a). With fewer workers operating in fewer plants, the overall average size of the plants rose, as did per-worker productivity. In short, the weakest and most marginal plants (often in textiles and apparel) closed, while in the border cities of Tijuana, Mexicali, and Ciudad Juárez the number of auto and auto parts plants grew. The crisis of 2000–2001 forced a dramatic restructuring of the maquila sector. How the crisis of late 2008–2010 will play out remains to be seen, but all current signs indicate that its effects will be graver and more far reaching, and not necessarily one-dimensional. With its race to the bottom strategy, Mexico will stand to gain from the collapse of the U.S. auto industry. Most of Mexico's auto plants are designed to build small, efficient autos. The U.S. auto industry is currently planning on maintaining many of these existing plants and even building more as the cost-cutting pressures continue to mount (as discussed in chapter 2).

But on a more general level, from the moment the current downturn began in September 2008 through June 2009, Mexico lost 114 maquila firms. The balance on July 1, 2009, was 2,600 firms in operation—30 percent fewer than in early 2001 (Colín 2009, 3A). Along the border, 70 percent of all firms had experienced sales declines from September 2008 through mid-2009. Hardest hit was the auto sector, where 91 percent of all firms found their sales dropping, followed by the electronics sector, where 82.6 percent of firms suffered reductions in sales (Colín 2009, 3A). Overall, in the first six months of 2009, total maquila exports fell by 26.1 percent on an annualized basis. Maquila exports fell faster than non-maquila exports. From the level achieved in the first half of 2007, FDI fell by 36 percent from January through June 2009 (Becerril and Saldaña 2009, 9). The rate of decline in FDI in the maquila sector was even greater. Employment was estimated to have fallen by 7 percent—or by 161,000 jobs—from its 2008 level. However, this statistic must be contextualized—a new approach to production slowdowns had been institutionalized in the context of the current crisis: *paros técnicos*—essentially, mandated layoffs of two, three, or even four days per week (or in some cases one or more weeks per month) became the chosen way to hold onto the workforce while simultaneously cutting the wage bill. The unemployment rate in the border states was above the national average in 2009, but it would have been far higher had it not been for the mandated temporary layoffs.

One major unintended consequence of the maquila program (and of the export-led model in general) has been to create a "three Mexicos" economic geography. This has displaced the long-standing dualism that had greatly privileged a Mexico City corridor, leaving the rest of the country (save the enclave of Monterrey) in penury. As careful econometric studies have demonstrated, under the export-led paradigm, the border and north central region of Mexico has steadily pulled away from the relatively better-off Mexico City region, now leaving the states to the south of Mexico City as a "third Mexico" with a markedly lower level of per capita income (Dávila Flores 2008). The north and north central regions have been the preferred site for both maquila and disguised maquila operations (as discussed in chapter 5), thereby raising the per capita income well above that of the national average.

In looking at the maquila sector, we can identify three simple stages: (1) *hesitant startup* from 1966 to 1982, (2) *dynamic acceleration* from 1983 to 2000, and (3) *stagnation and restructuring* from 2000 to 2007.[8] (It is likely that a fourth stage will be triggered by the devastating crisis that began in late 2008—but it is much too soon to know how this will play out.) Our analysis of the maquila sector will concentrate on the period from 1982 to 2007. Here we will situate the maquila sector within the broader theme of national economic development. In spite of the large and sometimes impressive changes wrought by the maquila program, we will demonstrate that it constituted a passive, failed development initiative. This result was due both to its own structure and to the policy rigidities imposed as a result of the neoclassical and neoliberal ideological blinders constraining the perspectives of the political and economic elite.

DWINDLING MANUFACTURING CAPACITY IN THE UNITED STATES

A confluence of factors contributed to the rapid growth of the maquila firms and consequently to the expansion of maquila employment from 1983 through 2000. On the U.S. side—which was essentially the *active* side in the process—it would be hard to overemphasize the frontal attack on labor unions and the general encouragement of deregulation engendered by the impact of President Reagan's policies from early 1981 to early 1989 (Kleinknecht 2009). The successful withering of labor's power had a dynamic effect—as union membership rapidly declined, labor had, year after year, fewer means to struggle against the shifting of plants to Mexico. The double-dip recession (January 1980–July 1980; July 1981–November 1982) pushed unemployment rates briefly to nearly 11 percent, signaling that the economy had entered depression territory. Job growth did not resume until late 1983. Perhaps, with another president, runaway plants shifting to Mexico in the midst of a vicious downturn would have engendered political resistance. Reagan and his advisors relished whatever processes (direct and indirect) might be found to undercut organized labor in particular and the working class in general. As a result, the share of the U.S. workforce represented by unions dropped from approximately 24 percent in 1980 to 18.5 percent in 1989 (Mischel et al. 2007, figure 3W).

Fear of "Japan as number 1" increasingly became a theme in the course of the 1980s—meaning that U.S. manufacturing firms sought methods to cut costs at every turn. Establishing production operations, particularly in nearby Mexico, was exceedingly attractive to hard-hit electronics and automotive firms. These were the industries where, by the 1980s, Japan increasingly set the standards for efficiency.

The strategy of offshoring production sites and decimating the U.S. industrial base did meet with a certain level of criticism: one of the most interesting, important, and ignored attempts to redirect the United States away from its emerging low-wage recovery strategy was a Council on Foreign Relations book, *Manufacturing Matters* (Cohen and Zysman 1987). Their analysis, running against the stream of neoliberal and neoclassical assurances that "the unregulated market always knows best"—the guiding light of the Reagan administration and soon to be the economic anthem of the Salinas administration in Mexico—pointed to the consequences that were becoming ever more apparent as the United States stepped back from its own history and the more recent lessons from Japan on the virtues and possibilities of strong, well-directed industrial policies. They succinctly illuminated the context in which U.S. manufacturers leaped over the border into Mexico in the 1980s:

> Until recently, [U.S.] firms dominated world markets; now they must adjust to them. Twenty-five years ago [the United States] produced about as many cars in a week as Japan did in a year. Europeans wrote books about the [U.S.] Challenge and the Secrets of the Giant [U.S.] Firms, while they fretted about technology gaps and insurmountable [U.S.] advantages in product, production process marketing strategy, and management techniques. Now the Japanese produce more cars per year than we do. (Cohen and Zysman 1987, 59–60)

Japanese executives, such as Akio Morita, the head of the Sony Corporation, were uncharacteristically blunt in their observations of U.S. indifference to the industrial base:

> Unless U.S. industry shores up its manufacturing base, it could lose everything. American companies have either shifted output to low-wage countries or come to buy parts and assembly products from countries like Japan that can make quality products at low prices. The result is the hollowing of American industry. The United States is abandoning its status as an industrial power. (Jones 1986, 59)

Decades later, Morita's criticism of the United States' "Mr. Magoo" approach to deindustrialization was echoed by a scion of Henry Ford's fortune. In a 2009 interview, William Clay Ford Jr. declared:

> One cannot find a healthy economy anywhere in the world that does not have a strong industrial base. . . . [The United States] seems to be the only country in the world that doesn't value that. Everywhere else Ford does business in the world the government and people understand it, and do everything they can to enhance it. . . . Manufacturing still has the greatest multiplier effect, in terms of job creation, of any sector in the economy. (Vlasic 2009, 14)

Cohen and Zysman used both quantitative data and theoretical analysis to demonstrate that the dominant, passive attitude of Reagan-era economists, that the United States could turn its back on manufacturing, was nonsense. Then as now, the neoclassical/neoliberal claim was that the United States could ascend to the next-higher rung—the service-based (or knowledge-based) economy. To lose manufacturing, Cohen and Zysman argued, was to forfeit technological capacity. If industry were offshored, a service-based economy would have no means to renew and expand the technological base of the U.S. economy.

But the United States had already traveled far down that road, opening an unprecedented large and rapidly growing deficit in the export/import balance of manufactured products beginning in 1982. Meanwhile, Japan's manufacturing trade balance had soared from $12.5 billion US in 1970 to an average of over $100 billion US in the 1980s. Germany's success was also spectacular, even as it trailed that of Japan (Cohen and Zysman 1987, 63). The U.S. share of world exports had dropped from 26 percent in 1960 to only 18 percent in 1980. From 1965 to 1983, U.S. manufacturing productivity (output per hour per worker) had risen by 40 percent, while Germany's jumped by 96 percent and Japan registered a 343 percent increase. From 1976 onward, both Germany and Japan maintained higher absolute manufacturing productivity levels than those of the United States (Cohen and Zysman 1987, 66). Unsurprisingly, the U.S. manufacturing industry's pretax profit rate fell from roughly 13 percent in 1963–1965 to only 7 percent in 1982. The United States, Cohen and Zysman proclaimed, suffered a crisis of confusion as it failed to grasp the nature and magnitude of the global industrial transition occurring in the 1980s. Cheaper labor was not the answer, they argued—Japan and Germany were meeting or exceeding the wage and work conditions of the United States. The United States could restore its competitiveness if it stuck to developing its manufacturing core, finding a combination of high-wage strategies based in industrial policy while revamping its national system of innovation (Cohen and Zysman 1987, xii, 81, 98–99).

With one very notable exception, the creation of the government/private sector consortium Sematech—which rescued the U.S. semiconductor manufacturing industries from near-certain oblivion, and opened the way for the information technology boom and bubble of the 1990s—Cohen and Zysman's bull's-eye analysis was shrugged off (Pages 1996, 89–108). The government's resuscitation of the semiconductor industry, as it was being overrun by the Japanese, was not driven by an abandonment of the free-market dogmas of neoliberalism and neoclassical economists. Rather, it was (for the most part) the exception that proved the rule. And it was also the latest application of the sub rosa industrial policy that the United States had effectively employed via the military sector since the days of World War II.

In lieu of steps advocated by Cohen and Zysman (and their energetic colleagues in the Berkeley Roundtable on the International Economy), U.S. policy makers and the corporate elite pursued the exact opposite course:

- Export capital and technology to low-wage havens.
- Build and maintain institutional structures to ensure that wages could not be appreciably raised in the new offshore manufacturing enclaves.
- Incorporate advanced production processes to attain productivity levels in low-wage havens that approximate those of the advanced industrial nations.
- Leverage the threat of the runaway manufacturing plants to push down wages in the United States and deprive U.S. workers of their productivity gains.
- Import low-wage workers to interface with what remained of the manufacturing industrial base, to add to the supply of desperate and therefore docile workers.

Here is a short, concrete example of how these forces began to exert their dark powers in the 1970s and 1980s: Work stoppages and strikes in the U.S. electrical industry had exceeded 100 per year in every year but one—when the number was 98—from 1956 to 1981. In thirteen of those years, stoppages and strikes exceeded 150 per year. But in 1982—with the Reagan administration in power—they abruptly fell to approximately zero, where they remained at least through 1986. Throughout the 1970s, the U.S. electronics industry steadily shifted production to Mexico, led by RCA, which had 5,600 workers in border towns in 1979 (Cowie 1999, 117, 124). The all-out labor offensive launched by the Reagan administration and the growing tendency to offshore electronics production to Mexico were the new structural conditions that led to a collapse of labor resistance, and therefore of wages, from the mid-1970s onward. This example, or something very close to it, was repeated in nearly every branch of the manufacturing sector.

Cohen and Zysman fervently championed their version of inclusive renewal at the very moment a new model of internationalized cheap-labor manufacturing was consolidating. Mexico, of course, was the locus for the largest realization of the new model, designed to maintain a competitive U.S.-controlled manufacturing base with the sole objective of restoring the profit rate.

Cohen and Zysman understood and articulated the recent emergence of a "manufacturing revolution" based in the merger of advanced electronics and computers, allowing for a variety of applications, including artificial intelligence, advanced robotics, programmable, automated machine tools, and so on. They termed the new era one of "programmable automation." The new wave of technologies would constitute the basis for a new era, ending the "Fordism" of dedicated machinery and equipment, and opening the door to a new era of "flexible" small-batch automated production techniques. They cautioned that the new technologies were far from a panacea: "The new equipment will either serve to remedy [U.S.] decline or entrench it" (Cohen and Zysman 1987, 162). For them, the crucial question was "integration"—could the United States get the combinations and proportions right, as had the Japanese?

U.S. industry in the course of the 1980s and 1990s—and forward to the present moment—has struggled with getting the combinations and proportions right. A major part of that effort has taken place in the maquila and disguised maquila firms (including in the Ford Motor Company's massive Mexican operations unmentioned in the interview of William Clay Ford Jr.). Ramping up production in the maquila industry in the 1970s was difficult because of major startup costs (such as the creation of an adequate infrastructure of industrial parks) and because the sense of overwhelming urgency on the part of U.S. manufacturers to restructure was only slowly growing in a cumulative manner over the course of the 1970s. At first, the run-ups in energy prices in the early 1970s and the deep recession of 1973–1975 were viewed as short-term factors momentarily diverting the United States from the strong growth path it had enjoyed from 1947 to 1971—often termed the "golden age." As the realization that the "golden age" had yielded to the "leaden age" and that the United States had lost its long-admired dominance in manufacturing, a new era of concern arose. But concern, as voiced by brilliant commentators such as Cohen, Zysman, Bennett Harrison, and a handful of others, was not enough (Harrison 1994). It is well to recall that the hallmark of economic thought in the 1980s was the economic quackery of supply-side economics and, in general, the odd concoctions of the Chicago School, whose views of the always beneficial outcomes yielded by a totally unconstrained free market became hegemonic (Heilbroner and Milberg 1995). And this was even truer in Mexico, and has remained so.

THE GLOBALLY INTEGRATED PRODUCTION SYSTEM

Getting the combinations and proportions right increasingly became a matter of shifting production offshore, particularly to Mexico, as could be seen in Ciudad Juárez: "[B]y 1990, the Parque Bermudez had grown to be the largest industrial park in the world; that corner of Juárez alone contained 46 plants, 49 companies and 35,000 workers" (Cowie 1999, 171). The conventional wisdom, at least in the 1980s, was that the maquila plants were limited to simple assembly operations where labor-intensive, low-productivity activities were relegated. This was and has remained true through the first decade of the twenty-first century, for perhaps 40–50 percent (or more) of the maquila plants, as discussed below. But for the rest, and for the disguised maquila plants examined in the next chapter, the technological and organizational production revolution noted by Cohen and Zysman had found its expression—at least to some considerable degree—along the Mexican side of the border.

> In the 1980s, several Juárez plants, particularly RCA,[9] began to move toward more capital-intensive forms of assembly production, more flexible forms of work organization, and a radical increase in efforts to retain well-trained and desirable employees. The electronics factories started to encompass high-technology investments, greater automation, quality circles, flexible production strategies, an increase in skill levels, a rise in the number of workers per plant, and a diversification of products manufactured. The new forms of work organization and product innovation also blurred the distinction between industrial work performed in the United States and that done in Mexico. (Cowie 1999, 171)

The trends mentioned by Cowie are quite important, but not for the reasons commonly stressed in Mexico. In Mexico, for the past twenty years, an enthusiastic group of researchers has repeatedly argued that as the capital and technology composition of the maquila industry has changed, the maquila industry has become a leading sector of the economy, capable of "pulling" along the rest of the economy (Carrillo and Rosio Barajas 2007). That is, not only has the maquila industry been outstanding in its growth (until 2000–2001) and in its capacity to attract FDI and create employment—its *quantitative dimensions*—far more important, it is a prime contributor to *qualitative change* in the Mexican production system. This is so, they have argued, because the "second generation" maquilas—as described by Cowie in the above citation—are a fount of technological spillover and learning effects. These issues will be discussed shortly.

What we seek to emphasize here is how these more advanced production processes need to be understood in their proper context. Whether or not the more technologically advanced production processes contribute to Mexico's economic development is a nonissue from the perspective of the U.S.-owned maquila operations—the origin of nearly 90 percent of all the FDI in the industry (Dussel Peters 2010, 59). The purpose of operating such advanced production processes, of course, has been to engage in a defensive struggle on the part of U.S. manufacturers who seek to address the forces of entropy that overcame them in the 1970s and 1980s. What needs to be emphasized is that the more highly capitalized plants were intended to be *complementary components* in a new *globally integrated production system*. This new system has been institutionalized from the late 1970s and early 1980s onward to the moment by nearly all the major manufacturers operating in the triad system.

In this transition *some* dependent and economically weak nations were sited into the new webs and networks of production. The process was far from homogeneous, or *global*. Mexico, for reasons of history, geography, political-economic pliability, and resource endowments (seemingly unlimited supplies of low-wage labor, yet to be exhausted), has been the most preferred locus for the global displacement of the United States' national production system—but far from its only locus. What this means is that, geographically, the U.S. national production system now includes a set of production *enclaves* in Mexico—particularly northern and north central Mexico. More than in any other industry, this "logic" of displacement has been driven by the strategies employed in the auto and auto parts industry (Dicken 2003, 355–98). For example, in a study of FDI in the Mexican manufacturing sector (including maquiladoras) from 1994 to 2005, Dussel Peters found that three of the ten most important areas for foreign investment were related to the auto sector (Dussel Peters 2010, 66). In total, the auto parts, auto assembly, and automotive electrical systems production areas accounted for 22.4 percent of all FDI and an overwhelming 45 percent of the top ten production areas receiving FDI. To put the matter into greater relief, the next-highest sector, accounting for a mere 4.82 percent of all FDI in the years sited, was devoted to the manufacturing of sodas (closely followed by investments in cigarettes).

How the globally integrated production system works in practice in Mexico does not yield to simple interpretation. Cutting through the accumulation of data, conjunctural, and institutional factors, Capdevielle has presented the most persuasive theoretical account of Mexico's dilemma: Mexico is now merely one of several important sites in a complex internationalized interactive web. The production system "is not the result of free international trade, although this is a requirement, but rather it is the strategy of productive organizations [e.g., TNCs] that define new global forms of competition and cooperation" (Capdevielle 2007, 52). In this new internationalized structure of production Mexico's role, as defined by the U.S.-based TNCs who are dominant in this structure, is to provide a strategically necessary component that cannot be easily or adequately acquired in the United States, that is, an abundant and seemingly inexhaustible supply of cheap, pliable, responsive, and quickly trained labor—a description that most recently defined 79 percent of the maquila labor force (Capdevielle 2007, 71).

The new system of production processes is fluid and often semiunique as measured from industry to industry and from nation to nation. The relationships established are not stable, and there is no one unique path of organization. The new structure is marked by a high degree of rivalry induced by rapid technological changes that generate swift obsolescence and changes in production processes. It is constructed through a symbiosis of both unregulated markets and planning initiatives instituted by the agents participating in the system. Capdevielle argues that the new system accounts for roughly 50 percent of all the Mexican workforce committed to manufacturing activities—involving both the maquiladoras and the disguised maquilas, or what has recently been termed the IMMEX sector (accounting for 81 percent of all manufactured exports in 2006).

The activities undertaken in Mexico by the TNCs are presumably highly profitable, yet the data available do not record the magnitude of the profitability. Capdevielle's analysis of this situation is the following: Maquiladora workers are much more productive than the numbers suggest. Through transfer pricing—the underinvoicing of the value of semifinished and finished products exported from Mexico and the overinvoicing of intermediate inputs coming into Mexico—the real profitable nature of the maquila industry remains obscured. Were this not the case, Mexico would have, and particularly Mexican workers would have, a legitimate claim on the value of their productivity. One compelling reason for this proposition is that maquila workers—in spite of the frequently high level of mechanization and sophistication of production processes—officially show virtually stagnant levels of productivity. Another reason is that under different schemes of accounting (which exclude transfer pricing), Mexican manufacturing sector workers (non-maquila) show significantly higher productivity levels (without equivalent levels of production systems). These sets of relationships—what might incorrectly be understood as anomalies or asymmetries—are, in fact, organic, central components of the globally integrated production system. In other words, set on a broader theoretical plane, the maquilas are a consistent and valuable generator of *unearned income transfers* for U.S.-based firms (and, of course, all other foreign investors who engage in similar practices).

The conventional understanding of the inner workings of the maquila system and the magnitude of the surplus transfer from Mexico is blurred by a series of complex arrangements leading to underpayment of workers, evasion of taxes, and chronic undervaluation of resources such as land and structures. The maquila regime deflects understanding of the magnitude of the potential technological economic rents that Mexico could partially capture under a distinct institutional structure guided by a national developmental consciousness that has been frequently exhibited in Asia:

> The concept of gross value added includes wages, taxes and the gross operating surplus, which includes both profits and the depreciation of fixed capital [machinery and equipment]. In the case of the maquiladora industry, wages are clearly included, but the accounting operations of the companies can be altered in regard to net profits and the payment of taxes due on them, and given the

[bookkeeping] method of entering consigned assets as if they were inputs, the measure of value added fails to account for the depreciation on these assets. The result is that due to the methods of operation of the maquila industry allowed under the current rules and regulations, the calculations of both the level of value added and the productivity based upon it are underestimated. (Capdevielle 2007, 76–77)

Still, in spite of the above considerations, the essence of the maquila industry is to free international capital from the obligation to pay wages that would presumably be paid in the advanced industrial nations, *even as the complex combinations of machinery, technology, and organization produce extremely high levels of labor productivity—permitting the realization of high-value-added activities to take place in the offshore profit centers chosen by the TNCs.* The new systems allow for the deconstruction and reconstruction of complex value chains—inserting cheap Mexican labor into advanced processes of production. All this allows for the realization of the returns on labor, capital, and technology to occur outside of Mexico. "This means that the [maquila] firms, paradoxically, can make intensive use of capital and cutting-edge technologies in the production of advanced products, without the implication of the payment of higher wages, or with a larger portion of local inputs" (Capdevielle 2007, 76–78).

It is worth recalling that national inputs into the production process—excluding packaging, transportation, electricity, and so on—amount to roughly 30 percent of the value of all inputs in the national manufacturing sector, but only 3 percent in the maquila firms. As Guillén Romo (2004, 186–87) notes: "Around the export pole are infrequently gathered 'backward linkage' or 'forward linkage' activities on the Mexican side—due to the weak integration of the entire export sector with the internal system of production—instead, above all, they exist on the U.S. side. This has created *regional production chains* of a transnational character, which have been substituted for national production chains."

CREATING AN ENCLAVE

The use of terms such as "dependent nations" and "enclave economies" has largely fallen out of fashion, particularly among most analysts focusing on the maquila sector. However, it is worth considering the concept of the enclave economy—long relegated to national economic systems dominated by plantations and/or mineral extraction—to understand the general long-term socioeconomic impact of FDI both in the maquila and non-maquila manufacturing sectors in Mexico. Focusing on the information technology

(IT) industry in and around Guadalajara (which began as a result of maquiladora investments), Gallagher and Zarsky found that "the FDI-led strategy has had limited success in stimulating the growth of Mexican firms either as competitors or suppliers to the multinationals. Instead, Mexican industry is being hollowed out and the economy as a whole has been bifurcated into a foreign 'enclave economy' and a domestic economy. Within the IT sector, a thriving domestic industry was largely wiped out and replaced by a foreign IT enclave" (Gallagher and Zarsky 2007, 1–2).

Their conclusions stand in stark contrast to the conventional wisdom that FDI is a fountainhead of transferable know-how. Among many others, the OECD gave vent to this approach in the following passage, cited by Gallagher and Zarsky: "Given the appropriate host-country policies and a basic level of development, a preponderance of studies shows that FDI triggers technology spill-overs, assists human capital formation, contributes to international trade integration, helps create a more competitive business and enhances enterprise development" (Gallagher and Zarsky 2007, 4). The portion of the above that must be emphasized—well known and long ago lost in high policy-making circles in Mexico—is *"Given the appropriate host-country policies. . . ."* Research on how effectively the developing nations of Asia have constructed policies to appropriate substantial portions of the spillover potentialities has been available for decades (Amsden 1989; Gereffi 1992). And, as we have shown in chapter 2, Mexico once demonstrated sustained capacity, not merely advantageous "host-country policies" but also endogenous industrial policies that either led or complemented FDI promotion.

Having made the above observations, Gallagher and Zarsky's case study of the IT industry led to a broad summing up that pointed exactly at the crux of Mexico's growing dilemma:

> Endogenous capacities for production and innovation held within domestic firms form the bedrock of sustainable industrial development. In most medium to large economies, local firms account for the bulk of industrial activity. An influx of FDI can quickly boost exports earnings and local employment. However, if [transnational corporations] are disarticulated from the local economy—that is, if financial, technological, knowledge, and human capital transfers are largely kept within foreign companies—local firms do not learn to undertake more advanced technological functions that enable them to move up the value chain. The benefits of FDI are captured primarily within the foreign enclave rather than diffused through the economy. (Gallagher and Zarsky 2007, 5)

The unlikely story of Mexico's IT industry began in the 1970s when Mexico's National Commission on Science and Technology (CONACYT) decided that the road to increasing national self-sufficiency in technology ran through the then-emerging computer industry. Seeking to build on established capabilities in the electronics industry, the state sought promotion of a new industry that would both supply the national market and exhibit strong export capacity. Only transnational corporations (TNCs) willing to accept (1) minority ownership up to 49 percent of capital invested, (2) the goal of achieving 70 percent national supply capacity in the computer industry, and (3) the expenditure of the equivalent of 3–6 percent of sales revenue on research and development were allowed to participate in the program (Gallagher and Zarsky 2007, 122–28). The program worked remarkably well for a time: By 1987, 56 percent of the demand for computers was being furnished by firms operating under the requirements of the program. More importantly, in light of the general goals of the program, an astonishing 50 percent of production was provided by wholly owned Mexican producers.

What happened? In 1985 IBM sought its first manufacturing plant in Guadalajara—but it balked at the 49 percent ownership cap. It wanted to establish Mexico as the private-sector alternative to state-led efforts in developing nations to build a computer industry. The Mexican government struck a deal exempting IBM from the national ownership rule. IBM established 100 percent ownership on the condition that it created a new center for semiconductor technology to train a cadre of Mexican professionals in the 1988–1994 period. Soon IBM "demanded and was given an exemption of the joint venture rule" of the IT program, and no reciprocal conditions (such as the establishment of the new center) were demanded of IBM (Gallagher and Zarsky 2007, 125). By 1987, other foreign firms were granted the same privileges without conditions, and the new policy of liberalization was instituted. President Salinas, by 1990, had begun to dismantle the domestic computer industry—the NAFTA negotiations sealed its fate. No longer would the government allow tariffs to promote national production and, equally important, the government ceased preferential buying from national suppliers. Local content and minimal R & D requirements were also abandoned.

Mexico still had a crying need for foreign exchange as the debt crisis of the 1980s hung over the economy. Dropping the state-led industrialization program in this sector was thought to be a way of attracting more FDI and creating much-needed foreign exchange. FDI went up by a factor of four in the electronic industry in general.

However, in the IT industry and elsewhere, Mexico suffers from the "missing middle" of local suppliers who are the recipients of diffused knowledge. In Asia these national firms possess a command of technological capabilities to the degree that these productive supplier firms can maintain global competitiveness and thereby help drive the export process:

Rather than contract with local Mexican firms, the global flagships [such as Hewlett-Packard and IBM] invited large, mostly US contract manufacturing firms (CMs) such as Flextronics and Solectron to co-locate in Guadalajara. The CMs, in turn, built their competitive advantage on managing a third tier of global suppliers, many in East Asia, on a razor-thin profit margin. Less than 5 percent of inputs were sourced locally. Far from generating broad-based growth, Mexico's "Silicon Valley" had been transformed by 2000 into a foreign enclave, and only a few of the original 50 Mexican IT firms were still in business. (Gallagher and Zarsky 2007, 7)

The failure of the Mexican IT sector was no minor matter—"More than on any other industry, Mexico pinned its post-NAFTA hopes for economic development on the local growth of a vibrant, export-oriented information technology industry" (Gallagher and Zarsky 2007, 71). The global IT industry, more concentrated than the global oil industry, was by 2000 plagued by overcapacity. U.S.-based TNCs reacted to this intensified competition by first crowding out Mexican supplier firms, bringing in their own preferred contract manufacturers (CMs)—who often had technological capabilities that exceeded top-tier producers, such as IBM. When this strategy failed to resolve the difficulties of the U.S.-based TNCs, their reaction was to shift production to Asia, particularly China. All this left Mexico farther away from the technological frontier, with fewer endogenous capabilities and national supplier/manufacturers than it had fifteen or twenty years earlier.

Using effective government leadership, Asian nations have been able to harness FDI to develop a national supplier base in the IT sector and elsewhere. The policies employed have facilitated the achievement of advanced technological processes in manufacturing and have created links with local universities to pursue a mutual research agenda. All this has created both viable and vigorous domestic firms and new national leaders capable of achieving their own export capacity. This optimal path has been found in Taiwan, China, India, Malaysia, and, to a certain degree, Korea. Mexico, on the other hand, embraced the neoliberal faith in passivity regarding markets and its hostility to public policies. From 1973 through 1989 Mexico operated within the guidelines set by the Technology Transfer Law, which attempted to ensure that Mexico could bargain constructively to acquire technologies from foreign sources under conditions that promoted national research and development and technology transfers. In 1990 President Salinas's reformulation of this policy allowed only the firms directly involved in FDI (e.g., the TNCs) to determine the scope (if any) of technology transfers. As a result of all of the above factors and policies, from 2000 to 2003 IT exports dropped by 60 percent, FDI fell precipitously, and 60,000 jobs left for China (Gallagher and Zarsky 2007, 71–88; 99–157).

EXPORT GROWTH WITHOUT EXPORT-LED GROWTH

Moreno-Brid and Ros aptly captured Mexico's dilemma with their pithy comment: "There has been rapid export growth, but no rapid export-led growth"
(Moreno-Brid and Ros 2009, 227). Let us recall the recent dimensions of the
centrality of Mexico's maquila-led transformation. Between 1994 and 2005
(before the levitation of oil prices), 72.3 percent of the growth of Mexico's
GDP was attributable to the increase in exports. From 1989 to 2005 the volume of national exports increased by a factor of six (Arroyo Picard 2007,
185). "Over the period 1985–2005, foreign investment grew by a factor of 7.
. . . Twenty-eight percent was in the form of mergers and acquisitions while
72 percent was greenfield investment" (Gallagher and Zarsky 2007, 54).
Exports of manufactured products as a share of total exports rose from 10
percent in 1980 to nearly 85 percent at the close of the 1990s. This export performance was more extraordinary than Malaysia's (19 percent to 79 percent),
Indonesia's (2 percent to 45 percent), Thailand's (25 percent to 74 percent),
and even Singapore's (43 percent to 86 percent) (Gallagher and Zarsky 2007,
85–86).

If manufactured exports and plenty of new FDI are a shortcut to economic
development, what explains Mexico's stagnant wages in manufacturing, the
troubling jobs deficit (more than one million per year), runaway emigration,
and staggering poverty levels? This question has been answered by many
perceptive analysts.[10]

It would be very difficult to improve upon the summary analysis recently
offered by Huerta Moreno, Maldonado, and Mariña Flores:

> The neoliberal modality of accumulation entails neither expansion nor de-
> velopment; it is, rather, a concentrator of income and wealth and therefore
> of the profitable opportunities for all economic spheres. . . . In the particular
> case of Mexico, policies of deregulation and the indiscriminate opening of the
> international sector have disarticulated the internal production chains, dein-
> dustrializing the country while maquilizing and concentrating the productive
> structure of the manufacturing sector increasing its dependence on imports.
> This dependence arises from the propensity to import both the capital goods
> and intermediate inputs of the manufacturing industry at a greater rate than
> exports expand, giving rise to well-known negative effects on the balance of
> payments. In relative terms, the importation of intermediate goods has grown
> in a significant manner as a result of the growth of maquila exports and due
> to *the progressive maquilization of traditional manufacturing*. . . . The de-
> creasing tendency to import capital goods shows us . . . that the anticipated
> modernization of technology has not occurred: Rather, during the period of
> neoliberal restructuring the business sector has sought to utilize labor in an

intensive manner, given the availability of cheap workers. (Huerta Moreno, Maldonado, and Mariña Flores 2007, 106)

The broad but accurate characterization of the Mexican economy under what these authors term the "neoliberal modality" deserves more extended consideration: First, consider deindustrialization—the national manufacturing sector shrank from 23 percent of GDP in 1988 to 17 percent in 2003 and has remained at that level through late 2008 (Garrido and Padilla 2007, 88; Dussel Peters 2009, 49).[11] At the same time, the weight of the maquila sector, expressed as a share of total manufacturing exports, went up remarkably. As noted above, the national manufacturing sector (excluding the maquilas) pays significantly higher wages—meaning that, overall, wage income has dramatically shrunk as the national manufacturing sector has shrunk while the maquila sector has grown (relatively in terms of employment, as well as in terms of value).

But, further, through programs instituted in the 1990s to promote temporary imports of inputs (discussed in the following chapter), a very large portion of Mexican manufacturers became similar to the maquilas in that they more and more depended on a rising tide of foreign-owned suppliers and imported inputs, including capital goods. Not only did this occur, but in addition, companies that were not export oriented came to increasingly rely on imported inputs for many reasons: In some instances their national-based suppliers were forced out of business due to the rapid drop in tariffs and other changes (such as the abandonment of local content legislation or the government's unwillingness to prioritize purchases of national products). Other companies folded during the downturn of 1994–1995 or because of abrupt changes in the exchange rate or due to the critical lack of availability of financing for small and medium-sized businesses. Domestic firms were unable to sidestep a variety of taxes, while maquila firms could and did.

Without attempting to locate an exhaustive list of factors that led to the deindustrialization, the point is that even firms that were not directly connected to the new "externalized" economy often ended up importing more inputs. For example, excluding maquila and disguised maquila firms, manufacturers increased their importation of intermediate inputs from 14.1 percent in 1980 to 21.8 percent in 1993 and 33.8 percent in 1998 (Flores 2004, 110). Indeed, with the exception of the crisis of 1994–1995, the trade deficit of the manufacturing sector has been steadily growing—by 2008 the manufacturing sector as a whole had a trade deficit of more than 30 percent (Dussel Peters 2009, 46). What this means is that the trade surplus of the maquila and disguised maquila firms—the sine qua non of the existing model based in the export of manufactures—is constantly undercut by the large and growing tendency for the manufacturers who are *not* exporters to import more and more of their intermediate inputs and luxury goods. In the final analysis, this has meant that Mexico has a trade balance (current account) that has hovered close to zero from 1994 through 2008. In short, Mexico exports more and more so that it can *import* more and more products that once were made nationally (or could be made nationally).

From the standpoint of the Mexican economy and the Mexican populace at large, the above noted tendencies appear to be, and are, perverse. However, the export-led model was never intended to be a facilitator of *Mexican* economic development. The model was intended as a *defensive* strategy on the part of large, often technologically advanced, U.S.-based manufacturing firms.[12] From this perspective, it is possible to view the maquila and disguised maquila sector—what has been termed the IMMEX sector since the beginning of 2007—as a success because it has generally met the strategic objectives of transnational (particularly U.S.) firms.

MEXICAN CAPITAL IN THE EXPORT MODEL

Regarding the Mexican *grupos* or conglomerates, the core of President Salinas's project was to "strengthen the business groups" (Vidal 2004, 57). Without the strengthening of the oligopolistic/monopolistic groups (who acquired most all of the privatized assets in the 1980s and 1990s, often paying pennies on the dollar value for these public assets), these conglomerates—in Salinas's own words—"would be [in] difficult [circumstances] to meet the competitive challenges of globalization, and Mexico would be left outside of the world markets" (Vidal 2004, 57). This did not mean, however, that Salinas foresaw that the *grupos* would have any considerable degree of manufacturing export capacity. Rather, they would be accommodated by virtue of the profitable niches they occupied within the Mexican economy, while facilitating the expansion of U.S. firms in various ways. Given their previous investments and their knowledge of national markets, the *grupos* could pursue nonmanufacturing activities—such as mining or real estate speculation—where economic rents were quickly and easily accumulated.

THE DEBATE OVER SECOND- AND THIRD-GENERATION MAQUILA FIRMS: "UPGRADING" OF PRODUCTION PROCESSES

Mexico's export-led model, then, would seem to generate (as Moreno-Brid and Ros noted) rapid export growth and no possibility of export-led *develop-*

ment. In short, it is functioning very well in terms of the conditions under which it was created and to which it has currently evolved. It is the logical result of *asymmetrical integration*. Because it does not and cannot create viable forward, backward, or lateral linkages, because it does not and cannot contribute to the capture of technological rents or spinoffs, it cannot be—under the current institutional and policy structure—more than, at best, a relatively trivial contributor to the advancement of the productive potentialities of the Mexican populace.

This, at any rate, would seem to be the consensus of a vast body of research. But it is far from the consensus due to the enthusiastic efforts of a school of researchers who have since the 1990s insisted that they have located systematic processes of technological transfers. These authors, clustered around the prolific work of Jorge Carrillo, have produced a stream of research material. On the other side of the dispute one finds not only many of the authors cited in previous sections of this chapter, but most especially the equally prolific Enrique de la Garza Toledo and his close research associates. This chapter closes with a consideration of the strongest arguments presented by the protagonists of the debate over the existence or nonexistence of the so-called second- and third-generation maquilas and the consequences pertaining to the hypotheses advanced by the protagonists, beginning with the views of Carrillo and his colleagues.

EVOLUTION AND UPGRADING IN THE MAQUILA PLANTS

An appreciable portion of the researchers who would seek to label the maquiladora program as a partial or total success for Mexico in terms of promoting or assisting economic development have adopted a "Schumpeterian" stance. J. A. Schumpeter, one of the greatest economists of the twentieth century, emphasized many things that are associated with the term "Schumpeterian," including the idea that economic systems "evolve"—rather than constantly diverting from and returning to some competitive equilibrium. It has become fashionable to recall one of Schumpeter's most important concepts—"the hurricane of creative destruction." To put the matter in a very compact form, Schumpeter believed that the search for profits drove the economic system to new heights as already-established industries dominating through the control of existing technologies were inevitably displaced by upstart firms, using new technologies that made the old ones obsolete. Thus destruction of the old constituted the *creation* of the new (and better). Front and center in any Schumpeterian analysis is technology—something that has always made neoclassical economists quite uncomfortable. And, more to the front and center—in Schumpeter's view—was the role of the entrepreneur as the striving innovator who drives the entire process of creative destruction and, therefore, economic growth.

It should be stressed at the outset that, prima facie, the association with Schumpeter is strangely selective because, clearly, the causal agent in Schumpeter's scheme is absent in Mexico. That is, aside from certain exceptions that prove the rule (usually associated with the Monterrey region), "Schumpeterian entrepreneurs" are virtually absent nationally, and they cannot exist in the maquila industry. Entrepreneurs cannot exist—or at least they certainly have never been found—in the maquila industry because the maquilas are the distant points of implementation of production processes that have been minutely predefined. Maquila plant managers, including all those we interviewed in researching this book, are order takers, not order makers. When, on rare occasion, maquila plants alter some aspect of production, this is not *innovation in the Schumpeterian sense*; when it is to be found at all, it amounts to incremental changes. In Schumpeter's theoretical construct the entrepreneur makes the decision to leap headlong into a new technological area, assuming massive risks and implementing structural changes in production and process technologies. Maquila managers are at the most distant end of the production chain—their task is to accept detailed direction from the top of the production chain. Any changes they are *allowed* to implement will be, by all accounts, marginal.

The idea that the maquilas are to be understood in the context of an evolutionary analysis has been advanced at least since the late 1980s (Gereffi 1992). A vast literature has emerged, and we will focus only on some of the accounts presented in two recent efforts. Jorge Carrillo and María del Rosio Barajas have assembled a collection of articles wherein Carrillo and Gomis assert that in the frontier region, "managers of foreign firms have been 'Mexicanized' and they undertake decisions that are increasingly autonomous from their headquarters" (Carrillo and Gomis 2007, 18). No longer, according to these authors and their associates, are the maquiladora firms mere assembly plants. Carrillo and Gomis locate five stages ranging from simple assembly to advanced design and engineering. This schema is collapsed into three "generations"—simple assembly, second-stage or "generation" maquilas where firms utilize *just-in-time* practices and "best practices" procedures, and the vaunted third-generation wherein the most advanced and complex aspects of production—design, engineering, research, and development—are located.

The fact is, there *are* a handful of such advanced centers along the border and in the interior of Mexico. The question, however, is what to make of it. At the moment, a few isolated sightings hardly constitute a trend and certainly do not suggest that plants that have moved beyond simple assembly will somehow evolve into R & D centers, generating endogenous technological advances. We can, therefore, essentially dismiss the idea that there is any third generation of plants or any evidence that such a generation will arise in the foreseeable future, given present policies and practices. In doing so, a major portion of the argument that maquilas are transmitting "learning" and "technology transfers" also falls to the ground.

What, then, of the so-called second-generation plants? Surprisingly, Car rillo and Gomis state: "[Here] wages do not rise with that of productivity, nor as modernization occurs; the substantive part of maquila activity continues to be assembly with a low-skilled labor force; integration with the national productive system is scarce" (Carrillo and Gomis 2007, 26–27). They subsequently state that 80 percent of the workers in the frontier region continue to be low skilled and that the number of technicians employed had hardly changed from 1980 to 2000 (Carrillo and Gomis 2007, 37). Still, they insist that along the border the plants are now "heterogeneous" in terms of their levels of technology and organization. Their research results "permit us to demonstrate the existence of a modern sector that has achieved advancement in the process of industrial upgrading" (Carrillo and Rosio Barajas 2007, 13).

Rosio Barajas and two associates introduce the concept of technoproductive structures, arguing that in the frontier region their categorization allows them to associate 51.5 percent of the plants sampled as exhibiting a "basic level," and 45.1 percent operating at an "intermediate level" (Rosio Barajas, Rodrí- guez, and Almaraz 2007, 164–66). Since elsewhere, this group of researchers locates only three "advanced level" plants, it is not clear how the authors arrived at the calculation that 3.4 percent of the plants—or approximately ten of the sampled plants—were in the advanced category. The authors' attempt to categorize on the basis of a technoproductive structure ends in a muddle when they acknowledge that large numbers of the *basic* plants use cutting-edge technologies—48 percent of those operating in the "basic level" claimed that their base technologies were comparable to the most advanced worldwide (Rosio Barajas, Rodríguez, and Almaraz 2007, 185).

Our research survey instruments, utilized in a study of the auto and auto parts sector in a central state in Mexico, indicated that these results cannot be easily duplicated. No plant managers interviewed in our study made such a claim. In any case, what Carrillo and his associates have documented is a *distinction without a difference*. Some plants, perhaps a considerable number, have restructured, and their production processes are now more advanced. But this does not mean that wage levels have risen, no substantial evidence of technological transfers or spinoffs has been documented, higher levels of complexity in production have not increased value-added activities in Mexico, nor has this change been associated with higher degrees of autonomy from headquarters operations (Rosio Barajas, Rodríguez, and Almaraz 2007, 148).

The second recent compendium summarizing a considerable body of research conducted by those who associate their work with an evolutionary approach focused on a number of related issues regarding learning and upgrading.Vera-Cruz and Dutrénit claim that there *are* knowledge spillover effects from the maquilas. However, they go on to note, this involves only a "very small" number of firms (Vera-Cruz and Dutrénit 2007, 244), which suggests that their findings are insignificant. In this second compendium Capdevielle would seem to have the final word: he acknowledges that the level of complexity of many plants has evolved, technical knowledge applied to the production process has improved, organizational structures and managerial capacities have become more sophisticated, many products produced are now more technologically advanced, yet two identical plants located in two distinct nations (such as the U.S. and Mexico) can yield distinct levels of value added (Capdevielle 2007, 83–86). It is therefore possible to draw the important distinction between *upgrading of production processes and upgrading of value*. In Mexico, while the production processes have been upgraded to some appreciable degree, the *appropriation* of value is based on the (external) ownership of the technology and capital equipment—meaning that Mexico's share in the globally integrated production process remains overwhelmingly merely the input of cheap labor.

ENRIQUE DE LA GARZA'S CRITICAL PERSPECTIVE

Enrique de la Garza's most recent attempt to capture the essence of the maquiladora operations is based in a very large empirical study known as ENESTYC 1999 and 2001. These are the most recent results available of the largest study ever conducted on the maquila industry. Based in this study (which also has been confirmed by FLACSO's research), de la Garza dismisses the very idea of the third-generation maquilas and contests the idea of the second-generation maquilas (Puyana 2008, 17–18). He points out that only 3.6 percent of the machine tools in the maquilas were "numerical control machines" and only 5.2 percent of the machine tools used were "computerized numerical control machines." In other words, then, more than 90 percent of the machine tools in the maquila sector were outmoded (de la Garza 2005, 49). Only 17 percent of the maquilas conducted any form of research and development. The dominant foreign firms devoted only 1.15 percent of their income to technology expenditures. Eighty-seven percent of this spending was for machinery and equipment, leaving 0.01 percent of income spent on R & D (de la Garza 2005, 51).

Backward and forward linkages—the interconnections that the new growth economics emphasized would be the mechanisms for learning and spillover effects—were found in only 2.8 percent of the maquilas who subcontracted with other maquilas—these subcontracting activities entailed only 5 percent of the value of production realized by the subcontractors (de la Garza 2005, 58). Nearly two-thirds (64 percent) of those employed in the maquila industry have three years or less of seniority, while on average workers receive only thirteen hours per year of training (de la Garza 2005, 61, 63). This suggests that learning effects will be minimal.

While the maquila plants have done relatively little to realize a thorough-going technological transformation of their production processes, de la Garza maintains that the effort at the organizational level has been greater. For the large maquilas (more than 250 employees), who account for the overwhelming bulk of maquila sales, organizational changes had been introduced by 64 percent of the firms by 1994, rising to 95.4 percent by 2001 (de la Garza 2007, 65).

Generally, those who share the *upgrading* perspective have argued that these changes in organization—involving a shift from "Fordism" to "Toyotism"—are part of the process of building a new *knowledge economy* in Mexico. But de la Garza, an expert on labor processes, also contests this notion. In effect, what he finds is that firms in Mexico practice an abbreviated and shallow form of production that blends early-twentieth-century Fordist elements of assembly production with late-nineteenth-century "Taylorist" forms of speedup and late-twentieth-century "Toyotist" organizational forms. In 2004, 77.3 percent of the maquila firms were of the old Taylorist-Fordist configuration—47 percent of them operating with average to low levels of (1) labor training, (2) technology, and (3) labor flexibility. Only 22.7 percent were operating with Toyotist practices (just-in-time, quality circles, continual upgrading of labor processes, flexible production, and so on). Of those firms that had undergone an organizational transformation, 75 percent operated with average or below-average technology, flexibility, and labor-training levels (de la Garza 2007, 70).

In short, even the advocates of the upgrading hypothesis have great difficulty establishing its existence and cannot demonstrate that it has reached a level of significance. Organizational restructuring, to institute best practices from the Toyota model, has likewise been wildly exaggerated. A careful examination of the trajectory of the maquila sector, unfortunately, points to the endurance of an old, tired French adage—*the more things change, the more they remain the same.*

Chapter Five

The Disguised Maquila
Sector and Beyond

This chapter focuses on the "parallel" maquila firms—those firms that have operated as high exporters yet have not been registered under the maquila regime. We begin by briefly summarizing some of the important general characteristics of these firms. We then focus the remainder of the chapter on a regional case study of the auto sector. This allows us to expand upon some of the crucial issues at stake regarding the continuation of current economic policies. An examination of these parallel maquila firms demonstates once again that the export-at-all-cost approach, as tied to a largely unregulated production process driven by and for transnational capital—overwhelmingly from the United States—has resulted in the marginalization of Mexico's dwindling industrial base. Unable, except in the rarest of instances, to participate in this production process, Mexico's endogenous technological capabilities have atrophied.

GENERAL CHARACTERISTICS OF THE
DISGUISED MAQUILA SECTOR

From 1985 onward, various governmental programs allowed foreign-owned transplant firms (and Mexican-owned companies) the option of both selling in the domestic market *and* the tariff exemptions and other privileges received by the maquila firms on imported components and parts—as well as machinery and equipment—when their production was exported. To exist in this category, a minimal level of exports had to be achieved and maintained. Such firms were then part of the PITEX program—the Program for the Temporary Importation of Export Items (de Maria y Campos et al. 2009, 37–41). The PITEX program began as part of the broad umbrella initiative known as PRONAFICE 1984–1988 (the National Program to Develop Industry and Foreign Trade), discussed in chapter 2. Intended to target ten key sectors—including the auto sector, where it had its greatest success—PRONAFICE was the last effort by the developmental nationalists to reinvigorate import-substitution policies during the 1982–1987 period (as discussed in chapter 2). PITEX firms were variously officially defined as corporations undertaking "indirect exports" and firms engaged in "sub-maquila operations." In 2002 they were required to export at least $500,000 US per year, or 10 percent of their production.

We have termed these high-export non-maquila plants the "disguised maquilas." These high-export firms operate with a significant portion of their production essentially devoted to processing imported inputs for re-export. Yet these activities, broadly similar in many respects to those undertaken by the maquila firms, were not—until late 2006—officially recognized in the discussion of the export-led model. That is, there is a vast literature dissecting almost every possible aspect of the maquila industry and a near paucity of analyses focusing on the more than three thousand firms operating in the *disguised maquila* sector. Over time the differences between the two diminished to the point that officially, in 2007, the two were merged under the Program for Maquiladora, Manufacturing and Export Services, or IMMEX. This program formally allowed the former PITEX firms the benefits that the maquila firms have received.[1] In short, there now are no differences of note between maquila firms and the disguised maquila firms in terms of customs duties, import-export laws, and internal taxes.

Figure 5.1 records the overall employment level in the disguised maquila (or PITEX) firms—including those workers *not* engaged in export activities. In most recent years the PITEX firms' overall employment level actually exceeded or matched that of the maquilas, according to the CNIMME, which compiles the data (as shown on the left axis).[2] The line in the figure pertains to the right-hand scale and measures the level of employment in the IMMEX firms (maquila plus disguised maquila) as a share of all formal manufacturing employment.

In early 2007 the IMMEX sector consisted of 3,620 PITEX firms and 2,795 maquiladora firms. (In mid-2009 there were a total of 6,120 IMMEX firms—295 fewer than in 2007.) These firms produced, as highlighted in chapter 1, 83 percent of all manufactured exports and 68 percent of total exports. But the exports of the maquiladoras exceeded those of the PITEX firms by $44.5 billion US ($96.8 billion versus $52.3 billion) in 2005 (Cañas and Gilmer 2007, 10). Furthermore, in the years 2000–2005, the maquila firms showed much higher export growth than did the disguised maquilas.

There are important geographical and other structural differences between the maquilas and the disguised maquilas. Even today 82 percent of the ma-

Figure 5.1. Employment in Mexico's Export Processing Programs, 2000–2008

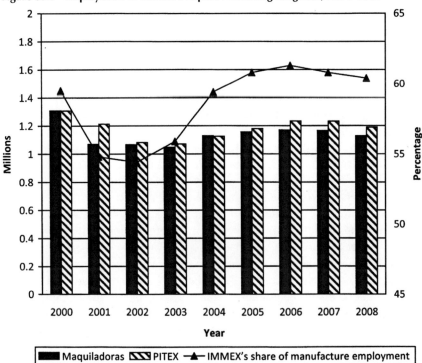

Maquiladoras PITEX IMMEX's share of manufacture employment

Source: INEGI "Maquiladoras"; CNIMME 2009. "Estadísticas" Indicadores Básicos de la Industria Maquiladora y Manufacturera de Exportación, Hoja 5d. Secretaría de Trabajo y Previsión Social. 2009. "Estadísticas del Sector."

quilas are clustered among seven border states. The disguised maquilas are predominantly older plants, only 35 percent of which are located in the border region. An equal number of the disguised maquila plants—35.5 percent of the total—are located in the old central industrial corridor in and around Mexico City—the State of Mexico, the Federal District, and the State of Puebla. But the tendency is unmistakable; future growth will mostly occur in the border region and in the north central states. Geographic location is important because it captures some of the distinguishing, essential elements of the disguised maquilas: these firms have older and deeper production systems (higher capital intensity, fewer low-skill labor-intensive operations) and their unions have a history of leadership and responsibility to their members that is only very rarely reproduced in the border states and north central states. Legacy union representation from the state-led industrialization era is important, but significant differences also exist because the major

TNCs generally accept a policy of industrial relations wherein payment of subsistence wages is not a goal (Cypher 2004a, 363). The disguised maquila production activities employ at minimum 500,000 workers, representing approximately 37 percent of all non-maquila manufacturing workers who are conventionally assumed to be working in the *national* manufacturing sector (Capdevielle 2005, 568).[3]

To the degree that plants in the north are currently producing identical products, such as autos, that have long been produced in the old central industrial corridor, the culture of pay and work is, if not exactly duplicated, of greater similarity than is to be found between a routine maquila operation and a disguised maquila operation such as an auto assembly plant. (This distinction does not carry over to all links in the supply chain: low-end auto parts suppliers serving the demands of the disguised maquilas make the most labor-intensive products with virtually no sizable innovation tendencies that would require capital deepening and retraining of the labor force and they offer the most basic of maquila wages and low-end benefits (Juárez 1999). The size of the pay differential between the two high-export sectors is difficult to calibrate and average—especially since the disguised maquilas have not received the attention from researchers that the maquilas have received. However, the results are likely to be striking, based on the spread recorded between apparel workers and electronics-sector workers (both overwhelmingly maquila operations) and transportation equipment–sector workers (heavily represented in the disguised maquila firms). Early in the twenty-first century apparel workers averaged $1.60 US per hour (including benefits), and electronics workers received $2.45 per hour (Ruiz Durán 2003, 61). In contrast, transport equipment workers averaged $4.99 per hour, with more extensive benefits.

Workers, regardless of the large differentials, are paid meager wages given the fact that (as noted) their productivity often approximates levels found in the (northern) industrial nations.[4] Frequently, the south/north wage differential (Mexico/U.S.) will be in the range of 1:7 in the parallel, or disguised, maquila sector (the auto differential is 1:6). This differential can be nearly double the 1:7 ratio in the maquila sector. The International Labor Organization found that for Mexican manufacturing workers *overall* (maquila plus non-maquila) in relation to U.S. manufacturing workers in 2003, the ratio was 1:11 (Howard 2004, 2). Even as foreign direct investment (FDI) has poured into Mexico throughout the NAFTA period, wages in the disguised maquila sector have fallen by more than 12 percent. In the maquila sector, in spite of some rising productivity, wages increased by only 3 percent or less from 1994 to 2003. In 2004, the daily wage of 3 percent of the lowest-paid maquila workers was $0.12 US.

More generally, as much as 38 percent of all processed/manufactured export output in recent years was undertaken via temporary import incentive
schemes—such as PITEX—and a similar program known as Altex (Capdevielle 2005, 564–65; Dussel Peters 2006, 83–85).[5] The disguised maquila
firms are, with rare exception, large transnationals (TNCs), usually from the
United States. They incorporate maquila-made parts and components (known
as "virtual exports"), or parts/components from the designated Mexican sup
plier web, and generate finished manufacturing products—often of a sophisticated nature, such as autos—which are then exported, primarily into the
U.S. market (see figure 5.2).[6] In addition, *the larger portion* of the processing
activities of the disguised maquilas consists of direct *temporary* importation
of parts and components, which are then re-exported after they have been
processed or assembled in the *disguised maquila* plants. A third aspect of this
"triangulation" structure is to export maquila products and then, perhaps with
further processing, to reimport products as inputs into the disguised maquila
sector—wherein they are then processed and again exported. Together the
disguised maquila and maquila firms accounted for 70 percent of all exports
in 2005, as shown in figure 5.2. In the entire NAFTA period through 2006,
the two maquila sectors (sometimes referred to as the *processing* sector) accounted for an average of 78 percent of all exports (Becerril 2006, 18; Dussel
Peters 2006, 75).

Figure 5.2. Mexico: Manufactured Exports by Type

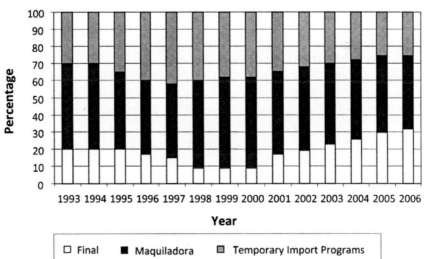

Source: **Bancomext 2005, *Atlas de comercio exterior, México;* Bancomext 2006,
*Sistema integral de información de comercio exterior.***

Frequently, this movement of inputs from the maquila firms to the larger TNCs constitutes intrafirm transactions since through joint ventures or direct ownership the large TNCs control many maquila supplier firms. Intrafirm trade:

> is trade within the boundaries of the firm—although across national boundaries—as transactions *between different parts of the same firm.* Unlike the kind of trade assumed in international trade theory—and in the trade statistics collected by national and international agencies—intra-firm trade does not take place on an "arms length" basis. It is, therefore, not subject to external market prices but to the internal decisions of the TNCs. (Dicken 2003, 52)

United States intrafirm transactions for imports in the auto and electronics sectors—the two largest export sectors for Mexico—stood at 75.9 percent and 67.5 percent, respectively, in 2002 (Duran Lima and Ventura-Dias 2003, 59). Progressively, Mexican exports have become intraindustry and frequently intrafirm transactions. For example, in the 1990–1994 period 55 percent of the growth in exports was accounted for through intraindustry trade. In the 1995–1999 period this portion explained 88 percent of the growth of exports (Leon González and Dussel Peters 2001, 657). This growth was concentrated in a narrow band of the industrial sector—9 percent of the eighty-eight industrial divisions accounted for 88 percent of the growth of trade, with the two largest areas being autos and auto parts and electronics. These tendencies had striking results in auto parts: between 1989 and 2001, 77 percent of the increase in auto parts imports into the United States came from the NAFTA countries, and 80 percent of the increase in exports went to the NAFTA area (PNUD 2004, 153).

Overall, by 1999, the level of intraindustry transactions had reached nearly 50 percent of the value of all Mexican exports, up from slightly more than 40 percent of all exports at the beginning of the decade (Leon González and Dussel Peters 2001, 664). By 2006 the growth in intraindustry transactions in at least one major area had increased significantly in relation to 1993: Using an index for intraindustry transactions in the auto industry, Jorge Alberto López and Óscar Robil found that such interactions had increased by 25.6 percent—the index rose from 0.78 to 0.98, meaning that virtually all auto and auto parts production was linked to cross-border intraindustry activities of some type by 2006 (López and Robil 2008, 98). The growth of intraindustry transactions means that firms operating in Mexico, either as U.S.-owned maquilas or disguised maquilas, or firms owned by Mexican business groups, are becoming (through enhanced FDI and varieties of joint-venture/strategic alliance operations) elements of a U.S.-Mexico globally integrated production system designed, in effect, to subordinate the Mexican production system to the dynamic needs of U.S.-based TNCs. More generally, the processes noted in the auto sector are also to be found at the macroeconomic level: for example, an industrial displacement index—measuring the degree to which national manufacturing production had been displaced by imports—stood at 29.5 percent in 1993–1994, rising to 43.7 percent in 2003 (Maria y Campos et al. 2009, 79–80).

In the disguised maquila sector, nationally produced inputs/components have fallen from 32 percent in 1993 to only 22.6 percent in 2004—a drop of 25 percent in only eleven years (Cadena 2005, 13). At least forty "production chains" that involved small and medium-sized Mexican-owned firms have been destroyed in this process—firms that supplied both the large exporters and the domestic market, according to recent research (Cadena 2005, 13). In one recent case study, the drop of national suppliers to the TNC Volvo was remarkable: in 1999 Volvo contracted with 430 Mexican suppliers, while in 2003 only ninety-nine remained. The remaining few Mexican suppliers provided Volvo with low-technology, low-value-added components (Ivarsson and Alvstam 2005, table 6). During these years a switch in major suppliers was achieved, and Volvo increasingly bought high-value-added inputs from other supplier TNCs who transplanted production operations to Mexico. In essence, these large export firms, such as Volvo (a disguised maquila), are progressively engaged in a process of shrinking Mexico's *national* industrial base as they substitute foreign inputs and foreign suppliers for Mexican-made components and producers. This situation largely leaves only the value of Mexican labor as the determining component of value added, since 77 percent of the inputs into the production process are imported. Furthermore, when Mexican-made inputs are extinguished, the impact is not limited to destroying supplier firms and jobs, but also the complex set of socioeconomic relationships and skills that have accumulated over decades. Once this web of relationships has been swept away, only long-term, systematic industrial policy can reverse these deindustrialization/deskilling effects.

The giant firms now engage in a higher degree of subcontracting, while they reserve for themselves the highest-value-added production activities. This has put new pressures on supplier firms: the TNCs now demand larger levels of output with higher quality and performance standards and expect improved production processes that demand greater levels of capital intensity. This organizational change has eliminated thousands of Mexican firms, whose production processes are now regularly turned over to other TNCs as suppliers. One study estimates that of the six hundred to eight hundred first-tier suppliers (discussed below) in the Mexican auto sector and the ten thousand second-tier suppliers in 2001, only twenty-five to one hundred first-tier suppliers and 2,000–4,000 second-tier suppliers (increasingly foreign-owned) would remain in 2010 (Mortimore and Barron 2005, 10).[7] Mortimore and Barron note that in this process, it is U.S. first-tier suppliers—subsidiaries of U.S. TNCs—that are dominating the auto parts industry (Mortimore and Barron 2005, 19). Enhancing outsourcing has collateral benefits in that the TNCs can sidestep or fragment unions by shifting significant portions of inputs production to captive (nonunion) suppliers—this practice has been well documented at the giant Volkswagen plant in Puebla that primarily exports finished autos to the United States (Juárez and Babson 1999).[8]

MEXICO'S AUTO SECTOR—THE VANGUARD OF THE EXPORT-LED MODEL

The global auto and auto parts industry is highly concentrated—in 2002 there were only 180 assembly plants and large-scale supplier companies that controlled 80 percent of worldwide sales (PNUD 2004, 21). In terms of its size, measured by the value of its exports, the auto and auto parts sector in Mexico was second only to the petroleum sector in the early twenty-first century. In fact, the export of auto parts amounted to 84 percent of the value of petroleum exports in 2008—the year when oil reached its all-time inflation-adjusted peak price (Durán 2010, 17). The industry is bifurcated: on one side, data for 2009 indicate that there are fourteen large-scale foreign-owned auto production/assembly corporations operating in Mexico, employing 45,000 workers (Cardoso 2010, 20). On the other side there were, in 2006, approximately 1,100 producers of auto parts—the majority small and medium-sized companies. Employment in auto parts reached a peak of 570,000 workers in early 2008, falling precipitously in the course of the crisis of 2009 (Cardoso 2010, 20). Including all supplier firms, in early 2008 over one million were directly employed in the auto and auto parts industry. Of the auto parts firms, an estimated seven hundred were owned by foreign capital, and these were the largest (Sievers Fernández 2008, 14). The large-scale production/assembly plants are completely state of the art, operating with a high composition of capital. One portion of the auto parts industry is directly linked to the assembly plants—these are termed "tier-1 suppliers." Tier-1 suppliers are technologically very advanced—frequently *more so* or on an equal level with the giant automakers. However, the grand majority of these supplier firms are not subsidiaries—most have no direct production, marketing, or ownership linkages with the giant assemblers.

Geography is an important factor in our understanding of the auto sector: from the 1920s into the 1970s the heart of the industry was located in the Federal District and in the nearby State of Mexico, serving the national market. At the beginning of the 1980s the U.S. auto industry reacted to the insurgency of the Japanese auto industry. Japan leaped from controlling 1.3 percent of the global auto market in 1960 to a peak of 26 percent in 1989 (Dicken 2003, 357). Its success was partly based in a variety of production techniques including just-in-time inventory control and *Toyotist, or lean, production* systems. The production innovations of the Japanese led to the restructuring of the U.S. auto industry, which introduced many of the Japanese innovations into its new plants—increasingly located in Mexico. Compared with the old-style "Fordist plants" installed in the central industrial corridor of Mexico, the new U.S.-owned lean plants in the north and north central regions of Mexico often were thought to use half the manpower, half the space, half the investment in machinery and equipment, and half the engineering to develop new autos in half the time.[9]

For the U.S. companies the principal innovation was to conceive of the industry as essentially mobile—in spite of the necessary massive investment in fixed capital. The first step was to push new assembly plants or significant components of production, such as engine plants, into the antilabor, low-unionized U.S. South. The giant producers shifted production out of the north central states, where the strongest, best-organized, and most successful unions had been located. But, having taken this important step, and under pressure from the youthful Japanese auto industry, it was not a radical move to shift production into the north and north central states of Mexico in the search for even cheaper labor (almost universally "represented" by passive and pliable "protection" unions).[10]

For the U.S. firms, the barriers to entering Mexico in the 1980s were some official "decrees" that reserved, in large part, the auto industry for a newly formed Mexican business elite. Most important in this now bygone nationalist and developmentalist environment was a 1977 auto decree reserving a high level of production content for national firms. For the U.S. firms this meant that Mexico would not be a viable alternative in their attempt to restructure and meet Japan's challenge unless Mexico would grant them "national treatment" for their transplanted operations. Condensing a long story that has received treatment in previous chapters, in the context of a prolonged and sharp economic crisis stretching through the "lost decade" of the 1980s, Mexico's once-famous nationalist spirit became relatively pliable. Little by little the laws and decrees that had reserved much of the auto and auto parts industry as a "national champion" for the national industrial bourgeoisie were changed. The coup de grâce for Mexico's autonomous industrialization aspirations (as we have emphasized in chapter 3) was realized in the negotiations and implementation of the NAFTA agreement.

As Alejandro Dávila Flores has noted, there is a high degree of evidence that NAFTA eliminated some of the tendencies to centralize industrial production in and around the Federal District—instead creating a certain premium for the frontier and nearby states (Dávila Flores 2008, 62). The Federal District corridor lost its hegemonic position as the central area of industrial production, and a heterogeneous process led the northeast and north central regions to become the locus of much production in order to minimize transportation costs into the U.S. market. Processes of agglomeration and *clustering* had the effect of continually elevating the regional per capita GDP, from 35 percent above the national average in 1993 to 48 percent in 2004 (Dávila Flores 2008, 62).[11] That is, Dávila Flores documented a linear tendency wherein this gap consecutively widened (Dávila Flores 2008, 62). The center for the most important industrial clusters was the State of Chihuahua—accounting for 40 percent of the northeast regional GDP in 2004 (Dávila Flores 2008, 63). Other areas where industrial enclaves driven largely by FDI were located included the states of Coahuila, Tamaulipas, and Nuevo Leon. This region has a high weighting in terms of the role of industry—being 16 percent above the national average (Dávila Flores 2008, 63). The association seems straightforward—a major portion of the differential between the north and north central states and the national average would seem to be due to the relatively high degree of industrialization. Factors of note regarding industry in this region are the presence of metal-using industries (particularly autos and auto parts), the "basic metals industry" such as steel-making plants that are derivative of the auto industry (backward linkages), and the chemicals industry (likewise demonstrating backward linkages). Public-sector investment is also a distinguishing characteristic of the general region: highway, gas, electrical, and water infrastructures are mutually supporting elements in the regional development pattern—as often argued by advocates of industrial policy (Dávila Flores 2008, 65).

Anticipating the arrival of the long-sought category of *national treatment* for the U.S. auto plants (achieved with NAFTA), at the beginning of the 1990s if not before, the giant automakers commenced massive investments in the north and north central regions of Mexico. The geographic investment pattern was partly tied to the already existing maquiladora industry located in the frontier states. In addition, and of greater importance in terms of this investment surge, were the new plants in the states of Querétaro, Guanajuato, San Luís Potosí, and Aguascalientes, which formed a new NAFTA auto corridor for the U.S. firms.[12] All of this investment was partly anchored in long-term efforts undertaken by both some states and the federal government of Mexico to build a vast infrastructure, consisting of well-designed industrial parks erected strategically in terms of their location to the U.S. market, which has received 87 percent of Mexico's auto exports. The industrial parks were complemented with an array of vital public services, particularly utilities, along with modern highway and communication grids. Complementing the conventional infrastructure, in 2009 Mexico operated an impressive grid of 260 industrial parks, which directly employed 500,000 manufacturing workers—with an estimated additional 1.5 million employed indirectly as a result of employment multiplier effects (González G. 2009, 27). The industrial parks, commonly housing TNC supplier firms, had been built through public-sector initiatives that involved subsidies from all levels of government—often with significant private-sector Mexican capital.

All of these factors and forces help explain the growing export intensity of the auto assembly operations in Mexico: in 2008 more than three of every four vehicles produced were exported (79 percent). This signified an important shift toward the external market in relation to the recent past. For example, in the period 1997–2004 the internal Mexican market absorbed almost one-third of vehicle production (Taboada Ibarra, Robles Rodríguez, and Velásquez García 2006, 103).

Today, anchored in the north and central regions of Mexico, the auto and auto parts industry is one of great scope, accounting for six of the ten largest foreign-owned firms in Mexico. Only 0.6 percent of all manufacturing firms were auto and auto parts producers, yet 12 percent of all employees in the manufacturing sector, along with 16.6 percent of the total wage and salary income received in the manufacturing sector, were derived from the auto and auto parts firms in 2004 (AMIA 2009). More significant, perhaps, was that this sector was responsible for 17.7 percent of total manufacturing production in 2004. The fundamental importance of the auto sector in the performance of Mexico's cheap labor–export model rests in the fact that in 2008 it was the largest single source of Mexico's manufacturing exports, accounting for 21.4 percent of the total. In 2007 exports of the auto and auto parts sector reached $41.9 billion US while imports of components, parts, and machinery for this sector were only $26.45 billion. The sizable trade surplus generated by the industry demonstrates its key role in sustaining the cheap labor–export model since this surplus is broadly used to cover the trade deficits in the many areas where Mexico's production system is inadequate.

In regard to this sector's impressive trade surplus, it is important to note that in 2004 the auto parts industry nearly reversed its long-standing trade deficit—which had tended to negate much of the stimulus generated by the trade surplus–producing auto assembly plants. In 2007 the auto parts industry had a small deficit—ten times less than that of 2001 (de Maria y Campos 2009, 84). In contrast, the trade deficit in auto parts was the equivalent of 114 percent of the value of auto parts exports in 1994 (INEGI various years, cuadros 3.3.8,

3.3.9). How was it possible, in the space of only ten years, to alter the long-standing deficit nature of the auto parts industry? One overwhelming factor was the expansion and restructuring of the auto parts industry in Mexico.

Currently, the auto parts sector is no longer dominated by a combination of U.S. capital and Mexican-owned firms noted for their production and technological backwardness. Mexican capital, virtually nonexistent in the assembly plants, now confronts marginalization in auto parts production. In 2007 it controlled only 23 percent of the total invested capital in the auto parts industry—thus we note a process of *de-mexicanization*. Due to recent investments, German capital is now the largest in auto parts production, followed by the United States (33 percent versus 30 percent). The new face of Mexico's auto parts industry is, apparently, the result of a large wave of FDI between 2003 and 2007. In those years the expansion of auto parts production was funded by an $8.125 billion US investment inflow in plant and equipment, as well as by mergers and acquisitions (INA 2008). During these years, foreign investments in the auto parts sector were more than four times greater than foreign investments in the much larger auto production/assembly operations.

Switching focus back to the production/assembly operations aspect of the industry, vehicle output averaged about one million per year in the 1993–1995 period. Five short years later, in 2000, production had almost doubled to 1.9 million vehicles per year. The production surge was the result of a sequence of plant expansions that began in 1995. In 2007 Mexico produced 2.02 million vehicles. Technically, Mexico reached record levels of annual production in 2008, when 2.1 million vehicles poured out of the foreign-owned plants. But in fact, this was not representative of the situation in 2008 because monthly output figures began to plummet from October onward as the U.S. market headed toward collapse. Based on figures from November 2008 through January 2009, we estimate that Mexican auto production for 2009 will fall by more than 25 percent, signaling significant excess capacity in Mexico. Based on the same period (November–January), exports for 2009 will likely fall by 28 percent, from the level of 1.662 million vehicles exported in 2008 (Taboada Ibarra, Robles Rodríguez, and Velásquez García 2006:103; AMIA 2009). Having been a "leading sector" for the Mexican economy in recent years and the leading example of success in manufacturing exports, the auto sector situation in 2009 verged on the catastrophic.

AUTO INDUSTRY COMPETITIVENESS AND STATE POLICY

The impressive run-up in auto production capabilities from 1997–1998 to 2007–2008 was the result of major investments that, surprisingly, do not fit well with the accepted wisdom regarding the pursuit of Mexico's neoliberal policies, particularly under President Fox (2000–2006). In late 2003 his administration issued the "Decree to Support the Competitiveness of the Auto Production Industry." The purpose of the decree was to

1. Create subsidies for this industry in order to increase FDI.
2. Reduce tariffs affecting this industry.
3. Create subsidies for the TNCs to import vehicles, conditioned on increased exportation of vehicles. (This allowed for more importation at cheaper prices of the large, luxurious vehicles coveted by Mexico's upper class and upper-middle class, as defined in chapter 1, table 1.1).
4. Authorize increased vehicle imports when there is a commitment to continue worker training programs, and/or expansion of the infrastructure of production, and/or the development of national suppliers, and/or the transfer of technologies to second- and third-tier suppliers (Miranda 2007, 223).

This decree had an important impact in terms of FDI directed to the industry. With this decree, very quickly, Toyota made major investments in the border region and Nissan significantly expanded its production facilities in Aguascalientes, while Volkswagen made similar commitments in Puebla at the same time that Chrysler, Ford, and General Motors expanded existing plants and/or built new ones in the north and north central states (Miranda 2007, 224). Ford, for example, announced $3 billion US of new investments in 2008—primarily to renovate its oldest foreign plant (Chavez 2009, 24; Duran 2009, 13). This plant will soon produce 324,000 vehicles per year—90 percent to be exported, primarily to the United States. This expansion will increase on-site plant employment from 600 to 2,300–3,000 and will likely increase Ford's overall purchases of auto parts in Mexico from $6 billion to $9 billion US per year. The renovated Ford plant will also employ 500 engineers by 2010. It is important to note, once again, that the cheap labor–export model is based on *relative*, not absolute, wages. In this case, the shifting of significant engineering capacities to Mexico will not be a sign that Mexico is upgrading its production capacities. Rather, Ford will control the flow of technology and learning while cutting its engineering costs by—most likely—a factor of ten.

Nonetheless, according to Arturo Miranda's analysis, in the new international order, Mexico was not competitive due to its inadequate infrastructure. As a result, while investment grew, it dropped behind the pace of expansion in many countries with the result that Mexico fell from the eighth-place producer in 2000 to the eleventh-largest producer of vehicles in 2004 (Kearney 2008, 1; Miranda 2007, 226). Vehicle production growth rates were spectacular from 1995 to 2000, when output expanded at a 15.6 percent annual rate (Kearney 2008, 2). But then the industry stagnated from 2000 to 2006, with average annual growth rates of only 0.8 percent. This process of falling behind larger (global) trends was even more acute in the auto parts industry:

> Where every day companies located in Mexico lose market share in the face of the incursion of the fabrication of vehicles with component parts imported largely from nations that correspond to the ownership of the Mexican-based foreign-owned plants using locally-based suppliers in these [foreign] nations whose levels of quality and productivity allow them to export parts to Mexico at competitive [i.e., lower] prices. (Miranda 2007, 226)

Although it is unquestionable that, as Miranda notes, the majority of national suppliers are producing with an undercapitalized and obsolete production system, there are some exceptions that suggest—with the assistance of a renovated national industrial policy—the possibility of facilitating a new structure of modernized national suppliers (Garrido and Padilla 2007; Cardero Garcia and Domínguez Villalobos 2007). But, more generally, there are very few participating firms among the six hundred producers of auto parts who have reached levels of competence in the higher reaches of technological capabilities and research and development—areas where, normally, Mexican businesspeople have not distinguished themselves. To achieve this level of competitiveness it has been necessary to form strategic alliances with U.S.-based firms. According to Alejandra Salas-Porras's comparative analysis, such alliances as have been formed in Mexico have not raised the level of performance to that realized by the *chaebols* of Korea. Nonetheless, she finds that such alliances have been important for some of the largest national firms in the auto parts industry:

> It is only in the petrochemical industry and, above all in the auto parts industry, that we can observe highly significant strategic alliances involving the development and distribution of products. Among those with the greatest importance we can locate the case of Nemak, a subsidiary of the ALFA [group] which in 1979 initiated an association with the US firm, Ford. From this alliance three research institutions were created in order to improve and develop engine heads as well as mono-blocks of aluminum and other auto parts. For its part the Desc group—through its subsidiary Spicer—initiated in the 1970s, in the context of the new Foreign Investment Law, an association with the US-based firm Dana Corp., which has been noticeably extended to include research and development projects as well as the distribution of products for the assembly and manufacturing of vehicles. (Salas-Porras 2007, 323–24)

Although the above-mentioned decree of December 2003 stimulated new investments, the overall slow level in the expansion of final demand and the structural weaknesses of the auto parts industry—the above exceptions not-withstanding—has called into question the future of the auto and auto parts industry as a leading sector in Mexico's manufacturing-led export model. The modest growth in demand has been far exceeded by the expansion of production facilities, which has left Mexico with a serious excess capacity problem reaching 40 percent by 2004 (Miranda 2007, 232). Production in 2009 will be less than that of 2004—and this level was approximately equal to production achieved in 1997–1998. Mexico's auto industry now confronts an alarming level of *overproduction/overcapacity*. All of this has taken place within a *global* context wherein total installed capacity is capable of producing 90 million vehicles while operating at a production level of only 66 million vehicles at the beginning of 2009 (Coy 2009, 25).

There is a lack of correspondence between the growth in the demand of autos in the United States and the supply of autos designed for the U.S. market in Mexico. Preferences in the U.S. market have been increasingly directed toward brand-name vehicles produced in Asia and Europe, while the largest part of Mexico's auto exports derives from U.S. brand-name vehicle producers (Miranda 2007, 238). Mexico's auto industry, then, is being technologically and structurally transformed—but not at the rate at which such changes are occurring elsewhere, particularly in Asia. U.S. auto giants have pursued a cheap labor path–dependent process in Mexico (the "lock-in" effect) while largely remaining "locked out" or falling behind in the most dynamic areas of the industry. For these reasons, Arturo Miranda concluded that "with the level of automation achieved throughout the auto sector and with the cheapening of technology, low labor costs will not be sufficient to justify the expansion of operations in Mexico" (Miranda 2007, 239).

THE TECHNOLOGICAL EXCLUSION PROCESS IN AUTO PARTS

The once-dominant nationally owned auto parts producers have been affected by a sustained process of structural change over the past thirty years. Today the giant production/assembly plants commonly incorporate new forms of modular production. They have adopted Toyotist practices, thereby achieving very high performance levels with their technology-infused machinery and well-trained workforce. This transition has passed to the first-tier suppliers—those firms that directly supply the production/assembly plants. In these restructured supplier activities, technical capacities for production are commonly on a par with those of the giant TNC auto production/assembly plants, *if not even higher*. To meet the demands imposed on the first-tier suppliers by the production/assembly plants, top-level suppliers today must exhibit considerable ability in the delivery of products constructed by way of deep technological, engineering, and design capabilities. Only firms that operate at the frontiers of international competitiveness can function as first-tier suppliers. Very few nationally owned auto parts firms (at best no more than the two mentioned above, and possibly a couple more) are capable of meeting these requirements.

It has not always been thus, and it is not necessary that the Mexican-owned auto parts producers remain on the periphery of the supplier chain relegated to be tier-2 and tier-3 producers. Second- and third-tier suppliers produce the more labor-intensive and/or low-tech products, including some of the most simple components. Such firms sell up the chain to the first-tier suppliers. Thus they are beholden to and dependent upon the strategies of the first-tier suppliers, whose activities, in turn, are determined by the giant producers/ assemblers. These low-level suppliers, particularly the tier-3 producers, pay lower wages and frequently suffer from very high labor turnover rates—often well in excess of 100 percent per year. Their technological capabilities are moderate to nonexistent. Mexican-owned firms operate in these low-value-added niches of the industry, if they exist at all. In our field research in north central Mexico, we encountered no Mexican suppliers, and only two first-tier suppliers—both operated by Japanese capital—in a sample of sixteen suppliers. For Mexican firms to re-enter this market it would be necessary to adopt a new industrial policy designed to both lead and assist the private sector in a manner once achieved in the era of state-led development.

In order to understand the current crossroad in the auto sector it is necessary to relate, in a very compressed form, some of the history of this sector. In the 1950s and particularly in the 1960s, during decades of rapid growth in the internal market, the auto industry was a leading sector of the Mexican economy. Unfortunately, the policies utilized to promote the auto sector had an antiexport character, which provoked a sector deficit in the balance of payments. Given that the original impulse to promote the sector arose from a policy of import-substitution industrialization, the situation of the 1970s was unbearable. Because of this situation, the federal government issued the Decree of 1977 (as noted in chapter 2), obligating the sector as a whole to become a net exporter (i.e., a generator of foreign exchange) in five years (Sosa Barajas 2005, 123). Ironically, it was almost at the same moment that the U.S.-based auto TNCs began to place new high-tech plants in the north of Mexico. With these new investments Mexico quickly became a net exporter in vehicle production. However, from 1976 onward until very recently, the auto parts industry showed a *greater* tendency to import. The policy focus remained on the giant production/assembly operations while largely neglecting the predominantly Mexican-owned auto parts industry. In fact, surging imports of new and replacement parts and components were such that the deficit in the auto sector was equivalent to 58 percent of the deficit for the *entire* economy in 1980. Although the need for an industrial policy directed at the auto parts industry was apparent, in the new environment of neoliberalism of the 1980s the ideological rejection of any and all policies of state-led industrialization was so thoroughgoing as to demonize such policy initiatives.[13]

Yet by 2005 the deficit in the auto parts industry had fallen to only $780 million US, according to the National Auto Parts Industry Association (INA 2008). The following year the auto parts industry operated with a small trade surplus. As the aggregate trade data indicate, the auto parts industry between the 1980s and 2006 had been completely transformed. This transformation has been due to the virtual collapse of the Mexican-owned auto parts companies and the rise of sixty (or so) foreign-owned tier-1 auto parts companies. The tier-1 companies often have, as noted, technological capabilities that can *surpass* those of the auto producing and assembly corporations. None of the research available on the restructuring of the auto parts industry in Mexico indicates that Mexican-owned supplier firms played any significant role in this process.

Mexican-owned supplier firms continue to be marginal participants in the auto parts industry, with the exception of those firms (Nemak and Spicer) mentioned above. This is attributable to the limitations these firms face in terms of modernizing their machinery and equipment, their inability to participate in the rapid advancement of technological innovations that are driven by the tier-1 foreign-owned corporations, and the lack of significant levels of financing from the banking system. They further face the problem that virtually all second- and third-tier firms confront outside of a few *clusters*—mostly in the border area. That is, those firms that are not part of the "globally integrated production system" attempt to survive in a production context where necessary ancillary support can often be virtually nonexistent. These firms exist in a broader environment wherein their day-to-day exigencies often simply cannot be met due to the lack of a supporting maintenance and repair network. Usually, backup repairs can be tackled only by artisan-style workshops. Small, simple but necessary parts and repairs often can be completed only by importing from the United States or sending work to larger cities such as Guadalajara. Except in larger border cities where export production has been long established, smaller suppliers confront the fact that they need a supporting supplier base of local, qualified firms that frequently does not exist.

Ironically, at both a national and regional level the gap between the large
TNC production/assembly plants and their associated suppliers operating on
tiers 2 and 3 has been growing in part due to taxation exemptions the Mexican state regularly grants to the top firms. For example, in 2007, General
Motors received more than $50 million US in subsidies when the govern-
ment waived the above amount of its tax payments. Meanwhile Chrysler
received more than $19 million US in tax subsidies, along with Volkswa-
gen's receipt of more than $12 million US, while the Monterrey-based Alfa
Group's Nemak subsidiary (partly owned by Ford) received approximately
$6 million US (Norandi 2008, 42). With such federal tax benefits available
to TNCs and joint-venture firms (often duplicated or exceeded at the state
level) and with the growing demands over the past two decades or so that the
first-tier suppliers have engineering, design, and related technological capacities that frequently *exceed* those of the giant automakers, it should come
as little surprise that a restructured and denationalized auto parts industry
substantially reduced its trade deficit by 90 percent between 2001 and 2007
due to large and continued waves of capacity-creating FDI in the auto parts
industry (de Maria y Campos et al. 2009, 84). In 2008, for example, Mexico
was to receive nearly $2 billion US of FDI in the auto parts industry (INA
2008). This strongly suggests that the tendency to displace auto parts companies from the United States and other nations into Mexico is a continuing
phenomenon.

In closing this section, it is necessary to contextualize the growth in the
automotive and auto parts industry in the past eight years. The increase in
the production of light vehicles, trucks, and auto parts has taken place within
the context of a profound process of deindustrialization in Mexico. In 2000
the manufacturing sector accounted for 35.4 percent of the jobs in the formal
sector of the economy. In 2008 this sector generated only 25.7 percent of
the employment in the economy—suffering an absolute decline of 886,000
manufacturing occupational positions from 2000 to 2008 (León Zaragoza
2009, 21). Consequently, while sales in the auto production, assembly, and
auto parts sector grew rapidly, and while employment levels have risen moderately in recent years (with auto parts producers adding 31,000 occupational
positions from 2001 through 2006), these effects have not had an impact sufficiently large to pull the overall manufacturing base in an upward direction.

THE AUTO INDUSTRY IN THE CENTRAL NORTH OF MEXICO

From 1997 onward, several states in the central north region of Mexico received a degree of support from the United Nations Development Program

and from the federal government due to the fact that 80 percent of the auto parts incorporated into autos assembled in this region were imported.[14] In 1997 the "Program for Productive Integration" in the region commenced with the objective of developing production chains while also creating a new "System for the Strategic Development of the Auto and Auto-Parts Industry" (PNUD 2004, 12). The objectives sought by the regional public-sector policy makers, auto plant and auto parts managers and owners, and leaders of regional business associations who participated in this project were:

> To demonstrate the disarticulation of the system of value creation for the small and medium-sized firms who confront the subsidiaries of transnational corporations who function through the structures of the global supplier network. This disarticulation can be understood in terms of the lack of formal linkages between the Mexican participants in this industry with the result being that there is a continual loss of competitiveness within the industry in the face of global dynamics. (PNUD 2004, 16)

Clearly, in the midst of the term of neoliberal president Ernesto Zedillo (1994–2000), the undertaking of the UN project was not to be anticipated. Yet the massive and comprehensive study reflects the significance of the auto industry at large and the desire by important elements of the power structure at a local and regional level to attempt to confront the forces that were destroying the national supplier base of this industry. Thus, the study represented a significant counterthrust to the "let the market solve the problem" ideology that was never stronger than during President Zedillo's term.

In the mid-1990s, according to data presented in the UN's study, the national structure of Mexico's auto industry was as follows: eight giant production and assembly automakers dominated the industrial pyramid. Below these firms were sixty very large key tier-1 suppliers (overwhelmingly foreign owned). Below them were some six hundred tier-2 supplier firms and one hundred tier-3 suppliers who remained very distant from the productive/technological frontiers of the tier-1 suppliers. In this hierarchy the national firms were left with the least profitable activities in the pyramid. According to the objectives of the program, promoting the industry was to be implemented by the export-promotion bank, Bancomext, and by the office of the secretariat of the economy. The objective of the program was to radically change the structure of the auto industry in the course of only four years. The idea was to *double* the number of tier-1 suppliers—adding thirty new Mexican-owned companies along with thirty new foreign-owned, high-tech entrants. In addition the program intended to stimulate the creation of 250 new tier-2 suppliers—150 being nationally owned firms, with the remainder foreign owned. Finally, the project proposed the creation of fifty new third-tier foreign-owned suppliers along with two hundred nationally owned firms (PNUD 2004, 20).[15]

Unfortunately, as important as the project would have been in terms of addressing one of the most critical issues relating to both regional and national economic development, it was never implemented at the regional level due to lack of sufficient funding. Without regard to the quite unrealistic time frame of the project, what is of interest is that at the level of policy makers in the states of the region, there has been for some time an acute awareness of the need to reverse the trajectory that has excluded more and more Mexican-owned firms from meaningful participation in the auto parts industry. It was understood and implicit in this project that it would be necessary to adopt some form of industrial policy in order to harness the developmental potential of the auto industry. That is, at the level of the policy makers of the region there was an awareness that spillover effects (in terms of learning effects and the transference of crucial technological capacities) arising from the auto parts industry will occur only if elements of industrial policy are in place to facilitate the realization and transference of benefits from the dynamic portions of the auto industry into the Mexican economy.

At the regional level, policy makers were attempting to adapt nationally owned firms to the difficult realities of a restructuring global auto industry wherein the production/assembly TNCs exercised growing leverage over suppliers in order to increase their demands for performance and capabilities. Every year, in order to be a participant in the production chain—even at the tier-2 or 3 level—the automakers demand that the suppliers be ever more competitive in large-scale operations while also being capable of making deliveries in "niche" markets (production of less than 200,000 units). In addition, the giant automakers, which effectively determine which firms are able to operate in the production chain, demand that suppliers be self-sufficient in the design of new components and have at their disposal the capacity to produce, mold, and fabricate basic primary materials such as plastics, steel, aluminum, fabrics, and glass, along with quality certifications such as ISO (PNUD 2004, 21, 23). For national suppliers to rise to this level of execution it would be necessary to significantly increase the training and specialization of the workforce and have within reach the possibility of significant technology transfers. Thus, in the 1990s, with their limited resources: "The fabricators of auto-parts in the region demanded means of support and consulting services that would permit them to update their systems of quality control" (PNUD 2004, 23). Another critical issue was that there was no process that would allow national suppliers to force cooperation in the transference of crucial technologies. In order to meet the expectations of the proposed strategic development project, parts fabricators maintained that there should be access to financing at preferred rates in order to purchase new machinery and equipment. The national suppliers also confronted the fact that the NAFTA agreement would shortly make matters even more difficult: From 1994 to 2003 they had a form of modest security since at least 20 percent of national value added in the auto industry was to come from Mexican producers. That support, along with a 10 percent tariff on imported auto parts, was eliminated in 2003.

The idea of the new promotion program was to privilege associations that combined Mexican fabricators and Mexican capital with foreign suppliers at the tier-1 and tier-2 levels. Behind the national promotion project was a new appreciation of the competitive advantage arising from the geographical proximity of the Mexican firms to the U.S. market.

This perspective, perhaps, seemed unusual or atypical given the exaggerated popularity of the concept of "globalization," which suggested that capital was entirely mobile, having little regard for falling transportation cost. But in our interviews with the Japanese TNC Nissan, at its Aguascalientes plant in the closing months of 2007, the "shrinking of space" concept, so popular in many interpretations of the "globalization" process, was not apparent. Due to time delays in delivery and high costs in transportation, it was part of Nissan's own plan for the promotion of its supplier base to expand the role of national firms (and/or national content) in its supplier chain. This means that companies such as Nissan, while recognizing that existing and potential Mexican firms within the supplier chain in the future operate with inferior technological capabilities—and at times with suboptimal skill and training levels in the workforce—*nonetheless* possess an important *latent competitive advantage* that can be realized through targeted industrial policies implemented at either the national, regional, or *firm* level. Nissan, recognizing that such a transition will not be completed given both the laissez-faire framework of national policies and the financial and coordination problems experienced at the regional level, has made the determination to attempt to expand its national supplier base sui generis. Such a policy may well form an important counterweight to the structural weakness in the supplier base and the deteriorating technological capabilities faced by national suppliers under the current model.

In response to Nissan's initiative and the needs of many other fabricators, the Mexican government and private-sector associations such as INA (the national auto parts association) created a new institution—the Alliance for Productive Articulation of the Auto Industry—in May 2007. The new entity was created in response to transnational producers, particularly Nissan, that petitioned the government to help solve the problem of a lack of a national supplier base in order to refrain from importing most of their inputs (Saldaña 2007, 18). The event was without historical precedent because it constituted a combined effort on the part of both the large assemblers association—AMIA and INA—and the government to work in alliance to create mechanisms to solve the weaknesses in the national supplier base. To date, details of the program, including its implementation, scope, financing, and achievements, remain scarce. It is apparent, nonetheless, that such a program (and there is at least one other focusing on creating an alliance to develop technology in the auto industry) is a considerable deviation from neoliberal policies and a major step toward the construction of an industrial policy in the auto sector.

There are many precedents within the large body of theoretical and empirical research that encompasses the field of economic development indicating the importance of privileging the national supplier base. Most recognized and continually applied is Albert Hirschman's breakthrough concept of the significance of forward and backward linkages (as mentioned in the previous chapter). Such linkages, either forward, toward higher levels of processing, or backward, moving ultimately toward the production of primary products, have been found to generate important "pull," spillover, learning, externality, and synergistic effects in less-developed nations—all working to lower production costs while enhancing efficiency, moving from firm to firm and linked industry to industry. In an economy where the FDI arising from assembly operations is the catalytic factor inducing the expansion of the supplier base, the importance of capturing and spreading these linkage effects throughout the manufacturing production system is of the highest priority. This is the case because, if the multiplier effects working through these backward and forward linkages are felt only in the nation that originates the FDI, or if these effects are limited to enhanced linkages between local enclaves dominated by foreign capital and linked production processes sited in the capital-originating nation, the host nation will be left bereft of the developmental effects noted by Hirschman.[16]

The dynamic effects highlighted by Hirschman cannot be attained in a system dominated by *enclaves of production*, as the Mexican case demonstrates. In an enclave economy, regardless of the products produced or the level of advancement of the production process, there are virtually no linkage or spillover effects or other related externalities because the inputs into the production process and the technologies utilized are imported—they are exogenous to the host economy. Whatever spillover or learning effects that may be gained are realized *endogenously* within the economy that researches, engineers, designs, and produces the inputs and machinery that are later used to produce the product. All this is independent of the nation where the assembly and processing sequences occur. The essential idea behind the System for the Strategic Development of the Auto and Auto-Parts Industry initiative was to stimulate the expansion of the national supplier base in order to overcome the enclave structure of the auto parts industry, thereby acquiring the advantages of virtuous circle effects of endogenous industrialization.

In the north central region of Mexico, due to the initiative of the producers associations and, in particular, the states' secretariats of economic development, there have been significant attempts to follow up on the basic ideas expressed in the above-mentioned regional initiative (i.e., the unrealized 1997 Program for Productive Integration). Several states undertook important em bedded initiatives bringing together auto parts producers, leading business associations, and state-level policy makers. In Aguascalientes one aspect of the follow-on process pursuing the broader goals advanced in the United Nations' regional project for the auto parts industry was an initiative focused on the development of a national supplier base for firms involved in the fabrication of auto engines and engine parts. Eighty-five percent of the value added in this segment of the auto industry was produced in Aguascalientes. Moreover, productivity in the auto industry in Aguascalientes was 1.6 times greater than the national average for the auto industry (PNUD 2004, 78–90). On the one hand, then, it seemed reasonable to focus on cooperative state/private-sector strategies that would allow nationally based producers in Aguascalientes to capture a greater share of the value added in order to realize some of the positive developmental effects stressed by Hirschman.

On the other hand, from the beginning of the 1990s onward, the relationship between the automakers and the tier-1 firms had undergone a radical transformation as the automakers attempted to confront a growing problem of over-production/excess capacity: instead of the pyramidal structure that had long functioned between the automakers and the suppliers at various tiers, *today the relation between the giant assembly corporations and the first-tier suppliers is much more horizontal than vertical.* First-tier suppliers are increasingly required to operate cutting-edge engineering and design centers in their areas of specialization. At the same time in the 1990s the automakers adopted the new modular system, constructing systems of common components for a production-receiving platform in many auto making plants. Thus, instead of making an engine gauge, with the modular system, an automaker might demand that a single supplier produce an entire dashboard, including all the required gauges, sensors, and other components. All of the massive changes introduced into the vehicle-making process carried important implications for supplier firms; now, instead of being one of several companies making one component, first-tier suppliers were expected to acquire massive economies of scale as well as design and engineering capabilities in order to be the single provider of a complex integrated system of components that would be installed by way of the modular system in the final production and assembly process. Obviously, this new—essentially horizontal—system introduced massive structural changes between suppliers and the automakers. Surviving suppliers were forced to attain a very high level of capitalization in machinery and equipment as well as acquire technological capabilities in the area of research and development. Tier-2 and 3 suppliers often became mere subcontractors or outsourced operations under the new schema. Under these new conditions, engine and engine parts suppliers in Aguascalientes now faced tremendous barriers of entry into the restructuring auto industry (PNUD 2004, 78–90). As the United Nations researchers noted, "The degree of collaboration and commitment between the vehicle fabricators and their suppliers under the current scheme has no precedent" (PNUD 2004, 93). They further added:

> The first tier supplier must offer a complete service to the automakers. It is an indispensable requirement to attain high volumes of production with zero defects, offer design and development capacities, make just-in-time deliveries, have costs based in productivity, achieve long-term cooperative agreements, and operate with continual improvement practices in both production and product development with worldwide delivery capability. (PNUD 2004, 93)

José Vieyra Medrano expands on the increasingly horizontal nature of the relationship between the vehicle assemblers and their suppliers—a relationship that can extend at least to the second-tier suppliers:

> Between 80 and 85 percent of the components required in a vehicle are manufactured outside of the final-stage auto assembly plants, thereby creating a high level of dependency on the part of the automakers with respect to the suppliers. This dependency is only apparent, because there is a high degree of integration between the suppliers and the final assemblers, with the latter firms being the ones who control the production process in general. In many cases, the major suppliers either are one-hundred percent owned by the same assembly firm or these firms possess a high ownership stake in the supplier to the degree that the assembly firm can control the "how, when and where" of the supplier in terms of the fulfillment of the assemblers necessities. The integration is so high that the agreement signed [between the assemblers and suppliers] demonstrate the freedom that the auto multinationals exercise to intervene, at the moment that they determine, in the supplier firms with the objective of adapting them to their own conditions and demands. (Vieyra Medrano 2000, 130)

The requirements for participation in the suppliers' network have been redefined, and the relation between automakers and the fabricators of auto parts has been restructured. Each and every one of the changes introduced manifests exclusionary characteristics for the marginal firms (overwhelmingly those operated under Mexican ownership) that can now exercise only one competitive advantage—a cheap labor force. If, then, these firms are not literally excluded, the requirement for survival for those who cannot make the leap into the new horizontal order, burdened with accelerating performance requirements and capabilities, is to operate with a lower (near zero) rate of profit. Under these conditions the marginal firms cannot gain the leverage needed to reinvest and modernize—either by way of their own reinvested profits or through financial credits—in order to achieve capacities allowing for average performance production levels. Making matters worse, the autonomy once exercised by the Mexican state and by the national states has been undermined in the new international framework that has been constructed as a result of the NAFTA agreement.

ENDOGENOUS GROWTH AND THE NATIONAL INNOVATION SYSTEM

With NAFTA Mexico forfeited a considerable degree of autonomy that must be rebuilt if restructuring of the productive apparatus, in the auto industry and beyond, is to be achieved. Consequently, the way forward points to a necessary rearrangement of key aspects of the NAFTA accord. The consolidation of this new structure served to marginalize Mexico in terms of the further evolution of its endogenous developmental capabilities. In a telling statement, the United Nations researchers summed up a core result of this new structural alignment: "The development strategy implemented by Mexico, as applied to the automobile industry, demonstrates that the nation has sought during the last decade [1992–2002] to consolidate itself *as a world trade center—not as a center for industrial development*" (PNUD 2004, 165, italics added).

The solution to Mexico's dilemma does not rest—in the final analysis—strictly or largely in a renegotiation of NAFTA. The limitations NAFTA imposes can be, to some degree, sidestepped and partially evaded. Ultimately, with or without NAFTA Mexico's dilemma will be resolved, or at least mitigated, if social agency is achieved by those actors who have both the will and capacity to construct a viable economic alternative. Such an alternative must be focused on a broad range of endogenous forces leading to, most fundamentally, the attainment of independent technological capabilities sufficient to foster a new era of embedded industrialization. That is, a new era of industrialization must arise through an interactive and interdependent process that will entail the active participation of professionally competent state managers, industrial associations, and industrialists. This relationship must be augmented through the active participation of a growing scientific cadre coming from the universities, government agencies, and large firms.

By current standards within Mexico, the previous paragraph would seem to advocate an earth-shattering transformation. But it does not. To some degree it merely reminds us of policies and social forces that helped spur Mexico to a high state of socioeconomic achievement from 1940 through 1982. This is not to argue, to any degree, that the way forward is through the past. The way forward, however, consists of building on successful past practices while incorporating needed new elements. Mexico need not invent a great deal; there are ample examples of successful development strategies that can be adapted and modified to national circumstances, such as current and past practices in Asia and, today, Brazil (Amsden 2001).

A key to solving the dilemma appears to be within reach, or not so far away, as our study of the auto sector indicates. That is, at the regional and state level—in business associations, in some firms, and within significant policy-making entities—there is both an awareness of the need to construct an alternative productive structure and a will to carry out the task. As yet, these forces have attained limited and nonsequential success. Nonetheless, an important finding of our field research has been to document that such forces do exist.

The task Mexico must confront is to direct development policy toward the enhancement of its national industrial base with an emphasis on "upgrading" into higher-value-added activities. To achieve such upgrading, industrial policy was successfully deployed in a range of Asian nations in the 1960–2009 period. A critical factor, not only in the case of developing Asian nations in the recent past, but more generally in Europe, the United States, and Japan in an earlier era, has been the realization of what the Schumpeterians refer to as the national innovation system. "[T]he term 'national system of innovation' is a broad concept designed to focus attention on the process of creation and diffusion of innovations . . . within specific national economies. It emphasizes how innovations are introduced and spread in a national context, why national economies differ and to some extent why innovations are important to economic change" (McKelvey 1994, 366).

The national system of innovation approach breaks with a long tendency in economics to assume a linear relationship between science and technology, which is then broadly applied to the production process, thereby fostering productivity-enhancing processes and leading to economic growth. The national system of innovation approach posits that innovations can be social, institutional, organizational, or technological. The production and application of scientific knowledge, while important, must share equal weight with national characteristics pertaining to the absorption and diffusion mechanisms specific to the institutional structure of a nation. One of the major contributors to the body of ideas behind the national system of innovation approach has been Christopher Freeman. He encapsulated the concept as "the network of institutions in the public and private sectors whose activities and interactions initiate, import, modify and diffuse new technology" (OECD 1997, 10).

In practice, the national system of innovation is frequently expressed in terms of the web of interactions and complementarities between firms, public institutions, and research institutions (OECD 1997, 9). Mario Cimoli has examined the general weakness and near absence of a national innovation system in Mexico. Cimoli notes that the limited elements of what might generously be termed to constitute Mexico's national innovation system are stagnant, while the distance between Mexico's technological capabilities and those in nations that operate on the frontiers of technological development is increasing. What little technological advance that does occur in Mexico is a function of imported technology embedded in machinery and equipment (Cimoli 2000, 285–92). Regarding linkages—the most important mechanisms of transmission of productivity-enhancing impulses—Cimoli finds that they "are increasingly replaced by an international integration process" (Cimoli 2000, 285). A much lower degree of knowledge and technological diffusion occurs because, "together with this [replacement] process, we can see a dramatic loss of articulation in the existing linkages and their domestic suppliers of inputs." In synthesis, we can sum up Mexico's patterns of technological evolution in figure 5.3.

On the vertical axis of this figure are indicators of production capacity, competitiveness, linkage effects, and technological capabilities. On the horizontal axis we note the time-path evolution through three recent stages: from 1940 through 1982 Mexico's economic dynamics were largely influenced and guided through the significant policy interventions of state-led industrialization. This was followed by a complex period of transition—1983–1993—analyzed in previous chapters. Subsequently, we encounter the current NAFTA period. The dashed line indicates that throughout the period of state-led industrialization there was a general rapid increase in both linkages and in the creation of an independent technological learning capability (ITLC). An ITLC entails borrowing existing technologies and adapting them to the conditions of the national economy. This means that a nation is achieving some limited technological autonomy. Acquiring and building upon an ITLC is an initial step that can, under the right policies, lead to the creation of technological *creation* capabilities. Mexico, of course, never came near this level of technological development. When the process of state-led industrialization confronted a crisis of continuance—when "light" or "shallow" industrial policies of import substitution might have been transformed into deeper forms of state-led industrialization—Mexico faltered. At that point—when Asian nations executed a crucial *strategy switch*—we find that Mexico remained locked into its shallow application/understanding of industrial policy. In

Figure 5.3.   Technological Capacities, Linkage Effects

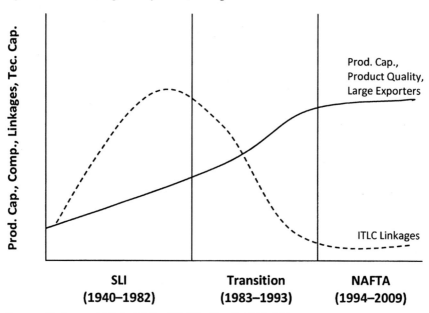

Source: Cypher and Dietz 2009, 425–29; Cimoli 2000, 286.

figure 5.3 the ITLC/linkages line commences now to trend downward. This trend proceeds on its downward trajectory to the point where disarticulation reaches critical dimensions. Then low-level stagnation (or disarticulation) ensues from the early 1990s.

In terms of technological capacities, Mario Capdevielle found that 80 percent of Mexico's manufacturing industry was engaged in "mature" production activities where little underlying technological development occurred (Capdevielle 2003, 455). Hence, the likelihood of technological development and spinoff effects was either low or nil in these dominant areas. Capdevielle's research revealed that Mexican manufacturing firms operated in the lower reaches of technological change—they remained restricted to *processes of adaptation* of existing (imported) technologies (Capdevielle 2003, 456). While the neoliberal model pivots on the expansion of FDI, one of Capdevielle's most significant (but unsurprising) findings is that *on average*, small and medium-sized firms spent more on research and development (R & D) as a percentage of their sales than did the large Mexican firms (including the powerful *grupos* or conglomerates), and that these large firms spent relatively more on R & D than did the transnational firms (Capdevielle 2003, 459). In an international comparative context, using the ratio of R & D expenditures/total sales as a proxy for technological dynamism, U.S. firms spent over five times more than did Mexican firms (Capdevielle 2003, 459).

There are, however, some areas of production in Mexican manufacturing that have a scientific component or "base" suggesting the possibility of dynamic technological effects. However, such growing areas of "technological opportunities" are not now necessarily more notable than they were during the closing decade of state-led industrialization (Capdevielle 2003, 455). According to a study conducted by Alma Rocha and Roberto López, there has been a "notable institutional erosion" from the import substitution era to the current neoliberal era, in terms of national technological/scientific policy (Rocha and López 2003, 126). In the previous era, such policy was directed at the formation and development of technological capacities. In the current era, expenditures have largely been focused on an enclave of theoretical or nonapplied scientific research, wherein government efforts have exhibited a consistent lack of continuity and feedback mechanisms. Within the state apparatus, government spending on science has been largely separated from and uncoordinated with efforts and programs of other agencies of the state.

Returning to figure 5.3, the solid line captures the ascendant process wherein Mexico's groups put great emphasis on the "light" aspects of competitiveness—such as quality control and improved managerial, marketing, and accounting techniques. Thus, light (or shallow) production capabilities improved dramatically until the early 1990s, after which they, too, have stagnated. Whatever elements of a national innovation system Mexico had initiated in the state-led industrialization era had long fallen into decay. As a consequence the large groups, or conglomerates, could not avail themselves of the multiplicity of positive external effects enjoyed by the transnational firms ensconced in Mexico whose production systems were largely a function of the national innovation systems in their country of origin.

Behind the statistics presented earlier regarding Mexico's deindustrialization is the constellation of forces we have analyzed in this chapter. Our focus has been on the auto industry because of its weight and significance in terms of both exports and the crucial variable of technology. We are not here proposing an *essentialist* interpretation of Mexico's industrial base. Technology is but one factor in the larger scenario. Its importance, however, is undeniable. And it enters too rarely, as does the manufacturing sector in general and the particulars of the processes of internationalization of capital, into analyses of Mexico's economic structure. This chapter has presented a synthesis of a number of elements which, taken together, reveal the fragility and incoherence of the neoliberal export-led model based in cheap-labor production processes.

Chapter Six

The Direct Exportation
of Mexican Labor

The purpose of this chapter is to discuss the context and features of the most recent phase of northbound Mexican emigration. We first intend to determine some of the factors associated with the maquilization of the Mexican economy, which effectively drives the engine of the new migration. We refer to the severe impingement on both the living and working conditions suffered by most of the Mexican population, as evidenced by the dislodgement of peasant or small farmers and urban workers as well as the weaknesses of the country's employment markets as a whole. Second, in an attempt to highlight the historical nature of Mexican migration, we sketch its most recent stages as they relate to the national accumulation process and the modes of incorporation into the U.S. economy. Third, based on these larger trends, we provide an overview of the most representative indicators of the quantitative and qualitative transformations that Mexican migration to the United States has undergone, with particular emphasis on the labor exodus. Finally, in order to assess the implications of Mexican migration for the U.S. economy, selected empirical evidence regarding the contributions of Mexican immigrants to the U.S. economy, and the costs of emigration for Mexico, is presented and analyzed.

The Mexico-United States migration process has recently undergone a structural transformation, particularly during the NAFTA era. Although the long history of Mexican migration to the United States began at the end of the nineteenth century, it was not until the past twenty-five years that it became particularly high—to the extent that Mexico became the largest source of migrants to the United States in the world. The change was not merely quantitative; more importantly, it entailed qualitative changes in social relations beyond the national boundaries. For Mexico, here is a brief list of these changes:

- A shifting of the economic structure in the United States, which created a new migration geography
- An exponential increase in migrant remittances to Mexico, making them one of the major sources of foreign income in the country
- An alteration in the preponderance of circular (temporary) migration and in the predominance of male participation in outflows
- Ascendance of Mexico to the top rank of countries with the highest migration rate in the world
- A troublesome depopulation trend in many regions of Mexico over the past decade

MEXICAN ECONOMIC COLLAPSE AND LABOR PAUPERIZATION: DUAL EFFECTS OF THE EXPORT DRIVE

As of the 1980s, and more intensely since NAFTA, a powerful macroeconomic policy implemented by Mexico favored the growth of exporting businesses to the almost complete exclusion of growth in other sectors. This export-led strategy brought about expansion of manufactured exports and an even larger increase in manufactured imports. In addition to the fact that it failed to generate production chains inside the Mexican economy, it also inhibited domestic growth rates. In turn, the growth of exports supported by an even higher growth of imports translated into an adverse trend in the balance of payments and in the economy as a whole. Since the advent of the NAFTA, Mexico has suffered a chronic trade deficit that in 1994 amounted to $21 billion, rising in 2007 to $30 billion (at constant prices for the year 2000). The disproportionality between the growth of the total economy and the foreign trade sector (exports plus imports) is well illustrated in the following statistics: from 1994 through 2008, GDP grew from $475 billion to $688 billion US (in constant, year 2000 dollars) while exports grew from $72 billion to $251 billion and imports from $93 billion to $281 billion US (World Bank 2008). That is, the foreign trade sector grew five times faster than did the Mexican economy as a whole.

An immediate effect of the macroeconomic policy seeking "structural change" and "economic stability" has been the relative fall in the internal market, along with the rise in structural unemployment, underemployment, and migration. The Mexican manufacturing apparatus has been progressively dismantled and restructured to service the foreign trade sector. As a consequence of (1) the dismantling of many manufacturing operations, (2) the lack of an export-investment nexus—particularly by the Mexican *grupos* or conglomerates, which would rather invest abroad or plow their profits into speculative activities, and (3) the repatriation of profits by the foreign-owned transnational corporations (TNCs) that dominate the export sector, Mexico stands out for its low growth rate and its structural inability to generate adequate sources of formal employment to improve the way of life of workers and their families. If we also consider that the anti-inflation monetary policy has operated under the hidden agenda of containing and reducing the price of labor, as the foundation of the cheap labor–export model, we find that it would *contradict* the basis of this model to actually improve the quality of work and the standard of living for the majority of the population. The new export-led manufacturing system thus engendered several important structural features of economic stratification, among them:

- *A set of foreign direct investment (FDI) enclaves* focused abroad that, in spite of being at the center of official policy, fail to operate as an engine of national development. These enclaves utilize cheap labor to cut down manufacturing costs through the *indirect* labor exports embodied in manufactured products exported through maquiladora and disguised maquila processing operations, as documented in chapters 4 and 5;
- *A declining and dissociated national production segment* oriented to the domestic market, deprived of government support to stay afloat and unable to energize national economic growth, which nonetheless refuses to give up on its job-creation task in spite of increasingly restrained and precarious conditions;
- *A survival sector*, such as the so-called informal businesses, that responds to a self-infused need to develop its own jobs given the precarious and inadequate opportunities for formal employment; and
- *A transnationalized labor sector* that has been increasingly active in the past decades in constituting labor migration or the *direct export* of the labor force.

Mexican neoliberal policy has featured the cancellation of economic growth opportunities. As discussed in chapter 2, in the state-led industrialization period, 1940–1982, annual per capita income growth averaged an impressive 3.1 percent. It subsequently fell to only 0.76 percent (or four times less than that achieved previously) from 1983 through 2008, as neoliberalism took its toll (Arroyo Picard 2007, 181; CEPAL 2008a, 120). This low growth rate in Mexico is both the product and outcome of a structural inability of the economy to generate enough high-quality formal jobs.

Table 6.1. Mexico: Labor and Employment Conditions, 1994–2009 (2nd Quarter)

Employment Categories (thousands)	1994	2000	2009
Economically active population[a]	34,594 (dec.)	39,043	45,709
Unemployed	1,200	988	2,365
Employed workers[b]	33,085 (dec.)	36,395	41,407
Workers with written contracts	21,349 (est.)	24,294	28,639
Workers with benefits	9,123 (est.)	12,905	14,729
Self-employed and unpaid workers	N.A.	12,089	12,768
Earning less than five minimum wages	N.A.	31,481	33,540
Agriculture (inc. forestry and fishing)	N.A.	6,678	5,644
Manufacturing index[c]	100	100	75.2[d]

Sources: Avendaño Ramos and Gutiérrez Lara 2007; INEGI, Banco de Información Económica, "Indicadores económicos de coyuntura"; "Indicadores estratégicos de ocupación y empleo" (INEGI 2009b).
[a]Includes employed workers with written contracts, self-employed, unemployed, employers, unpaid workers, and those who receive nonwage payments.
[b]Excludes employers and the unemployed.
[c]1993 = 100.
[d]August 2009.
N.A. = Not Available.

Formal employment in 1994–2009, defined as workers with retirement and health benefits obtained through their enrollment in the social security system (or a similar program for government-sector employees) grew by only 387,000 jobs per year (see table 6.1).[1] This figure is equivalent to the employment with benefits of only, roughly, 38 percent of those young individuals who left the educational system to enter the labor force. The sluggish increase in formal employment fell dramatically below the potential expansion of the labor force, which had been in excess of 1–1.2 million per year in most of the previous years. The gap between the two is commonly known as the *employment deficit*. These circumstances necessarily result in unemployment, underemployment, precarious employment, and migration, all forces stalking Mexican society.

The workings of the formal labor market are quite erratic. In 1990–1993—the period immediately preceding the launching of the NAFTA—the number of new jobs grew slightly, but then plummeted in the crisis of 1995. A fast recovery took place from late that year until 2000. As noted in the row labeled "Employed workers" in table 6.1, from late 1994 to 2000 more than 3.3 million jobs were created. From the row labeled "workers with benefits" we find that 3.8 million employees were enrolled by the social security system (IMSS)—or related systems (IMSS 2009).[2] This period was framed by a boom in *indirect* labor force exports due to the increased number of jobs offered by the maquiladora and disguised maquiladora firms. The year 2000 was a turning point for the cheap labor–export model; recruitment dropped in the maquila and indirect maquila firms, while *direct* labor exports, migration, surged.

CHARACTERISTICS OF THE MEXICAN LABOR FORCE

Using as reference the official quarterly surveys of the national statistical institute, from December 1994 through the second quarter of 2009, employment increased by roughly 8.32 million (including job growth in the informal sector, but excluding employers) (Avendaño Ramos and Gutiérrez Lara 2007, 13; INEGI 2009b). Table 6.1 presents a quantitative panorama of the elements that highlight the precarious employment conditions of much of the workforce. (In the table, the various categories, such as "self-employed and unpaid workers," are representations of various qualitative aspects of the workforce—hence they are not additive components.) Conditions of labor vulnerablility would apply to all workers employed without a written labor contract—some 12.8 million, or 31 percent of the total employed in 2009. Using official data, we estimate that the "nonprotected" portion of the workforce—those who receive no retirement, health, or other benefits whatsoever from their employment—amounted to almost 64 percent of the employed workforce.[3] Some observers would also apply the term "informal sector " to all such workers: Dr. Enrique Dussel, editor of Canacintra's *Monitor de Manufactura Mexicana*, calculated that in the period 1994 through 2008, only 37.7 percent of the new entrants into the labor force were incorporated into the social security system as permanent workers with full benefits (Canacintra 2009, 17). The remainder of the population leaving the school system in hopes of employment "has been forced to find it in the United States or in the informal sector [as workers] that are not enrolled in the Social Security system" (Canacintra 2009, 17).[4] Since, in 2009, only 10.7 percent of the workforce earned more than five minimum wages per day (or more than $21 US), while 63.5 percent earned less than three minimum wages per day, it is hardly reasonable to anticipate that any significant number of workers without employer health coverage could buy it on their own (INEGI 2009b).[5]

The category with the largest growth was that of the unemployed, whose ranks grew from 989,000 in 2000 to 2,365,000 in 2009—an increase of 137 percent. The 2.4 million unemployed were, by definition, part of the increasingly precarious working population, since Mexico's unemployment insurance is minimal in amount and scope. Low-income workers grew by roughly 4 million from 2000 to 2009—81 percent of the new jobs created paid less than five times the minimum wage, or less than $5,976 US per year in 2009.[6] These workers—if they were the sole source of household income—would overwhelmingly be located in strata D- and E in table 1.1 (chapter 1), pertaining to the bottom 50 percent of the household income distribution.

Sectorwise, the loss of 1.03 million agricultural jobs in 2000–2009 (a 15.5 percent decline) was driven by (1) an indiscriminate trade opening in agricultural products resulting from the NAFTA; (2) market control exerted by large transnational agribusiness companies; and (3) suspension by the state of most promotion actions oriented toward this sector. Likewise, the drop in the manufacturing sector index registered the dramatic decline between 2000 and August 2009 of roughly 1.3 million manufacturing jobs (one of every four jobs), as a result of both the shrinking domestic market and the stagnant export-processing operations of the maquiladora and disguised maquiladora firms.

This brief statistical overview of Mexico's employment structure outlines the general characteristics of a growing pauperization process that constrains the growth in formal sector employment while driving large portions of the labor force to seek occupation alternatives in Mexico and abroad. The following paragraphs are a brief review of conditions and processes of labor pauperization in the context of shrinking employment opportunities:

1. *Loss of an employment dynamic in the maquila sector.* Both the maquila and disguised maquila operations are supported by cheap labor, low (or practically no) legitimate union representation, high labor turnover, and employment insecurity (de la Garza Toledo 2007; Gambrill 2008; Puyana 2008). Although the maquiladora sector had been important (before 2000) in terms of creating new formal jobs, the assumed competitive advantage of a cheap workforce has not endured (even theoretically it is conceived as a static competitive advantage). A case in point is the relative stagnation of Mexican maquila operations from 2000 onward, caused by the relocation of numerous low-skill operations to China and Central America (discussed in chapter 4).

2. *Fall of wage income in the manufacturing sector.* In spite of the fact that the manufacturing sector operates as the pivot in the industrial restructuring process asymmetrically linking the United States and Mexico since the early 1990s (that—according to official discourse—is supposed to lead the development trend), 2008 real wage levels were down 3 percent as compared with 1994 in non-maquila manufacturing. This stood in sharp contrast to labor productivity, which increased in the period by 71 percent, according to Banco de México's data (Banxico 2009a). With wages essentially stagnant and productivity soaring, unit labor costs fell by more than 40 percent. This opened a broad and deep channel wherein profits flowed to the home base of TNCs, particularly the U.S.-based TNCs, as well as to those few Mexican *grupos* or conglomerates that remained proficient in manufacturing.[7] This relationship between real

wages and productivity generally follows the wages drop/productivity rises pattern in the United States—as we have shown in chapter 3, figure 3.1. (In contrast, the maquiladora industry, starting from a much lower base, experienced some modest catch-up in wage levels vis-à-vis the non-maquila manufacturing sector while recorded productivity stagnated, if official data sources are representative. In chapter 4 we noted why official data probably do not capture the cross-border accounting practices in the maquila sector and, hence, do not allow for a solid estimate of labor productivity.)[8]

3. *Workers' loss of purchase power.* The wage share of GDP fell from 35.3 percent in 1994 to 32.3 percent in 2007 (Moreno-Brid and Ros 2009, 274–76). In the same period (1994–2007), average overall (economywide) real average wages fell 24.2 percent. In terms of the distribution of income for the working population, following official figures, by the first quarter of 2009, 8 percent of the working population had no income; 13 percent earned the minimum wage or less (the official minimum wage was $4.15 US per day in 2009); 22.5 percent earned one to two minimum wages; 20 percent earned two to three; 17.8 percent earned three to five; and 10.7 percent earned more than five minimum wages (INEGI 2009b).[9] This means that 41 percent do not earn enough—two minimum wages or less—to ensure minimum levels of family well-being, while only 11.1 percent earned more than five minimum wages ($2.60 US per hour), which is the estimated value of the basic goods and services needed to maintain "decent" living standards (called the basic income).[10]

4. *Persistence of high poverty levels.* According to official figures, poverty in Mexico dropped from 52.4 percent in 1994 to 42.7 percent in 2008, and extreme poverty from 21.2 percent to 18.2 percent in the same period (CONEVAL 2008). This apparent diminution in relative but not absolute poverty levels[11] most likely reveals the impact of the exponential growth in migration over this period and the key role played by migrant remittances as a household survival strategy.

The general conditions of labor pauperization in Mexico arise from the inadequate creation of formal employment positions as well as the power of both the Mexican *grupos* and the TNCs to hold wages dramatically below increases in productivity. This is manifested by the abundance of self-employed people, people working in roofless microbusinesses, and the significance of both short workdays and workdays that surpass legal or customary limits. Moreover, it is necessary to take into account the sweeping weight of non-protected workers—encompassing informal workers, subsistence agricultural workers, and domestic and formal workers without benefits—revealing the emergence of new scenarios of extreme labor pauperization associated with the expansion of subcontracting chains beyond the boundaries of the increasingly restricted formal labor market.

In synthesis, under the influence of neoliberal policies, Mexico is undergoing a progressive dismantling of its manufacturing operations dating from the end of the ISI period (1982). At play in a parallel fashion we find mechanisms that to a fair extent resemble David Harvey's interpretation of the "creative destruction processes"—such as the expulsion of the Mexican peasantry from the countryside and into the migration stream (or the informal economy) due to the surge of cheap basic foodstuffs imported from the United States due to the NAFTA (Harvey 2007, 34–35). In such a context, a wide channel opened to reorient the economy toward a peculiar form of export-based production utilizing cheap labor while much of the labor surplus was simply expelled via migration.

HISTORICAL OVERVIEW OF RECENT MEXICAN MIGRATION

Since the end the nineteenth century, the labor force exodus into the United States has occurred with different intensities and features. Consequently, a variety of conceptions and policies emerged to encourage, contain, and repress population displacements according to the economic dynamics of both the United States and Mexico. In each stage, migrant workers have played a particular role. Contrary to interpretative approaches that postulate that migratory processes, once initiated, develop their own dynamic, we maintain that there is a close and decisive link between migration and the current accumulation model of cross-border regional integration. In recent years a qualitatively and quantitatively *new dynamic* underlying migration has taken place. Below, we truncate this important history, beginning with the Bracero Program mentioned in chapter 4.

1. *The Bracero Program* (1942–1964): The labor shortage in the United States caused by World War II created new conditions calling for the recruitment of Mexican laborers. In spite of the high growth rates achieved in Mexico in this period, there was a surplus of agrarian workers who did not find jobs in cities or industrial sites. This caused the first negotiation of the migration process between Mexico and the United States. The Bracero Program favored a predominant circular migration pattern of temporary workers. Toward the end of the period, the number of visas for farmhands was cut down, triggering the rise of illegal immigrants (Massey, Durand, and Malone 2002, 34–41).

2. *Illegal migration* (1964–1985): At the close of this period, a decline of the state-led industrialization model took place, undercutting employment opportunities. Meanwhile, in the United States, the demand for migrant laborers continued to grow in pace with the enlargement of the country's vast internal market, the growth of its export sector, and the emergence of an all-out attack on the organized U.S. labor force. Because of the constrained legal channels for entry into the United States, there was a substantial increase in undocumented migration, which was quickly stigmatized by criminalizing the immigrants (Delgado Wise 2004). Far from stopping under these circumstances, migration continued, enabling U.S. employers to hire cheap Mexican labor. Migrants exhibited a high propensity to return, making the net inflow of undocumented migrants modest, in terms of future migration: 4.9 million over a twenty-year period (Massey, Durand, and Malone 2002, 64). In these years, the Mexican government assumed a passive, indulgent attitude, tacitly instituting what García y Griego defines as "the policy of no policy" (García y Griego 1988, 147).

3. *Massive migration* (1986 to date): In 1986 Mexico signed the GATT, launching nonrestricted, open investment and trade processes later consolidated by the NAFTA—discussed in detail in chapter 3. These institutional changes constituted a powerful engine, forcing massive numbers of Mexicans to migrate to the United States—400,000 per year from 2000 to 2005, according to recent estimates by the United Nations Population Division (United Nations 2006). The unprecedented legalization of 2.3 million Mexicans under the IRCA (Immigration Reform and Control Act of 1986) in 1987 was unable to contain the new migration drive—particularly its high illegal component. In this context, the attempt to negotiate a migration agenda with the United States at the beginning of the administration of President Fox (2000–2006) was frustrated by 9/11, which brought about a tougher immigration policy. On the Mexican side, given the visibility and growing strategic significance of emigration, a policy was adopted that Durand calls "damage repair," oriented toward the protection of the migrant population (Durand 2005, 24).

When the cheap labor–export model was established as the pivot of a nationwide "accumulation" strategy, the migration policy underwent a sort of "courtship of the diaspora," with the purpose of ensuring monetary remittances from migrants and rendering migration a core element of macroeconomic stability. This was the case, given the crucial impact of money transfers as a source of foreign exchange in the trade balance. As well, the policy helped maintain social stability since roughly 1.6 million Mexican families depend on remittances as their main source of income (Canales 2008, 210–18). In this sense, although not an overt part of the Mexican policy, the fact is that labor exports have become an *implicit* element of the reigning cheap labor–export model and of the government policies that support it.

Finally, we should stress that this model is starting to show signs of unsustainability. This is so because of (1) the present economic crisis that affects both the United States and Mexico; (2) the distortions engendered in Mexico's production capacities and processes under the umbrella of this model—as detailed in chapters 4 and 5; and (3) the emerging signs of *backwash effects*, such as the surfacing of a strong depopulation trend in a large portion of the Mexican territory (as documented in the following section) accompanied by the abandonment of national manufacturing businesses as the internal market stagnated or declined.

THE NEW MIGRATION DYNAMICS

The Mexico-United States migration system is exceptional—being one of the oldest, most complex, and most active in the world. Although its profile is shaped by several factors, there is no doubt that the spinal column of the current migration flow is driven by underemployed and unemployed Mexican workers (Durand and Massey 2003, 45). We refer to the direct labor export process that coincides with the two indirect export production processes we have analyzed in chapters 4 and 5—the maquilas and the disguised maquilas.

Currently, Mexican migration has reached record proportions, particularly due to the NAFTA. In the past thirty years, the native Mexican population residing in the United States grew nearly sixfold, from 2.2 million in 1980 to 11.8 million in 2009 (CONAPO 2009). While Mexico has become the top exporter of migrants in the world, second place goes to China (390,000 per year), and third place to India (280,000)—both nations with populations more than ten times greater than Mexico's. Concurrently, the United States has the highest immigration rate in the world (absorbing 20 percent of the world's total), of which Mexicans constitute a majority—27.6 percent (CONAPO 2009).

As illustrated in figure 6.1, the extent of this trend is quite expressive: in 2008 native Mexicans estimated to be residing in the United States exceeded 30 million, including both immigrants born in Mexico (11.8 million)—legal or not—and United States citizens with Mexican ancestors (first, second, and further generations).

In line with the above figures, Mexico underwent a process of exponential growth in terms of migrant remittances, climbing to second place in the world below India and China (World Bank 2009). For 2007, money transfers totaled

Figure 6.1.   Mexican Natives Residing in the United States

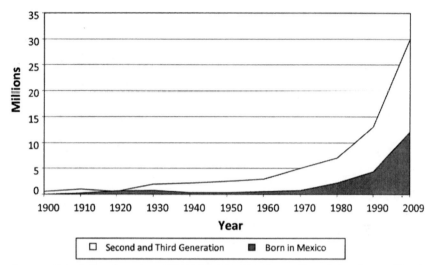

Sources: Calculations based on CONAPO 2009; *U.S. Current Population Survey*, March 2009.

$26 billion US (Banxico 2009b). Notwithstanding, we should add that for 2008 the figure fell to $25 billion US, the first decline since the advent of the NAFTA, as a result of the U.S. recession (see figure 6.2).

The following major qualitative changes are evident over and above those features that account for the quantitative growth of migration:

- There has been international migration from practically all over the Mexican territory, involving 96.2 percent of the municipalities in 2000. This spread of migratory participation entailed both new departure and destination zones of migration flows (Zúñiga and Leite 2004). Concurrently, the number of Mexican natives residing in the United States—regardless of their prior concentration in a few states—has expanded across the country in the past few years. Among other places, immigration flows are expanding into the eastern and north central United States (Zúñiga and Hernández León 2005), precisely where some of the most active industrial restructuring centers are located (Champlin and Hake 2006).
- Education-wise, 39.3 percent of the population aged twenty-four or older born in Mexico and residing in the United States in 2008 had high-school or further education (See table 6.2). In contrast, the average for Mexico in 2005 (last available year) was 30.7 percent (U.S. Census Bureau 2009). This means that, contrary to common belief, more skilled labor is leaving rather than staying in Mexico. Furthermore, considering schooling

Figure 6.2. Mexico—Remittances: Amount and Annual Growth Rate

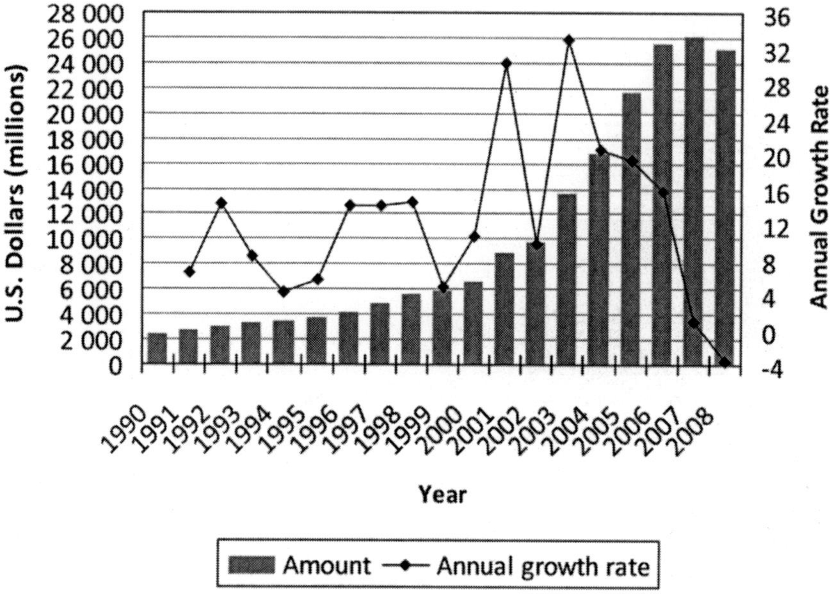

Source: Calculation based on Banxico 2009b.

from 1994 and 2008, we find an evident progress in the growth of skilled migration. It should be noted, nevertheless, that as compared with other immigrant groups, the Mexican population of the United States has less education. This circumstance illustrates the severe education lag prevailing in Mexico (OCDE 2005).

• We also find evidence of a hardly visible type of displacement that does not fall under any labor migration stereotype regarding Mexicans—those residing in the United States with a B.A. or a graduate degree. In 2008 these exceeded 533,000, all born in Mexico, including 9,550 with Ph.D. degrees (U.S. Census Bureau 2009). Far more revealing is the number of

Table 6.2. Increase in Educational Levels of Mexicans Living in the United States (24 Years of Age and Above)

	1994	Percentage	2008	Percentage
High school and above	1,336,889	29.37	3,773,087	39.28
B.S. and above	205,402	4.51	533,526	5.55
Graduate degree	53,553	1.18	158,264	1.65
Ph.D.	5,873	0.13	9,550	0.10

Source: Calculations based on the U.S. *Current Population Survey*, March 2009.

highly skilled Mexicans who migrate to the United States as compared with those who stay. If the number of Mexicans living in the United States is considerable (a little over 10 percent), the highly skilled portion of this population, huge in relative terms (a little over 30 percent), is an even greater cause for concern (U.S. Census Bureau 2009, table 6; INEE 2008) This brings up the "brain drain" process—an alarming issue that warrants serious consideration.

- All these changes have been accompanied by a significant transformation of the migration pattern: from a predominantly circular pattern, it shifted to a predominance of migrant settlers. Although this trend is usually the outcome of evolution and maturing of migration flows, it has been accompanied by unilaterally closing the border which, contrary to the purpose of containing a population exodus, has locked in the migrants. This is due to the risk of returning, causing Mexican immigrants to opt for extending their stay indefinitely (Massey, Durand, and Malone 2002).
- Finally, the shift in migration patterns and the fall in domestic birth rates led to a growing and preoccupying depopulation trend between 2000 and 2005: Out of 2,435 municipalities in the country, 1,243 (one in every two) experienced a negative population growth rate (INEGI 2006).

THE ROLE OF MEXICAN LABOR IN THE U.S. ECONOMIC RESTRUCTURING PROCESS

The quantitative and qualitative description of the burgeoning Mexican migration into the United States is obviously incomplete without a glimpse of the role that Mexican labor plays in the U.S. economy. These are issues that to a fair extent are kept invisible and have been practically absent in the political debate on migration.

NAFTA and the general neoliberal restructuring of the Mexican economy that began in the 1980s have had a profound two-way impact on the U.S. production system. Notable in this process has been the shifting of U.S. investment into Mexico, as discussed and analyzed in previous chapters. At the same time that increasing capital mobility undermined the rate of capital formation in the United States, a countertendency was created through the increasing portion of the Mexican economic surplus that was displaced to the United States as profits rose from the Mexican operations of U.S. transnational corporations. This countertendency was reinforced as Mexican immigrants flowed into the United States and into the industrial sectors, lowering production costs and raising profits. Thus, the impact of capital shifting to Mexico fell on the U.S. labor force, particularly organized labor, while the U.S. restructuring process created two significant avenues to increased profits (available repatriated profits and lower wages), with these benefits flowing to a small percentage of owners, managers, and stockholders located in U.S. manufacturing and finance.

The U.S. economy receives a certain type of stimulus from Mexican emigration to the degree that new investments occur because of substantially different consumption patterns arising from the 7.5 million Mexican immigrant workers and their dependents living in the United States in 2009. This is to be noted in the so-called migration industry—that is, the migrant-related economic activities that have increasingly turned into a profitable business for large transnational corporations, such as transportation, telecommunications, money transfers, and so on (Guarnizo 2003).

Shifting capital to Mexico destroyed jobs in the United States, as did the sizable trade deficit the United States developed with Mexico once the NAFTA agreement had been consummated. But bringing more of Mexico's economic surplus back to the United States stimulated the economy, and the influx of millions of Mexican immigrants helped push down labor's share of national income to a record low. The net effect was to create a new "social structure of accumulation." This constituted a leaner and meaner social environment for all workers, emigrant or not, and a corpulent, more contented business elite in the United States, now better positioned to meet foreign competitors by either locating portions of production processes in the United States or in Mexico (or elsewhere), as profit maximization strategies indicated.

Improving the macroeconomic relationships of the U.S. economy, however, was an unintended consequence, not the determinant factor in the repositioning of U.S. capital to Mexico. Viewing the matter from the standpoint of the restructuring of the U.S. production system, a separate microeconomic logic—driven by the desire to maximize profits and outperform the competition—prevailed: under this logic, shifting capital to Mexico could enable U.S. firms to purchase labor processes at as low as 10 percent of their cost in the United States, while accepting that productivity per hour might not be quite as high as that in the United States. From this level of the microeconomics of the firm—assuming the stability of final demand for products exported from Mexico to the United States—shifting capital to Mexico to achieve "labor efficiencies" was a logical step in many instances. In highly oligopolized industries, such as autos, the available research indicates that the cost-saving production processes adopted in Mexico were taken as profits—not in price reductions benefiting U.S. consumers (Cypher 2001). In less capital-intensive industries, such as apparel, where brand identity is strong, similar profit-enhancing results are to be anticipated.

Shifting production to Mexico made credible the threat of further production shifts, thereby weakening all U.S. labor, particularly organized labor. The stagnation in U.S. production workers' pay (constituting 80 percent of the U.S. workforce) as documented in chapter 3, figure 3.1, is broadly correlated with the increasing tendency of U.S. corporations to move their production operations to Mexico (and elsewhere). In the process of restructuring the U.S. production system—a perceived necessity during the course of the 1980s—a complex, mutually reinforcing, triple movement began. First, significant elements of U.S. capital shifted to Mexico, thereby lowering their costs of production. Second, U.S. firms often *threatened* to move to Mexico (but did not, or did not to the extent anticipated). Using a cudgel that did not exist until the 1970s when capital mobility commenced in earnest, employers strengthened their bargaining power over labor in many ways—including by defeating union elections or by reducing the rate of growth of wages (or lowering wages) through hard bargaining (Bronfenbrenner 2000; Cowie 1999; MacArthur 2000). Third, growing numbers of workers were displaced by the production shifts to Mexico, thereby reducing the portion of the labor force in unions. This process reduced the collateral impacts union labor generally generates to push up wages for all workers (except those near the minimum wage). That is, the union wage was for decades the standard and the "target" for nonunion workers with similar skills and responsibilities. When the unions' power declined, so did the "target"—thereby effectively pulling down wages for almost all production workers.

THE UNITED STATES' DEMAND FOR MEXICAN LABOR

The *Current Population Survey*'s occupational data show the strategic function of migrants in the U.S. labor market. The country generated about 23.2 million new jobs between 1994 and 2008; 46.2 percent of these were filled by the immigrant population (see table 6.3). Mexicans comprise the largest workforce-providing immigrant group, obtaining 3.8 million jobs between 1994 and 2008. This was a third of the immigrant population's total labor supply and 16 percent of all U.S.-generated employment—that is, one in every six employment positions. In these years Mexican immigrant employment grew by 106 percent, while total employment rose 18 percent.

The role played by Mexican migrants in the U.S. job market is even more evident when approached in relative terms: Mexican immigrant employment has grown at the fastest annual rate—7.6 percent—throughout the NAFTA era. This is nearly ten times higher than the rate of growth of the nonimmigrant population.

Compulsive Mexican migration to the United States is molded by processes of cross-border regional integration, but it has very different impacts in each country. The receiving country benefits from an increased labor supply

Table 6.3. Employed Population in the United States According to Migration Status, 1994–2008

	1994	2008	Difference	Annual Average Growth Rate (Percentage)
Employed population	129,714,943	152,986,375	23,271,432	1.3
Employed native population	116,753,126	129,266,308	12,513,182	0.8
Employed immigrant population	12,961,817	23,720,067	10,758,250	5.9
Employed non-Mexican immigrant population	9,323,008	16,226,064	6,903,056	5.3
Employed Mexican immigrant population	3,638,809	7,494,003	3,855,194	7.6

Source: Calculations based on U.S. *Current Population Survey*, March issue, 1994–2008.

in certain sectors of the labor market, which reduces labor costs and increases benefits to capital, as discussed above. This process is not simply regulated by the free play of workforce supply and demand; in many ways, it is also managed via deliberate corporate strategies that seek to reduce labor costs through the massive replacement of native workers in certain sectors of the U.S. economy. The behavior of the manufacturing industry is paradigmatic in both labor restructuring and corporate strategies, where migrants play a key role. These strategies certainly facilitated the process of workforce substitution, as can be seen in table 6.4. Between 1994 and 2008, the native workforce in the manufacturing sector decreased by 4.28 million, while immigrant employees increased by about 812,000. Of these, some 300,000 (40 percent) were Mexican. While nonimmigrant manufacturing employment dropped by 23.6 percent, Mexican immigrant employment leaped by 40.2 percent. Certain immigrant groups in this sector, particularly the Mexicans, receive extremely low salaries. Table 6.4 shows the very significant salary gaps between native and immigrant salaries in relation to those of Mexican manufacturing workers. Mexican immigrants were employed at a 48 percent discount to the wages of nonimmigrant manufacturing workers in 2008.

We see that not only is the wage differential significant regarding Mexican immigrants and U.S. natives employed in manufacturing—it has also increased from 42 percent to 48 percent since the NAFTA commenced. These data demonstrate one aspect of the precarious employment process taking place within the U.S. economy. This process consists, inter alia, of the replacement of workers, the instability or fragility of employment, and the escalating decline of labor standards in a context of deunionization. This process operates within

Table 6.4.   Manufacturing Sector Employment According to Migration Status, 1994–2008

Employment and Salary	1994	2008
Total employed in the manufacturing sector	20,340,523	16,868,190
Average annual salary (USD prices 2008)	$37,079	$48,910
Total native population employed in the manufacturing sector	18,119,790	13,835,048
Average annual salary (USD prices 2008)	$37,784	$50,361
Total immigrant population employed in the manufacturing sector	2,220,733	3,033,142
Average annual salary (USD prices 2008)	$32,396	$42,198
Total non-Mexican immigrant population employed in the manufacturing sector	1,412,495	1,900,300
Average annual salary (USD prices 2008)	$38,519	$51,572
Total immigrant Mexican population employed in the manufacturing sector	808,238	1,132,842
Average annual salary (USD prices 2008)	$21,795	$26,360
Native versus Mexican salary difference	$15,989	$24,001
Non-Mexican immigrant versus Mexican immigrant salary difference	$16,724	$25,212
Percent of employed native population in relation to total manufacture-employed population	89.1	82.0
Percent of employed Mexican population in relation to total manufacture-employed population	6.9	11.3
Percent of employed Mexican migrant population in relation to total manufacture-employed population	4.0	6.7

Source: Calculations based on U.S. *Current Population Survey* data, March issue, 1994–2008.

the broader context of national deindustrialization/transnational restructuring, demonstrating the fundamental role of the Mexican workforce export model (Delgado Wise and Márquez Covarrubias 2007).

In short, immigrants in general, and Mexicans in particular, contribute to the restructuring of the U.S. economy in the following five ways:

1. *Cost reduction effects.* A cheap, flexible, and disorganized workforce contributes to cost reductions in the labor process, both in low-skill and highly qualified sectors.
2. *Displacement effects.* Migrants are used to replace better-paid and unionized labor contingents since they are willing to work under more exploitative and demanding conditions (Levine 2001; Passel 2005).

3. *Complementarities effect.* Given the decreased population growth rate, migrants provide the required workforce to maintain accumulation and economic growth rates.
4. *Replacement effects.* The internationalization of production and new global commodity chains displace jobs to underdeveloped or peripheral nations with an abundance of cheap workforce. (These processes were examined in detail in chapters 4 and 5.)
5. *Devaluation effects.* By contributing to labor cheapening, displacement, complementarities, and replacement effects, and (further) by working as domestic laborers and in activities that produce wage goods, migrants also contribute to the general devaluation (or cheapening) of the workforce in the global framework of capitalist restructuring. That is, the *maintenance and reproduction costs of the workforce are reduced.* (This we highlighted in chapter 3, figure 3.1, wherein wages of production workers failed to rise for more than thirty years in spite of productivity increases—a relationship never before existing in U.S. history for any significant period of time, let alone for more than three decades.)

CONTRIBUTION OF MEXICAN IMMIGRANTS TO PRODUCTION AND CONSUMPTION IN THE UNITED STATES

To begin, we must take into account the fact that the vast number of Mexican migrants working and residing in the United States strengthens both national production and consumption. Their contribution to the U.S. GDP has increased by two-thirds from 1994 to 2008, from 2.3 percent to 3.8 percent. In 2008 this amounted to $531.6 billion US (or 46.5 percent of the Mexican GDP).[12] The U.S. economy grew by $4.148 trillion US in real terms between 1994 and 2008—using 2008 prices (BEA 2009). Mexican immigrants contributed $312 billion US, or 7.5 percent of this increase. And, in spite of their having the lowest income levels, their consumption also played a significant role in energizing the U.S. internal market. In fact, they contributed $400 billion in 2008.[13]

EDUCATIONAL AND SOCIAL REPRODUCTION COST TRANSFERS FROM MEXICO TO THE UNITED STATES

The reigning discourse on migration and development tends to portray migrants as a fiscal and social burden on the United States. This, however, is unfounded if one considers all the relevant factors involved, as we discuss below. Labor inclusion accompanied by social exclusion is the preordained path for most Mexican immigrants in the United States. This is particularly true for the undocumented migrants: according to Passel, 46.5 percent of Mexican immigrants were undocumented in 1990; this number rose to 52.2 percent in 2000 and 56.4 percent in 2005 (Passel 2005). The plight of the immigrants (documented and undocumented) is characterized by at least three factors:

1. *Restriction of social mobility.* Precarious labor conditions, social exclusion, and the need to send a fraction of their income to Mexico mean that migrants' consumption capacity is minimal, as are their opportunities for social ascent.
2. *Stigmatization of migrants as human merchandise.* Immigrants are reduced to the status of cheap labor force: their exploitation must incur the least social spending and earn minimal rewards. In addition, they are, of course, disposable.
3. *Subsidization of the state.* In addition to living under superexploitative conditions, immigrants transfer a part of Mexico's social capital, subsidizing the accumulation process in the United States while being stigmatized, criminalized, and segregated.

Migrants' labor insertion into the U.S. labor market entails a transfer of resources derived from the educational and social reproduction costs of the workforce. These were covered by Mexico through educational, social subsistence, health, and welfare programs. Seen from another angle, labor migration saves the United States considerable social expenditures, most particularly because the age profile of the migrant population is inordinately correlated with years of maximum labor force participation. These costs for the creation and reproduction of the labor force are considerably lower in Mexico.

By taking into account the educational level of Mexican migrants upon their arrival in the United States and the costs this represents for the Mexican public education system, we estimate that between 1994 and 2008, Mexico transferred $83 billion US (at 2008 prices) to its northern neighbor (U.S. Census Bureau 2009; INEE 2009).[14] These preliminary calculations, conducted by a research consortium known as SIMDE, were made using the peso costs of distinct levels of public education in Mexico. These expenditure estimates were then converted into 2008 prices and then into U.S. dollars at the average exchange rate.

A second calculation was made, based loosely on the methodology of purchasing power parity (PPP). Had these same educational levels that Mexican migrants brought to the United States been instead attained in U.S. public schools, the estimated social cost would have been $613 billion US of educational expenditures (at constant 2008 prices) over the same time span. Using this method, if remittances by Mexican immigrants to Mexico are considered a drain of resources from the United States, their total would constitute only an estimated 30 percent of the total amount of the educational surplus transferred to the United States by the Mexican immigrant workforce from 1994 to 2008.

In addition to the educational costs, migration involves a transfer of resources in terms of social reproduction—that is, the upkeep costs of the individual before emigration. These costs involve a variety of expenses, including public welfare, social programs, and the family expenditures used to support and develop those who eventually emigrate (including a substantial portion of remittances, which contribute to the formation of a new emigrant workforce). These costs, difficult to measure, constitute the socioeconomic outlays for human capital formation. Taking the cost of the basic food basket estimated by the National Council for the Evaluation of Social Development Policy as an expression of the cost of living, SIMDE has provisionally estimated that Mexico transferred $257 billion US (at 2008 prices) to the United States between 1994 and 2008 (CONEVAL 2008). This is 1.4 times the total amount of remittances received during this period.

When we add up the estimated educational and social costs—excluding the issues of PPP and the quality differentials in public education—we come up with a total transfer of $340 billion US, 1.8 times the full amount of remittances sent to Mexico in 1994–2008. This estimate is certainly very low—because it values the services provided in Mexico in peso prices rather than in terms of the opportunity cost of these services in the United States. In U.S. prices, as we have seen, the value of the educational transfer leaps by 7.4 times from the $83 billion US estimated by SIMDE for the years 1994–2008.

The calculations of the "burden" of immigrants that we have reviewed begin with the immigrants already in the United States. That is, the educational costs and socioeconomic reproduction costs incurred in Mexico are not part of the calculation. If they were, and if these transfers from Mexico to the United States were part of a calculation adjusted properly in terms of their value in U.S. dollar equivalent purchasing power, it would be evident, we assert, that Mexican society *currently subsidizes* the U.S. economy via labor migration.

While it is frequently claimed in public discourse that immigrants are a net fiscal burden on the United States (lifetime taxes paid < public benefits received), all these studies ignore the wealth transfer made by Mexico to the United States in terms of the social costs of raising and educating the Mexican immigrant workforce. Nevertheless, even when these crucial factors are ignored, a recent analysis of several widely cited studies by economists on the theme of the "burden" of immigrants concludes that

> The consensus among most economists seems to be that, over the long term and averaged across all immigrants (including illegal ones, who pay less in taxes and receive less in benefits), immigrants more than pay their way in the U.S., in that their tax contributions exceed public spending on them. However, it seems that the benefit is largely received at the federal level rather than the state level. (Bolin 2004, 6)[15]

It is clearly beyond the scope of this chapter to present a detailed discussion on all aspects of the taxes paid and public economic benefits received by Mexican immigrants. Our primary focus is elsewhere—on the extraordinary profit-making opportunities that Mexican immigrants afford (directly and indirectly) to U.S. capital. Thus, no matter how the debate over the fiscal burden is resolved, it is clear that the funding of the public programs available to immigrants does not come primarily from the large and medium-sized U.S. corporations that enjoy the financial advantages flowing from their Mexican immigrant employees. In their method of calculation—which is profit and loss—there can be no doubt that the migration component of the cheap labor–export model constitutes an important transference of value from Mexico to U.S. capital operating in the United States.

REMITTANCES AS A MEXICAN DEVELOPMENTAL POLICY?

Remittances are often portrayed as a strong form of currency that sustains Mexico's external accounts; a money supply endowed with expansive, multiplying effects; quality resources for local development; philanthropic contributions to impoverished communities; or a river of gold flowing into Mexico, creating waves of progress. These are nothing but a series of ideologically based statements promoted by the World Bank and the Inter-American Development Bank—an attempt to depict migrants as sources of wealth or capital, successful entrepreneurs, the new heroes of development in charge of performing the duties of capital and the state. This apologetic discourse masks the mechanics of asymmetric regional integration underlying the cheap labor–export model followed by Mexico.

Even though there is no empirical proof or theoretical foundation to the claim that migrants' remittances can be used as tools for development in countries of origin, this idea would appear to be factual and unquestionable given the number of reports, articles, and speeches that intone, over and over, this new mantra of development (Gosh 2006; Kapur 2004, World Bank 2006). The problem behind this political and ideological concept is that the context, and all involved processes and agents, are essentially ignored. We are provided with a romanticized vision of migrants as heroes of development, even though most of them are excluded workers striving to support themselves and their families. This approach ignores the root causes of migration, ignores the Mexican immigrants' contributions to the U.S. economy, and exaggerates and idealizes the power of remittances in pauperized, increasingly desolate and underdeveloped places of origin: ghost towns where productive activities have been abandoned, populations have been uprooted, and despair is part of the landscape.

In addition to asking ourselves what remittances are, we must find out how they are produced. Migrants send part of their income to dependents still residing at home in order to cover basic family needs (Márquez 2007). The remaining sum must ensure their own subsistence and that of any dependents living with them in the United States. We must then assess the living and working conditions of migrants and their dependents, both at home and in the receiving country, in order to understand the nature and function of remittances. Such a comprehensive approach will show that, while remittances comprise an income transference from the United States to Mexico, this drain is insignificant when compared to the resource transferences that enable it—as we have demonstrated in the previous section. Remittances, in short, are framed by a context of unequal exchange and the new international division of labor generated by neoliberal globalization, which undermines growth, accumulation, and development processes in Mexico.

Migrants' remittances come from a salary that is, essentially, a subsalary. That is, it is apparently higher than what the person would earn in Mexico but lower than that of other—similarly employed—workers in the United States. In fact, it is often below the socially demarcated minimum level of basic subsistence, reproduction, and recreation in the United States. In short, it is a salary constructed under conditions of superexploitation and social exclusion. This structure allows for only modest remittances, which clearly cannot be expected to foster a development process.

Chapter Seven

The International Political Economy of Capital Restructuring

Beyond its specificities, the Mexican labor export-led model illustrates a major trend in the process of capital restructuring characterizing contemporary capitalism: the dual process of the exportation of embodied labor power in manufactured products and the direct exportation of the workforce via migration. Our empirical and conceptual findings regarding the Mexico-United States case are crucial guidelines for understanding key aspects of the current global context, its driving forces and main contradictions.

During the past three and a half decades, labor constraints became one of the main obstacles to worldwide capital accumulation (Harvey 2003). In order to overcome this obstacle, the challenge, especially for large transnational corporations (TNCs), was to cheapen labor, resulting in deteriorating conditions for workers, particularly in the industrially advanced nations. Notably, the new strategies took the following interrelated forms: (1) the displacement of capital to peripheral regions with an abundant low-cost workforce, (2) the promotion of technological advances, especially those associated with the construction/expansion/deepening of global commodity chains, and (3) the luring of a peripheral immigrant workforce to developed nations in order to employ this massive surplus population as a source of cheap labor (Gereffi 2001).[1] The latter process simultaneously increased competition for jobs at the point of production, thereby dramatically holding down wages for all workers while productivity levels rose.

Under these circumstances, high-income nations, led by the United States, have developed a complex, worldwide capital restructuring strategy for the benefit of large transnational capital. In this context, capital mobility has increased, with serious consequences: the U.S. manufacturing sector shed more than six million employment positions from 1990 through mid-2009, according to the U.S. Bureau of Labor Statistics—a drop of over 33 percent

(*Economist* 2009, 38). Among the main elements of this process of restructuring are

1. The internationalization of production;
2. The implementation of neoliberal structural adjustment policies aimed at reinserting peripheral countries in the new global accumulation dynamic under asymmetrical and subordinate conditions;
3. The incorporation of massive contingents of labor from both the ex-Soviet Union and China into processes of internationalized production;
4. The transformation of innovation systems in the major developed nations in consonance with capital's internationalization strategy; and,
5. The massive expansion of speculative/financial capital. (The latter registers a vastly superior dynamic to that of the so-called real economy, also accelerating the processes of capital concentration and centralization, thereby distorting the functioning of the global economy as a whole.)

These strategies have been supported by the militarization of international relations and the commercialization of a vast range of natural resources. The mechanisms behind the new global political economy triggered an extensive and contradictory project of capitalist expansion founded on the massive incorporation of cheap labor. As we have shown throughout this book, the direct and indirect exportation of the Mexican workforce has become a key element in this process. The results offer stark contrasts: an exacerbated concentration of capital, a steep increase in asymmetries between nations (particularly across the north-south boundary), and an unprecedented growth in social inequality. Moreover, since the summer of 2007, this internationalized system has entered a profound and multidimensional crisis. This crisis is one that not only promises to be deep and long lasting; it also seriously questions the strategy behind the neoliberal capitalist restructuring project.

LANDMARKS OF CONTEMPORARY CAPITALISM

Within this broad framework, some particular structural features should be noted:

1. *Oversupply of labor*
   - With the incorporation of the ex-Soviet Union, China, and India, the labor supply for capital potentially increased from 1.46 to 3 billion in 2000 (Robinson 2008, 24).

- To this should be added the dislocation/displacement of labor via massive international migration from the periphery to the advanced industrial nations as a result of neoliberal structural adjustment programs.

2. *The vulnerability of labor*
   - Instead of the "win-win" upward convergence between north and south wage earners—as predicted by the economic models that drove the process of "free-trade" agreements, we find increasing divergence in some instances and in other situations a process of "downward convergence," or "lose-lose" for industrial workers.

3. *Increased south to north labor migration*
   - The number of migrants has nearly tripled since 1975.
   - Increasing flow of remittances: These reverse flows have produced a new development mantra—the "golden river," which has no basis in fact.

4. *Growing social inequalities*
   - Social polarization, narrowing of middle classes, dismantling of the welfare state.
   - In the case of the United States, by the early twenty-first century income inequality had reached levels not seen since the unregulated years of the 1920s. The richest 1 percent of the population received 21.7 percent of all income, while the top 20 percent obtained roughly 62 percent (Cypher 2007a, 15).

5. *Low growth rates—another important indicator*
   - In contrast with the postwar U.S. growth rates of GDP in the "golden age" from 1948 to 1973 of 4.01 percent per year, capitalism in the United States (and elsewhere) has been marked by declining dynamism in the past thirty-six years:
     - 1970–1999: 2.95 percent per year
     - 2000–2009: 1.8 percent per year (BEA 2009, table 1.1.1)

UNEQUAL DEVELOPMENT AND THE EXPORTATION OF THE WORKFORCE

The nature of contemporary capitalism is inaccurately portrayed by the anodyne notion of globalization, which merely traces the international flows of capital, information, technology, and the workforce. Beyond this poorly descriptive view, which rests on blind faith in a self-regulating free market that can ostensibly achieve a fair and equal global society, we find that the past three and a half decades have been defined by a project of capitalist expansion that has delivered brutal consequences in the areas of development and social justice. The concept of unequal development is particularly useful for describing and analyzing this situation, since it refers to a historical process of economic, social, and political polarization among regions, nations, and classes, all of which are a consequence of processes of capitalist accumulation, international labor divisions, and class conflict on a variety of planes. The most evident result is the expansion of social inequality, embodied in the concentration of capital, power, and wealth in the hands of a small elite. At the other extreme we note an abundant process of transformation and growing inequality, excluding Asia. In Asia, as we have noted, many nations (including most importantly China and to some degree India) successfully pursued national development projects through the initiation of state-led processes of industrialization, following strategies decried by the Washington Consensus (Cypher and Dietz 2009, 294–95). More generally, at the level of the world capitalist system there is a profound differentiation among core or developed nations and most peripheral, underdeveloped or dependent ones—leaving aside the short-term impacts of the commodities boom of the early twenty-first century on several resource-abundant nations (Cypher 2009).

It is not our intention, however, to characterize the development of capitalism as merely a dichotomous process, nor do we advance a simple Manichaean vision. Rather, we have sought to document the particulars of the general process of the internationalization of capital in the case of Mexico and the United States. The essence of this internationalization process in the periphery and in the advanced industrial "core" nations is in the economic elite's seizure of the economic surplus.[2] Relations of domination, exploitation, and uneven exchange have developed between the core and the periphery with varying degrees of intensity, depending on the historical periods of colonization, postcolonization, and the modern period of the internationalization of capital (Baran 1957).

In order to understand the process of unequal development at work under contemporary capitalism, and to dissect the mechanisms behind labor exportation (both indirect and direct), we have sought to demonstrate (on the basis of a case study of the transnational integration of the Mexican and United States economies) that the periphery's present role is to provide the developed world with a cheap workforce. Neoliberal structural adjustment policies are designed to foster the following three processes in peripheral economies (Delgado Wise and Márquez Covarrubias 2007): (1) dismantle and rearticulate their economic structure; (2) restructure the labor market to effectively generate a growing surplus population, and (3) induce an outflow of this surplus labor (migration). These processes, in turn, establish the contours of a new international labor division with the following characteristics:

1. *The reinsertion of peripheral nations into the global capitalist system as appendages of the global commodity chains.* Under the aegis of the global capital restructuring and the pressure of the international financial institutions (IFI), Washington Consensus policies based on outward orientation, deregulation, and privatization have frequently been implemented in peripheral nations. In Mexico, these fundamental structural changes (occurring crucially in the 1980s and early 1990s) were willingly introduced and sometimes initiated by state policy makers who worked closely with, and drew their inspiration from, peak business organizations, such as the Business Coordinating Council (CCE). The capstone piece of legislation for both Mexico and the United States was the passage of NAFTA, disguised as a "free-trade" agreement while being, in reality, fundamentally an *investment* accord to create more options for foreign direct investment (FDI). More generally, these structural programs have led to the reinsertion of peripheral nations (including some from the former socialist bloc) into deeper processes of internationalization of capital led by large TNCs.
2. *The exporting of cheap workforce.* Reinsertion leads to a new international division of labor where a significant form of exchange between the center and the periphery is the marketing of the workforce on the international market, thus converting this labor into a fundamental merchandise, feeding polarizing economic growth and the disarticulation of the periphery.

The export of the cheap labor workforce (as we have demonstrated throughout the course of this book) takes two interrelated forms: (1) the indirect or disembodied type, exemplified by assembly plants that are located in peripheral countries but form part of global commodity chains, and (2) the direct type, also known as labor migration. In the first case, large TNCs are able to access a cheap peripheral workforce by displacing part of the global production process to underdeveloped countries. But, crucially, this all occurs without creating structural production linkages in the host nation. In fact, as we have demonstrated—particularly in the case of the auto industry—the process of internationalization disrupts, deforms, and ruptures structural productive linkages within the host nation. New enclaves of advanced production lead to the undermining and displacement of the national supplier base, as first-tier suppliers are increasingly TNCs that employ advanced technological processes that match or exceed the innovational capabilities of those firms that undertake and coordinate the final processing/assembly of manufactured products for export. These periphery-based enclaves generate the appearance of a strengthened export platform for host nations. That is, nations such as Mexico highlight the growth of their manufacturing capabilities—not merely of "labor-intensive" products such as apparel—but of advanced products and even, to some degree, "hi-tech" products. Nevertheless, upon close examination we find that this process actually entails an economic regression because the national contribution to this internationalized accumulation process is limited essentially to low salaries and, in the best of cases, a restricted multiplier effect through consumption. Under the cheap labor–export model, the peripheral nation serves to transfer net profits abroad. This is oftentimes done via intrafirm operations that tend to be largely tax exempt—or even subsidized—and often free from any fundamental responsibility regarding potential environmental damage. Because of the proprietary nature of intrafirm activities, the magnitude of these net profit transfers can be easily hidden and impossible to accurately measure.

Direct workforce export, on the other hand, is a response to cheap labor demands in central nations, which not only seek to satisfy a need the receiving country cannot itself produce. More important, this serves as a means to cheapen the cost of the *entire nonprofessional* workforce (with the process increasingly spilling over into the professional cadres) in core nations. In this regard, rather than being a blind market-driven phenomenon, it represents an intentional, institutionalized corporate-driven strategy.

This new feature of the international division of labor is based in a process that systematically undermines the living and working conditions of the majority of the employed population (and their dependents) and entails a growing devaluation and cheapening of the workforce, including under conditions of superexploitation for immigrant workers. The Mexican labor export-led model firmly exemplifies such a trend and its consequences: severe regression in the national development process under a process of asymmetrical regional (transnational) integration.

As we have already pointed out, the new global architecture includes an overflow of speculative financial capital and environmental destruction, which worsen the system's inherent contradictions and highlight its proclivity toward social deprivation while frequently fostering impoverishment.[3] Under these circumstances, the landscape of unequal development is tainted by growing social chasms, including the unprecedented widening of income gaps between many if not most nations and within nations—particularly in both Mexico and the United States.

THE EMERGENCE OF NEW FORMS OF UNEQUAL
EXCHANGE AND LABOR DEVALUATION

Workforce exporting has led to two new modes of unequal exchange that are much more disadvantageous than previous methods, for example, the exchange of primary products for industrialized ones.[4] On the one hand, the indirect exporting of the workforce arising from the participation of peripheral nations in global commodity chains leads to a net transfer of profits and a simultaneous disarticulation of the productive sphere of the economy in the periphery. It is an extreme form of unequal exchange and the most disadvantageous of all, preventing any kind of consistent, integral, and endogenous economic development and growth in the periphery. On the other hand, direct workforce exports in the form of economically forced labor migration (the exclusion of labor from the production process and the expulsion of labor via migration) involves the nullification of the future anticipated benefits arising from formative and reproduction social expenditures and the loss of the sending country's most important resource for capital accumulation (its working-age populace). The growing "brain drain" of a highly qualified workforce exacerbates this problem and seriously reduces the sending nation's ability to generate self-beneficial, innovative, and technology-intensive development projects. Analyzing these new modes of unequal exchange poses a theoretical, methodological, and empirical challenge, as it requires changes in the perception and characterization of categories conventionally used to interpret contemporary capitalism. Contrary to neoliberal postulates, the cheap labor–export model does not lead to local, regional, or national development. Rather, this model has been shown to be another instance of peripheral subjugation, attesting to a process of increasing disarticulation and distortion of the productive apparatus in the nations that operate within this model.

Further, we find that the idea that migrants are the new agents of development is a fantasy that obscures the nature of contemporary capitalism. It makes migrants responsible for improving their living and labor conditions in spite of the root disadvantages posed by their exploitation at home and abroad. Moreover, it eschews any kind of proposal regarding the type of structural, institutional, and political changes required to achieve substantial social transformation. It also obscures the important role played by migrants in the economy of destination countries, satisfying existing labor demand and reducing the cost of production processes. Instead of publicly recognizing these contributions, migrant-receiving countries engage in a discriminatory discourse that criminalizes migrants and portrays them as social burdens and security risks. The stigmatizing of the migrant workforce contributes to its devalorization. Developed nations demand ample multinational contingents of qualified, moderately qualified, and less-qualified workers, whether legally incorporated or not; their states play a fundamental role in the regulation of migration flows and do so in accordance with the interests of the dominant classes and corporations they represent. But since these factors are obscured, migrants become the scapegoats of choice in the eyes of the public and are blamed for a variety of evils, including the dismantling of the welfare state, the disappearance of the middle class, unemployment, and precarious labor conditions, to cite a few.

In the context of unequal development, peripheral countries are reinserted into global accumulation processes under highly disadvantageous conditions. Those that embrace the neoliberal ideology of the Washington Consensus deliver their key sectors into the hands of the grupos and foreign capital, in the process dismantling much of their limited system of social welfare. All of this is designed to increase the transference of surpluses created in the internationalized production/assembly processes along with the delivery of both natural and human resources to the national elite and to the center of the system.

It would appear that labor-exporting countries benefit in this setting: They can channel their surplus population, ease structural unemployment, decrease the risk of social conflict, and find a new currency source in remittances. In short, the new internationalization structure creates certain "safety valve" effects. In the case of remittance flows, they would seem to ease the poverty of the dependent family members and paint a human face on the neoliberal system. But, in fact, migrant-sending nations are losing resources that are essential for their sustainability. As stressed, the workforce is the main source of all wealth, and the educational and social costs of this workforce are not met by the nations that eventually employ it.

The economic burdens generated by the neoliberal restructuring process heighten and deepen the asymmetries between a significant portion of the northern and southern hemispheres, thus leading to labor expulsion, thereby feeding migration flows. It is clear that the reigning discourse distorts reality and creates the illusion that migrants and remittances (conceived as an eternal source of monetary resources) can and should contribute to the development of the countries of origin. In order to demystify what is an essentially ideological approach, we must reveal the mechanisms behind it: the structural causes of migration, the social and economic contributions made by migrants to receiving countries, and the forms of economic, social, and population transference that make up international migration. As far as the causes are concerned, we must keep in mind that the internationalization process depends on the cheapening of labor as well as the export of the workforce from peripheral and former socialist nations to center countries. That is, the periphery is economically disarticulated and excluded at the same time that it is asymmetrically reassimilated into the orbit of center nations, to which it remains subordinated.

FINAL REMARKS

The theoretical and empirical analysis presented above comprises a large and complex set of elements. Among them certain components stand out in terms of their sharp contrast with the widely disseminated image of Mexico under NAFTA.

First, the actual model deployed by Mexico is not a triumphant example of outward-oriented industrialization; instead it is typified by a very basic form of "primarization." Many Latin American nations have taken a step backward into specializing in low-value-added exports of commodities or undifferentiated resource-based industrial products—most notably Argentina (Cypher 2009). Mexico has taken "two steps backward," reverting even further, offering up as its absolute advantage cheap, usually modestly trained labor in an institutional setting wherein this labor can be deployed with few constraints posed by unions, in terms of benefits, labor rights, legal recourse to adverse health effects, or severance protections. In our first chapter in particular, and elsewhere, we have made adequate reference to the need for a dramatically different national economic policy—industrial policy—based in a renovation of development concepts and principles advocated by policy makers throughout Latin America in the 1940s, 1950s, and 1960s. Such an approach cannot be, however, reducible to a *revival* of past practices. Import-substitution programs were, at least in the case of Mexico, sufficient to yield strong results for decades. Nonetheless, they were *shallow* attempts at state-led industrialization that were demonstrated to be inadequate when Mexico began to face systemic difficulties in the 1970s. Much progress can be made, in the structuring of an alternative and sustainable model, through a careful study of how and why East Asian nations were relatively successful in recent decades while Latin America—particularly Mexico—has fallen behind (Kay 2002; Storm and Naastepad 2005).

At that crucial crossroad, peak business organizations, such as the CCE, commenced a campaign to become much more autonomous—opposing and escaping their subordinate corporatist past (Valdés Ugalde 1997). Through the decades since then, the relative power of the large business groups, or conglomerates, has increasingly been a primary formative force in the creation of economic policy (Puga 2004). The debacle that Mexico today faces, then, is a *constructed* debacle—one in which the peak business organizations

bear a high degree of responsibility. At this critical historical juncture it is
not sufficient that prominent voices within the now-fracturing political elite,
backed by small and medium manufacturing business interests such as Canacintra (who are largely dependent on the internal market), are finding promise
in a turn toward industrial policy. As we have pointed out in the first chapter,
achieving coherence with such a policy requires the existence of *state capacity* (Kohli 2004). The deliberate deconstruction of state capacity has been a
prime focus of the neoliberal policies introduced through a new state formation that congealed in the late 1980s, as we have shown in chapters 2 and 3.
From that moment forward, policy parameters have been *codetermined* by
both Mexico's peak business associations and the prime agents of the Washington Consensus—particularly the U.S. government, the U.S. corporate
elite, and two key multilateral institutions heavily under the influence of the
United States—the World Bank and the IMF. Mexico is now farther from
having the required state capacity to engineer a constructive turn toward an
endogenous process of restructuring than at any time since the 1930s.

Nations, however, can and do sometimes rise to the demands of the occasion—even nations such as Mexico, which has co-constructed a new, stronger
cage of economic dependency through its cheap labor–export model. A structural, paradigmatic transformation, should it come, cannot be merely change
from the top (Cypher 2007b). A realignment of the political elite backed by
some prominent forces at the level of the production base will not suffice.
Rather, such a change will, of necessity, be a function of renewed resistance
to the reigning model, *from below*. Just as capital has achieved new institutional coherence in an era of internationalization, so must organized labor
and other groups pushed to the margin by the cheap labor–export model.
This means that constructive change must be based on broad social participation—at the national level and at the point of production.

In order to attain a new national project that is *nonexclusive*, transnational labor unions will have to be an important part of a new constellation
of social agents framing socioeconomic and institutional transformation
initiatives. In the United States, where union power has been decimated
by the runaway shop and an all-out offensive by the state—and in Mexico,
where union power means "protection unions" who vigilantly protect the
interests of business—the idea of emergent union participation in national
policy seems quixotic. Yet history sets an example: it was precisely in the
1930s, while workers were desperate for employment and logically prone
to seeing their fellow workers as their competitors and not their allies, when
they rallied and coalesced—both in Mexico and in the United States. Today
workers face not only the challenges of disunity they faced in the 1930s,
but the greater leap into transnational organizing. Yet Mexico's dilemma

can be solved only if it acts to curtail the prerogatives given to national and transnational capital by the NAFTA. Creation of a new elite transnational institution—NAFTA—was a momentous step that demonstrates the necessity of further forms of transnationalization that could be constructive for the underlying population.

Second, Mexico is undergoing a process of *labor devaluation and national disaccumulation*—the labor force employed is offered subsistence wages under working conditions that frequently lead to (1) job-related injuries and overwhelming economic insecurity coupled with (2) the failure of the model to create an economic surplus that remains for Mexico's deployment/ reinvestment. Instead, this surplus is transferred to the grupos and to the United States (or elsewhere), where it serves to expand the production base and assist in the restructuring of the economy. The anticipated host country effects of the subordinated integration process in the form of backward and forward linkages, process upgrading, technological learning, and so on, fail to arrive. Instead, a new nefarious form of profit transfer, centering on the disembodied export of cheap labor, gives rise *to the debilitating export of revenues derived from the transnational productive/assembling process.* This is a process that reaches far beyond the vitiating relationships described by the dependency writers of the 1960s and 1970s who tended to maintain their focus on external flow relationships rather than on internal production processes and power relationships (Munck 2000).

Third, we have demonstrated that the NAFTA process was not in any fundamental sense a trade-based policy, leading to a benign and mutually beneficial process of economic specialization through economic competition on both sides of the border, as portrayed in the textbook models of "free trade." Rather than trade, let alone "free" or competition-based trade, the neoliberal program was constructed to serve the ends of oligopoly power—the control of markets—by displacing significant portions of the U.S. production system to Mexico. In short, NAFTA was an investment/ production restructuring agreement—not a trade agreement—that enabled U.S. firms to shift production to Mexico. U.S. firms doubly benefited as the processes unleashed by NAFTA's arrival also displaced the Mexican peasantry who flowed in unimagined numbers into the U.S. labor force, lowering labor costs in the United States. U.S. firms were allowed to expand their production in Mexico without the previously emplaced national benefits of domestic content legislation, or export quotas, or restrictions on the repatriation of profits, or technology sharing agreements, or any other constraints on the use of their capital.

For the United States, the potential dynamic impacts of the cheap labor export-led model are based on lowering production costs in Mexico and/or the United States through the insertion of cheap labor into the production process. With the increased profits arising from this model, U.S. firms then can

1. fund greater R & D spending, conceivably leading to greater levels of innovation and, subsequently, technological diffusion across much of the U.S. industrial system and
2. fund investment in the modernization of machinery and equipment, labor/managerial organizational restructuring programs, and labor training programs.

Additionally, to the degree that lowering of production costs in Mexico and in the United States is partially passed on to U.S. consumers via some lower prices, the labor export-led model serves to lower the reproduction costs of U.S. labor. This process enables U.S. corporations and businesses to operate with lower wages than otherwise would be necessary, thereby (once again) enhancing the competitiveness of the U.S. production system while raising profit margins.

In Mexico, however, this new form of asymmetric integration has clearly not been associated with new possibilities for economic growth, let alone development. Stagnating or dropping wages, rising unemployment, and informal activities have constituted the environment that has necessitated the explosion in migration, involving millions. The lack of linkage effects in the Mexican economy has negated the potential dynamic spillover effects that, according to the new growth theory, would spread across much of the production system due to enhanced foreign investment under NAFTA. On one hand, this has meant that Mexico has become increasingly dependent upon remittances in order to stabilize the macroeconomy and society at large—to the point where (1) remittances, (2) net export earnings from oil (even during a boom in prices), and (3) the net export earnings of the maquila sector have all converged for the first time. On the other hand, the uncontrolled leap in emigration has called into question the sustainability of the *cheap labor–export* model—particularly in terms of the depopulation effects in many parts of Mexico. With increasing marginalization and poverty, the pressures to emigrate escalate, and this could very well collide with U.S. policy, given the desires of the U.S. citizenry to guarantee their "security."

Hence, given the cheap labor–export model's incapacity to dynamize the Mexican economy—to increase salaries, to create employment positions, to encourage advancements in technological know-how, to incorporate national supplier firms into the matrix of production relationships—we find the model to be unsustainable. Consequently, to escape from this treadmill, vast and fundamental changes will be necessary in Mexico. In particular, the implications here center on and arise from the form in which economic integration has thus far been conceived and orchestrated.

In the final analysis, socioeconomic development has never been achieved by a nation as a result of exogenous forces. A premise, based in the theory and in the history of economic development, is that the responsibility for initiating and maintaining a process of economic development fundamentally rests in endogenous social forces, particularly in the ability of the state to mount and sustain a national project of accumulation rather than reaching outward and adopting policies that are generators of asymmetric accumulation processes, such as NAFTA. Overcoming Mexico's dilemma, or even acknowledging its existence, will demand coherent and consistent efforts that go far beyond merely a reformulation of NAFTA. It demands strategic and structural changes grounded within a renovated and critical perspective of development, both in theory and in practice. A political economy approach is fundamental for understanding the nature of the current problem faced by Mexico and for envisioning the key role that agents of social transformation must play. Specifically, addressing a centuries-old structural deficiency—the absence of independent technological learning and creation capabilities—will have to become a first-order priority. Emergence from underdevelopment or relative economic dependence has always pivoted on the capacity to constructively borrow and adapt technologies to the particularities of national economies and cultures. Creation and *institutionalization* of a national innovation system will demand massive restructuring of both the organizational capacities and the cultural practices of Mexican business, the Mexican state, and Mexican workers.

None of this can be approached without a restructuring of the relationship between state and capital in Mexico. In abandoning the existing model, a new set of institutional structures must be created. Such structures, long in place in successful nations, would conform to the concepts of the "developmental state" as sketched in figure 1.1, chapter 1. That is to say, there is a need for state empowerment, based in the creation of a new national development project. After decades of demonizing the state under the guidelines of the Chicago School, such a transition will be arduous. Pursuing a developmental strategy demands policy *coherence and discipline capability*, the latter being the ability to enforce performance compliance on capital as a form of reciprocity for the promotion of strategic sectors. The lack of such compliance under import-substitution industrialization meant that the state was incapable of discontinuing unnecessary benefits provided to the private sector. The lack of *embeddedness* with the private sector was another, greater weakness. In the final analysis, then and now, *competence* is too often lacking—with high-level functionaries and their close subordinates securing their positions by way of family and social connections rather than by way of merit. A professional civil service, rigorously trained and merit based, is a prerequisite for any forward movement in terms of national policy.

These are but two of many important steps—although perhaps they are the most fundamental—that will be required to confront the present failed model of development. To express such objectives may be considered fanciful. But it is even more unrealistic to anticipate, as does the current economic and political power structure, that the status quo of asymmetric accumulation and accelerating dependence can be prolonged through the strengthening of the neoliberal program.

Notes

CHAPTER 1

1. It is a common occurrence to encounter unqualified negation, in the press and in scholarly literature, of the idea that Mexico's exports are today in any meaningful degree tied to cheap labor. One totally irrelevant but frequent assertion is that there are several countries where labor is cheaper. This is undeniably true but less than meaningful when the frame of reference is one wherein U.S.-based firms can commonly exploit a wage differential of 1:10 (or near that ratio) when they shift to Mexico. Further, Mexican productivity needs to be considered — and it is commonly quite high in relation to other nations that seek to attract firms on the basis of cheap labor.

The second argument that is commonly advanced is that Mexico has ceased to anchor its exports in labor-intensive activities such as textiles and apparel or shoemaking. This is again true, but irrelevant. Mexico's two major export sectors, (1) autos and auto parts and (2) electronics, are based on the advantages of *relatively* cheap labor along with a generally satisfactory infrastructure supporting export activities. Some authors cite the fact that Mexican engineers or other highly skilled workers are sought out by the export firms. This is true, and once again it is true because Mexican engineers are *relatively* cheap. Our argument regarding the cheap labor–export model is in no way tied to the notion of *absolutely* cheap labor-intensive production processes that involve the lowest possible skill levels. Rather, it rests on the concept that Mexican labor is *relatively* cheaper and that the wage differential between the United States and Mexico is overwhelmingly significant. In any case, the AlixPartners 2009 Manufacturing-Outsourcing Cost Index registers Mexico as cheaper in most manufacturing components than either China or India (AlixPartners 2009, 9).

2. Aside from the overwhelming emphasis on "trade liberalization," some of the major elements to be adopted by nations following the Washington Consensus included privatization of state-owned enterprises, deregulation, reduction of public sector spending, and tax cuts for corporations and wealthy individuals.

3. IMMEX firms include all of those formerly under the maquila program plus all other high-exporting firms (e.g., the disguised maquila firms) that had previously been part of several programs that allowed for the temporary importation of inputs exempt from tariffs and value-added taxes if they were later exported in manufactured products.

4. We have been unable to confirm beyond doubt the accuracy of the high-end estimate. In spite of several attempts to clarify the matter with entities such as the Consejo Nacional de la Industria Maquiladora y Manufacturera de Exportación, or CNIMME, INEGI—the national statistical institute—and qualified researchers, we have not received a definitive response. We harbor some doubts on the overall employment figures commonly utilized in Mexico regarding the IMMEX firms. The problem, we believe, rests in the fact that the high-export firms that are outside of the calculations for employment of the maquila sector operate as both high exporters *and* as producers who sell significant portions of their output in the internal market—such as the auto producers. Maquila firms, until recently, were mandated to export their entire production. When the transition to the IMMEX regime took place, it appears that *all* employment in the high-export non-maquila firms (or the disguised maquila firms) was swept into the IMMEX employment calculation, without regard to whether these workers were employed strictly in export activities or not.

5. The attempt to impose the 15 percent IVA tax on food and medicine failed. But the regressive IVA tax was raised from 15 to 16 percent on October 31, 2009.

6. On the Economic Solidarity Pact and its policy implications, see Cypher 1990, 195–96. Regarding the signing of this pact, Agustin Legorreta, then the head of the peak business organization, the Business Coordinating Council, or CCE, stated that it was a result of the actions between the president and a "very comfortable little group of 300 people [who] make all the economically important decisions in Mexico" (Cypher 1990, 2; Schamis 2002, 118).

7. In general, MUNDOS found 71 percent of the respondents in families with debt that severely limited current household expenditures and curtailed any purchases of significance (up from 48 percent a year ago). Of this 71 percent, the increased level from previous studies was almost all located in social market categories C and D, with most located in C− and D+ (see table 1.1).

These two segments (C and D) compose 53 percent of the population and are the key to the current internal market. They are also the core of public political participation in voting and other citizen dynamics at the present time. Even more tightly focused, the roughly 25 percent of the population located in C− and D+ are the key to electoral politics. It is this segment that first broke with traditional family voting habits in the mid- to late 1980s; as its young men and women have come of age they have been the most fluid in voting for different parties since 1997.

This group gave (neoliberal) President Fox his victory in 2000, as well as (leftist) Manuel López Obrador the mayoral position in Mexico City that same year, and was the most disputed sector of the election in 2006 (MUND Group 2009, 2).

According to their analysis, the 20 percent remaining in group C—"the remaining middle class"—and the 33 percent in group D (the working sectors), constitute a mercurial majority now under siege who could be the swing factor in a dramatic policy shift in Mexico that would bring to the foreground the needs of domestic producers and consumers while forcing the jettisoning of the cheap labor–export model.

There are, then, both (a) mass popular and (b) serious and articulate technocratic and professional cadres who are pushing for the abandonment of neoliberalism. As the MUND Group report notes:

> What does exist now are dozens of small eruptions all over the country, sometimes persistent, often momentary. Ordinary citizens are protesting, along with small farmers, indigenous groups and environmental-action community organizations. Buildings are occupied in protest over water rights and services; highways are blocked in protest over electrical rates and services; demonstrations are mounted to petition for unresolved grievances, especially transport service hikes.
>
> Social explosions are occurring in all parts of the country, many of them not in the easy view of the media in Mexico City. The question is whether this maze of local frustrations would turn into a critical mass of national expression. (MUND Group 2009, 1)

CHAPTER 2

1. At the same time that the Monterrey group became a central force in the political struggle between state and capital, the Monterrey conglomerates also demonstrated that they (and a few other conglomerates) were then on the threshold of a new phase in Mexico's industrialization. Part of the fierce opposition to Echeverría's policies arose from the fact that the capitalist cadre in Monterrey had (through their investments in both the modernization of their productive systems and scientific research and technological development) reached another stage wherein they could be competitive in the international markets without the forms of direct support (such as tariffs, subsidies, and directed credit) that had been used to incubate Mexican industrialization in the past. The Monterrey group, then, sought (but failed to receive) state policies that would encourage export-led development strategies at a time when neither the state nor most Mexican firms were prepared in the least for such a transition (Davis 2004, 328–31).

2. Unlike Southeast Asia's, Mexico's auto industry was not developed by Mexican business interests. Instead, some of the largest transnational corporations created Mexico's auto sector, whereas in some Asian nations, particularly Korea, the auto industry flourished through national strategies designed to capture the external benefits of incubating this industry in the national economy. The advantage for policy makers of such an arrangement as was developed in Asia is that a deep ISI strategy constitutes a barrier to the imposition of restructuring policies through the influence of the transnational corporations.

3. CEPAL's numbers were in constant prices, with 2000 as the base year. The incoming FDI was converted from nominal dollar amounts provided by the secretariat of the economy to constant dollar amounts using the U.S. consumer price index. This

method is not without some weakness, but it should serve as a largely accurate guide in permitting us to express these inflation-adjusted data.

CHAPTER 3

1. It is certainly the case that some sections of the Mexican business elite sought the NAFTA accord for trade-oriented reasons—because it would give them open access to the largest market in the world. In several instances, prior to the NAFTA accord, U.S. policy makers used portions of their arsenal of weapons to block or reduce Mexican exports. Mexican business leaders and state policy makers erroneously assumed that nationalist U.S. policy would be overcome with the passage of NAFTA.

But this interest in trade on the part of the Mexican conglomerates has turned out to be a relatively minor consideration for two reasons: first, with the important exception of (a) some mostly resource-dependent Mexican firms such as Cemex (cement), Gruma (wheat flour), and Tamsa (steel pipe), (b) firms that can understandably exploit the Hispanic market in the United States, and (c) a few that prove to be *the exceptions*, such as auto parts transnational Grupo San Luis and the ever-agile, restructured, Monterrey-based conglomerates (the three largest being the above mentioned Cemex, FEMSA [soft drinks], and Grupo Alfa [petrochemicals, food products, and steel]), Mexican firms were not sufficiently competitive to play a major role in expanding Mexico's exports to the United States; second, while Mexico's exports grew at an extremely strong rate from 1993 onward, this was primarily a result of the U.S. project to invest heavily in Mexico (particularly in the auto sector) in order to export manufacturing products produced with cheap Mexican labor as a major input.

In 2008, excluding PEMEX, the top six exporting firms were all transnational corporations. The top five of the six were manufacturers, in the following order: General Motors, Nissan, Chrysler, Volkswagen, Ford, and Coca-Cola. The two following firms, Grupo México and Industrias Peñoles, are mining conglomerates whose export success was simply a function of the commodities boom that swept Latin America from late 2003 through late 2008. Only one Mexican manufacturing company, Mabe, appeared in the list annually published by the magazine *Expansion*. Mabe, operating since 1987 in a strategic alliance formed with General Electric Corporation, is a legacy of the ISI era, tracing its origins to state-led industrialization initiatives commencing during the era of President Cárdenas (1934–1940).

2. Overall, production worker employment rose from 1.977 million in 1994 to 2.763 million in 2000. But the entire wage bill increased only 8.8 percent (in real 1994 pesos), since virtually all the growth occurred in the maquila sector (Cypher 2004a, 362–63). The growth in the maquila sector shifted wage earnings to the border region. Most, if not all, of the 8.8 percent increase in the wage bill leaked into the U.S. economy since the large net increase in border-area workers meant more routine shopping on the U.S. side.

3. Recently, Ackerman and Gallagher have critically reviewed the "state of the art" of the CGE models (Ackerman and Gallagher 2008). They found that some of

the fanciful results predicted by those who modeled the NAFTA accord have now been toned down through the modification of some of the most unsubstantiated assumptions: "Although the results of global trade modeling are often touted as evidence of large gains available from further trade liberalization, the most widely discussed CGE models now make surprisingly small estimates of the benefits of liberalization of merchandise trade. The estimates are especially small for developing countries, particularly under realistic assumptions about the likely extent of future trade liberalization" (Ackerman and Gallagher 2008, 51). They further note: "The limits of the most recent global CGE trade model predictions goes deeper than their inability to produce the expected huge forecasts of benefits for developing countries. . . . They fall short of offering a useful, comprehensive framework for thinking about and measuring the important effects of trade. . . . The theoretical apparatus ironically enforces arbitrary, undesired simplifications, . . . [such as] the central flaw of ignoring employment effects by design. The employment-related questions that policy makers care most about cannot be answered within the standard CGE framework, because they cannot even be asked. Instead, attention is focused on a narrower analysis of interindustry shifts, often starting from the assumption that the total number of jobs in each country cannot be changed by trade policy" (Ackerman and Gallagher 2008, 74).

4. There are only thirty-six members of the Mexican Businessmen's Council (CMHN). In 1992 these individuals were in control of approximately $67 billion in assets owned by their conglomerates, then equivalent to 22 percent of the GDP. Their firms employed 450,000—a considerable portion of the entire private-sector workforce in the formal economy (Montesinos 1992, 114). According to Ben Ross Schneider, "The CMHN is the only institutionalized direct channel between Monterrey's biggest business leaders and their counterparts in Mexico City" (Ross Schneider 2002, 92). Among its other accomplishments, the CMHN is commonly credited with the selection of Carlos Salinas to be Mexico's next president at a secret meeting it held in 1987 (Ross Schneider 2002, 92).

5. For a similar application in the case of Mexico, see our comments on the Monterrey group in note 1, chapter 2.

6. President de la Madrid privatized 537 state-owned firms, while Salinas inherited 618. At the end of his term, Salinas had sold 160, liquidated 152, extinguished 51, merged 17, and transferred 11. Only 216 state firms remained (Concheiro Bórquez 1996, 76, 82). Of this remaining number, only seventy were industrial or commercial firms. In addition, "the Federal Government placed at the disposition of the private sector 893,392 hectares in 24 zones of mineral reserves, which had already been explored and proven by government technicians" (Concheiro Bórquez 1996, 83).

7. CEMAI (Consejo Empresarial Mexicano Para Asuntos Internacionales), the Mexican Business Council for International Affairs, had been the primary advisor to the CCE on international economic issues until the creation of COECE. From the time of its organization the CEMAI had been the most influential force pushing for an opening to international investment. It was the most experienced business organization in creating cross-border joint ventures and "strategic alliances" with both the

Mexican consortiums and transnational corporations. The directors of CEMAI arose from these consortiums and transnational corporations (Puga 2004, 133).

CHAPTER 4

1. This chapter is not intended to be a detailed study of the origins and history of the maquila sector. There is a vast and important body of research on these themes that can be consulted (Gereffi 1992; Kopinak 1996, 2004).

2. Maquila firms are also present to a much lesser degree of concentration in many of the interior states; 78 percent of output occurs in the border region.

3. These numbers are representative only to the degree that the CNIMME estimate of the job multiplier is accurate. See our table 6.1 for the total growth in national employment over the period.

4. The new growth theory of the 1980s posited impressive dynamic effects from greater trade and foreign investment, particularly positive externalities due to learning effects, technological diffusion, and the applications of new forms of production and administrative organization.

5. Backward linkages are the forms of economic interdependence that tie a producer of a product to suppliers. If the suppliers are national, the economic impact of buying more inputs is felt within the national economy. Forward linkages are those economic interdependencies that may exist between the producer and the final consumer. For example, the steel industry will generate forward linkages if output is used as input in the construction of a national rail system. The rail system, in turn, is but an intermediary in the transportation of final products. Backward, forward, and horizontal linkage effects are considered key elements in any project of national economic development because they serve to transmit a variety of spillover effects and crucial multiplier effects—including employment and final demand multiplier effects.

6. In 1996 Carlos Tello maintained that Mexico's manufacturing export boom consisted of no more than the export of cheap labor power, but subsequently the implications of his comment were not formally pursued (Tello 1996).

7. On that date the maquiladora firms were subsumed under a new regime known as IMMEX. IMMEX firms include all of those formerly under the maquila program plus all other high-exporting firms that had previously been part of several programs that allowed for the temporary importation of inputs exempt from tariffs and value-added taxes if they were later exported in manufactured products. (The non-maquila high-export firms were previously known as PITEX firms, and, to a much lesser degree, ALTEX firms.) IMMEX firms can also import machinery and equipment, free of tariffs or other impediments, for the duration of the IMMEX program (which is unspecified). The reason for the creation of this new regime may have simply been to rationalize and unify several government programs that facilitated and subsidized Mexico-based participants in the globally integrated production system. The transition to the IMMEX regime generated little comment in Mexico. Under certain circumstances, non-IMMEX firms can function as subcontractors to IMMEX firms, thereby

both increasing the web of firms engaged in "in bond" manufacturing processes (i.e., maquila-type operations) and also, conceivably, increasing cost advantages and furthering the profit-driven logic of the maquila/IMMEX export sector. For analysts such as the authors, the importance of the IMMEX decree is that it is now impossible to have accurate time-series data for the maquilas that go beyond 2006, thereby diminishing their capability to offer precise, current evaluations of this program.

8. This periodization corresponds, in general, to the jump in direct foreign investment in the 1980s over that of the 1970s. Annual FDI in 1971–1978 grew from $168 million to $383 million. Skipping the oil boom injections from 1979 to 1981, FDI grew from $627 million in 1982 to $3.157 billion in 1988 (Nacional Financiera 1995, 347). Clearly, some of the jump in FDI was due to privatizations that attracted foreign investors. And, clearly, only a part of FDI went to the maquila (and disguised maquila) manufacturers.

9. For roughly seventy-five years RCA was a leading consumer electronics firm in the United States. Noted for its deep technological capacities, RCA was nonetheless not able to keep pace with international competitors, particularly Japanese, as the pace and direction of cutting-edge technologies changed. In the 1980s it had the largest production facility in Parque Bermudez. RCA was taken over by the General Electric Corporation in 1986 and subsequently sold to the French conglomerate Thomson.

10. Greenfield investment, as opposed to the takeover of already existing plant and equipment by foreign investors, is a new addition to capital formation. In conventional economic analysis, greenfield investments should raise the capital/labor ratio, increase labor productivity, and raise wages and consumption while engendering multiplier effects in a widening virtuous circle of growth and development. Wages fell from 1975 to 2002 by roughly one-third in the manufacturing sector and about 10 percent in the maquila sector (Gambrill 2008, 65).

11. This measure excludes the maquila firms but *does* include the disguised maquilas that temporarily import inputs duty free and tax free.

12. Vidal, a specialist in the area of the Mexican conglomerates, notes that "only a few" Mexican-owned firms, notably auto-parts makers Desc and Grupo Satillo Industrial, have been either willing or able to participate in the surge in exports (Vidal 2004, 57).

CHAPTER 5

1. In November 2006 the Mexican government decreed that the juridical difference between the maquila and disguised maquila sectors would cease to exist. In 2007 all formerly maquila firms and all firms operating under special provisions as temporary importers of inputs (the disguised maquilas) were to be registered under the same decree known as the "Decreto para el Fomento de la Industria Manufacturera, Maquiladora y de Servicios de Exportación." The combined areas (maquila plus disguised maquila) are the IMMEX sector, and at the official level the term "maquiladora" ceased to be used (Saldaña 2006, 19). Aside from eliminating a familiar term, the

decree appears to impose no substantive changes either on labor or on capital. Since the issuance of the decree, data gathering, crucial to this and the previous chapter, has largely been held in abeyance through late 2009. According to government sources, the data bank regarding the IMMEX firms will not directly correspond to the methods used in officially accounting for the maquiladora industry.

2. The data from CNIMME are not specific as to whether the former PITEX firms' employment figures are simply those of all workers, or that portion of a firm's employees who produce for the export market. Other comments lead us to believe that figure 5.1 employment numbers for the former PITEX (now IMMEX) firms may exaggerate the numbers involved in the export of manufactured products (see note 2, chapter 1, for further comment on the strength of these estimates).

3. We are referring to formally registered workers as defined by coverage under the social security system as tabulated by the secretary of labor. All maquila workers are included in the formal manufacturing labor force.

4. On productivity, see Shaiken for an early account, and Mortimore and Barron on findings that productivity in auto assembly production in Mexico is equivalent to U.S. levels (Shaiken 1990, x–xi; Mortimore and Barron 2005, 48).

5. Altex stood for "high-export firms." In 2000, according to the secretariat of the economy, there were also 3,600 supplier firms that produced inputs exempt from the value-added tax when they provided inputs to either the maquilas or the disguised maquila firms.

6. The category "final exports" (or *nonprocessed exports*) has risen significantly due to the commodities boom since 2002 and the fact that many items listed under manufactured exports are scarcely transformed raw materials, such as cement, that are primarily produced by the Mexican-owned conglomerates. The general significance of these national conglomerates (or *grupos de poder*) was briefly introduced in chapter 1.

7. Mortimore and Barron offer a clear description of the hierarchical tiering system of supplier firms providing the 15,000 parts and components needed to produce a vehicle (Mortimore and Barron 2005, 47). Regarding Nissan's productivity in Mexico, see note 9 below.

8. Fragmenting unions is also a transnational tactic employed by the U.S. auto producers, which in the face of an unprecedented crisis of overproduction in 2006 decided to decimate the United Auto Workers—letting go 113,000 workers via buyouts at GM-Delphi and 75,000 workers at Ford. Most of these jobs were going to Mexico, where wages were then $3.50–$4.60 per hour versus $27 per hour in the United States. Since 2006, the UAW has been crushed by the bankruptcy of General Motors and Chrysler in 2009 and the leverage exerted by Ford in what is perhaps the ultimate round of restructuring for the U.S. auto giants. This restructuring continues to favor expansion in Mexico: in 2009 GM completed a large greenfield plant located in San Luís Potosí, employing 1,800 workers. Ford is planning to open a new plant in Mexico while expanding its two existing plants and its engine plant. Chrysler will inject $1 billion into its operations in Mexico. Further U.S. investments will flow to the auto parts sector, where 430,000 were already employed in 2006 (Malkin 2006,

C1, C4). The major portion of these recent investments ($4 billion from 2005 to mid-2006) was channeled into the disguised maquila sector.

9. With easy access to the U.S. market, particularly after the passage of NAFTA, the Japanese also relocated some of their production to Mexico. Lean production in their foreign-owned plants could, in fact, improve on the once astonishing levels of productivity achieved in Japan. For example, the Nissan plant located in Aguascalientes has been rated by the corporation to be its top plant in the world in terms of labor productivity.

10. To be sure, not all production went to this region—Chrysler stood out for its dedication to the Toluca region near Mexico City and its attempts to gain efficiencies through agglomeration effects in the old central industrial corridor of Mexico (Lara Rivero, García Garnicia, and Trujado 2004).

11. We will discuss, below, the clustering concept and its implications.

12. Of course, the auto industry in this region is not restricted to U.S. firms. Most notable are two highly competitive Japanese plants—the Nissan plant in Aguascalientes referred to in the text and the Toyota plant in Baja California. Nissan's plant was originally focused on expected growth in the Mexican market. It now fits well within the disguised maquila concept, having switched its emphasis to exports. The Toyota plant was designed to export to the U.S. market after the passage of NAFTA. Toyota sought to take full advantage of a deep web of maquila firms clustered along the border to gain production economies.

13. For further details, see the section "The Auto Sector" in chapter 2.

14. The states included in the UN program were Aguascalientes, Colima, Guanajuato, Jalisco, Michoacán, Nayarit, Querétaro, San Luís Potosí, and Zacatecas. We have broadened out the UN's focus in this section to include some details pertaining to the auto sector in the bordering state of Coahuila.

15. As is frequently the case, the data from various sources are not consistent as to the number of tier 1 suppliers in Mexico. Various authors have insisted that there were nearly 350 tier 1 suppliers in 2005 or 2006. If there were, in fact, sixty first-tier suppliers in the mid- or late 1990s, it is impossible to imagine that there could be 350 such firms—all giant, internationally competitive, leading-edge companies—operating in Mexico in 2005. The difficulty, we believe, is that when one moves from source to source, there is no strict, conventionally agreed upon definition of what constitutes a first-tier supplier. The common and conventional definition is that of a supplier that works directly with an auto-making corporation providing medium-term delivery of relatively complex subsystems, such as engines or drive trains, to the automakers. Thus, having a contract for direct delivery to the auto production plant for a minor item does not allow for the inclusion of a low-tech company (delivering hubcaps, perhaps) to define itself as a tier 1 supplier. Automakers today frequently go to their tier 1 suppliers to solve technological difficulties that they are incapable of solving.

16. Beyond the direct and indirect effects stressed by Hirschman, a more recent body of research known as the *new growth theory* has found an even larger range of potential effects suggesting *increasing returns* to be gained through the process of economic growth, whether or not it is induced through FDI (Cypher and Dietz 2009,

239–70). Emerging in the 1980s and 1990s, this theoretical framework places central emphasis on the possibilities of capturing a range of *positive externalities* through learning effects or via technological spillovers.

CHAPTER 6

1. This estimate (workers with benefits/employed workers) is based on the exclusion of employers from the numerator and the denominator from the foregoing ratio. Since, on average, 4.4 percent of the "economically active population" (known as the PEA)—excluding the unemployed—were employers, we assumed that the total number of the PEA who were employers with health benefits was equal to the share of their representation (4.4 percent on average from 2000 to 2009) in the PEA. Hence, we used INEGI's estimate, which includes (1) the insured government-sector workers (members of ISSSTE), (2) the workers insured under the social security program (IMSS), and (3) a small number who are in other programs such as one for PEMEX workers, and then reduced that number by 4.4 percent to estimate the number of *workers* with benefits.

2. This calculation is based on IMSS data plus data from ISSSTE's *Anuario Estadistico*. www.issste.gob.mx/issste/anuarios/.

3. The Mexican government estimated in 2009 that 50 percent of the population had no access to health care services either through employment or through government programs of public assistance. The Comisión Nacional de Protección Social operates a massive program—free to the poorest 20 percent of the population—known as "Seguro Popular." Data on the state of Oaxaca offer a sense of the scope of the program: in 2008, 1.292 million citizens of the state of Oaxaca (36 percent of the population) were enrolled in Seguro Popular. See www.seguro-popular.salud.gob.mx.

4. The estimate made by Enrique Dussel Peters is slightly different from our calculations based on INEGI data because, first, ours is an estimate using the number of employed workers, while Dussel Peters used the entire labor force as the base number for his calculations. Second, the INEGI database uses a definition of workers with full health benefits that includes the government-worker health program ISSSTE, the health program established for PEMEX workers, and some other small programs, while Dussel Peters used only the enrollees of social security. Allowing for the different methods and databases, the two estimates are consistent.

5. These numbers must be interpreted with great care. Within the total are 1.94 million employers. Thus, the numbers are not confined to those who earn wages and salaries. More important, these are the distributional figures for "base" pay. Depending on the employment situation, workers may receive sizable Christmas and vacation bonuses, "stimulus" or "incentive" payments (that can in some instances double base pay), seniority premiums, payments for punctuality and for a low frequency of absences, as well as numerous other forms of payment. In short, base pay could represent as much as 100 percent of total earned income or less than 50 percent. But this applies only to the small percentage of workers with benefits.

For the rest, 63 percent of the employed, any premiums and bonuses are an optional item from the employers' perspective—they largely do not exist. Hence, the "base" pay numbers in the text are an accurate portrayal of income received for nearly two-thirds of the workforce.

6. An additional 8 percent of the employed workforce was officially registered as having a "nonspecified" level of income (INEGI 2009b).

7. Labor costs, of course, are but one of many factors determining the profit rate. Directly, at the point of production, and indirectly—through the purchase of inputs—labor costs will be the largest of all. Regarding other factors of importance in determining the profit rate, it was only at the close of the period—from 2006 through mid-2008—that rising materials costs, due to the commodities boom, played a significant role.

8. On this point, however, Mario Capdevielle has made an important observation that calls into question the official figures regarding maquila productivity:

> Maquila firms frequently operate with capital goods that are imported for a limited period of time, being property of the home-based firm or a foreign contracting firm which operates the equipment on consignment, and for this reason in the accounting process the depreciation of these machines is not registered [as value-added in Mexico]. This process makes it difficult to accurately measure value added and the level of capital utilized. (Capdevielle 2005, 569)

In all likelihood, the rate of growth of maquila productivity is higher than registered—currently it is calibrated at only 27 percent of the level achieved in non-maquila manufacturing—because the maquilas do not necessarily register all value-added when the maquilas report the value of their exports: the level of value added and the profits received from maquila activities are not calculated from market prices; rather, they are registered through transfer prices, prices that are determined within the organizational structure of the transnational firms. These firms can underinvoice or overinvoice their purchases and sales, according to their desires in terms of minimizing taxes (Capdevielle 2005, 659).

9. See notes 3 and 4.

10. The *canasta básica* is made up of eighty goods and services grouped into eight categories: food, beverages, and tobacco (22.7 percent); clothes, shoes, and accessories (5.59 percent); housing (26.4 percent); furniture and household appliances (4.9 percent); health and personal care (8.6 percent); transportation (13.4 percent); education and entertainment (11.5 percent); and other utilities (6.9 percent). The data were computed by the Consejo Nacional de Evaluación de la Política de Desarrollo Social (CONEVAL).

11. In contrast with official figures, Boltvinik, one of the top Mexican experts on poverty issues, estimates that in 2000–2004 poverty grew by 8.1 percent and extreme poverty by 2.1 percent (Boltvinik 2006).

12. These estimates were generated by SIMDE (Sistema de Información sobre Migración y Desarrollo), a nonprofit statistical research consortium based at the Universidad Autónoma de Zacatecas. SIMDE's as yet unpublished estimate of the

contribution of Mexican immigrants to U.S. GDP is based on disaggregated data from the U.S. *Current Population Survey* (March supplement) regarding the participation of Mexicans in thirty-four activities and sectors of the U.S. economy, multiplying them by the corresponding average sector productivity figures provided by the U.S. Bureau of Economic Activity (1994–2008). The magnitudes of the Mexican population residing in the United States allow the implementation of this direct estimation of the GDP with a high degree of statistical confidence. For the data and methodology, contact rdwise@estudiosdeldesarrollo.net. For further information on SIMDE, see http://maremival.sociales.unam.mx/~migracion/Seminario/mesa8/ZUNIGA_SISTEMA %20DE%20INFORMACION.pdf.

13. SIMDE's estimates, based on USCPS and BEA data. Consumption estimates are based on desegregated (thirty-four activities and sectors) average income earnings of Mexican immigrants provided by the *Current Population Survey* (March supplement), considering their annual income-consumption spillovers in the U.S. economy (1994–2008).

14. These calculations were based on expenses at each educational level as issued by the Instituto Nacional para la Evaluación de la Educación (INEE) in combination with *Current Population Survey* data regarding the level of education of Mexican immigrants upon their arrival to the United States (U.S. Census Bureau various years; INEE 2009). Dr. Héctor Rodríguez Ramírez, director of the doctoral program in public policy at the Monterrey campus of the Instituto Tecnológico y Estudios de Monterrey, coordinated the statistical analyses that resulted in the SIMDE estimates cited. No adjustment for educational quality was made.

15. A recent study of the California economy tends to support these conclusions. Taking a long-term frame of analysis, the study found that the net average fiscal impact of immigrants was positive, but negative at the State of California level (Center for the Continuing Study of the California Economy 2005, 45–46).

CHAPTER 7

1. Although we refer to Gereffi's concept of global commodity chains, we do not share his optimistic view of globalization. Specifically, we do not find that these integrated systems of production have played a developmental role for nations such as Mexico.

2. The economic surplus is the difference between the value of total output and the socially necessary expenditures needed to reproduce society—particularly the labor force. All societies produce an economic surplus. The surplus can be used to improve present and future conditions of a social system, or it can be squandered in conspicuous consumption, conspicuous display, and conspicuous waste, as Thorstein Veblen emphasized in his numerous writings. In peripheral societies, the social surplus is relatively greater than in core nations—although such a result may seem counterintuitive. Such is the long-term result of an institutionally constructed matrix of power and hierarchy (usually created under colonialism and later perpetuated) whereby the

socially determined necessary expenditures to reproduce society can be held near the physical minimum necessary for survival (Baran 1957).

3. Natural resources in the biosphere have been increasingly incorporated into market logistics. Since the goal is to obtain a maximum amount of profit in the least amount of time, these resources have been unscrupulously damaged. Many scientists and institutions have called attention to serious phenomena such as global warming, climate change, and loss of biodiversity, as well as the current imbalances in social metabolism, that is, in the interactions between humans and the environment and the reproduction of human life on the planet.

4. This system was originally analyzed by specialists at the Economic Commission for Latin America and the Caribbean (ECLAC) such as Raúl Prebisch and Celso Furtado (Mallorquín 2007; Bresser-Pereira 2007). The many variants of dependency analysis and theoretical work on the hypothesis of unequal exchange have not, to date, resulted in a rigorous and definitive body of thought (Brewer 1980, 208–32; Munck 2000). Hence, our usage of the term "unequal exchange" is limited to our empirical observations that units of labor in the south, at equivalent levels of productivity, and in the same industry, can be bought at a ratio of between 1:6 and 1:12 to units of labor in the north. The evidence of productivity equivalents (or near equivalents) between many production operations in Mexico and those in the United States has been well established for decades. On productivity, see Shaiken for an early account, and Mortimore and Barron on findings that productivity in auto assembly production in Mexico is equivalent to United States levels (Shaiken 1990, x–xi; Mortimore and Barron 2005, 48). We also have noted, in chapter 6, the magnitude of unequal exchange of labor units between immigrant Mexican and native-born U.S. workers.

References

Ackerman, Frank, and Kevin P. Gallagher. 2008. The shrinking gains from global trade liberalization in computable general equilibrium models: A critical assessment. *International Journal of Political Economy* 37, no. 1 (Spring): 50–77.

Ahumada, Consuelo. 1996. *El modelo neoliberal*. Bogotá: El Áncora Editores.

AlixPartners. 2009. *2009 Manufacturing-outsourcing cost index*. Chicago: AlixPartners.

AMIA (Asociación Mexicana de la Industria Automotriz). 2009. Estadisticas. www.amia.com.mx/estadisticas.html.

Amsden, Alice. 1989. *Asia's next giant*. Oxford: Oxford University Press.

———. 2001. *The rise of "the rest": Challenges to the West from late-industrializing economies*. Oxford: Oxford University Press.

Arés, Mathieu. 2007. El estado empresario: Nacional Financiera durante la industrialización por sustitución de importaciones (1934–1994). *Foro Internacional* 188 (April–June) (vol. 47, no. 2): 201–43.

Arroyo Picard, Alberto. 2007. Política salarial compatible con la elevación del bienestar y la preservación de los equilibrios macroeconómicos. In *Empleo, ingreso y bienestar*, ed. José Luis Calva, 177–94. México, D.F.: M. A. Porrúa.

Aspe, Pedro. 1993. *Economic transformation the Mexican way*. Cambridge, Mass.: MIT Press.

Avendaño Ramos, Eréndira, and Aníbal Gutiérrez Lara. 2007. Indicadores económicos: Saldo sexenal. *Economia Informa* 343 (November–December): 127–36.

Babb, Sara. 2001. *Managing Mexico*. Princeton, N.J.: Princeton University Press.

Bancomext (Banco Nacional de Comercio Exterior). 2005. *Atlas de comercio exterior*. www.bancomext.com/Bancomext (retrieved March 3, 2005).

———. 2006. *Sistema integral de información de comercio exterior*. www.siicex.gob.pe/siicex.portal.

Banxico (Banco de México). 2009a. Remuneraciones y productividad. *Indicadores Laborales*. www.banxico.org.mx/polmoneinflacion/estadisticas/laboral/laboral.html.

———.2009b. Balanza de pagos. *Estadísticas*. www.banxico.org.mx.

Baran, Paul. 1957. *The political economy of growth*. New York: Monthly Review Press.

Barberán, José. 1988. *Radiografía de fraude*. México: Nueva Imagen.

BEA (United States Bureau of Economic Affairs). 2009. *National income and product accounts*. www.bea.gov/national/nipaweb.

Becerril, Isabel. 2006. Marco regulatorio del comercio exterior, un obstáculo. *El Financiero* (September 4): 18.

———. 2009. Riesgo de estallido social: Empresarios piden reformas. *El Financiero* (August 26): 1.

Becerril, Isabel, and Ivette Saldaña. 2009. Capata México IED por 10 mil mdd. *El Financiero* (August 20): 9.

Becker, Guillermo. 1995. *Retos para la modernización industrial de México*. México, D.F.: Nacional Financiera.

Bizberg, Ilan. 2008. *Alianza público-privadas, estrategias para el desarrollo exportador, y la innovación: El caso de México*. LC/MEX/L.866 (June 17). Santiago, Chile: Comisión Económica para América Latina.

Blair, Calvin. 1964. Nacional financiera. In *Public policy and private enterprise in Mexico*, ed. Raymond Vernon, 193–238. Cambridge, Mass.: Harvard University Press.

Bolin, Tim. 2004. *The economic and fiscal impacts of immigration*. Newport Beach, Calif.: Merage Foundation, 1–22. www.meragefoundations.com/Occasional Papers/ EconomicandFiscalImpactsofImmigration(Bolin).pdf.

Boltvinik, Julio. 2003. Welfare, inequality, and poverty in Mexico, 1970–2000. In *Confronting development: Assessing Mexico's economic and social policy challenges*, ed. Kevin Middlebrook and Eduardo Zepeda, 385–446. Stanford, Calif.: Stanford University Press.

———. 2006. Los fracasos de Fox/II. *La Jornada* (June 2). www.jornada.unam .mx/2006/06/02/index.

Boltvinik, Julio, and Enrique Hernández Laos. 1981. Origen del a crisis industrial: El agotamiento del modelo de sustitución de importaciones. In *Desarrollo y crisis de la economía mexicana*, ed. Rolando Cordera, 456–533. México, D.F.: Fondo de Cultura Económia.

Brailovsky, Vladimir. 1980. *Industrialization and oil in Mexico: A long-term perspective*. México, D.F.: Secretaría de Patrimonio y Fomento Industrial.

Bresser-Pereira, Luis. 2007. Method and passion in Celso Furtado. In *Ideas, policies and economic development in the Americas*, ed. Esteban Pérez and Matías Vernengo, 9–30. London: Routledge.

Brewer, Anthony. 1980. *Marxist theories of imperialism*. London: Routledge and Kegan Paul.

Bronfenbrenner, Kate. 2000. *Uneasy terrain: The impact of capital mobility on workers, wages and union organizing*. Ithaca: New York State School of Industrial and Labor Relations, Cornell University, 1–76.

Cadena, Guadalupe. 2005. Manufactura, en la ruta de la "desindustrialización." *El Financiero* (August 16): 13.

Cameron, Maxwell, and Brian Tomlin. 2000. *The making of NAFTA*. Ithaca, N.Y.: Cornell University Press.

Canacintra. 2009. *Monitor de la Manufactura Mexicana* 5, no. 7 (March): 1–50.

Canales, Alejandro. 2008. *Vivir del Norte: Remesas, desarrollo y pobreza en México*. Mexico, D.F.: CONAPO.

Cañas, Jesus, and Robert Gilmer. 2007. Mexican reform clouds view of key industry. *Southwest Economy: Federal Reserve Bank of Dallas* (May/June): 10.

Capdevielle, Mario. 2003. Composición tecnológica de la industria manufactura mexicana. In *Innovación, aprendizaje y creación de capacidades tecnológicas*, ed. Jaime Aboites and Gabriela Dutrénit, 451–70. México, D.F.: M. A. Porrúa.

———. 2005. Procesos de producción global: ¿Alternativa para el desarrollo mexicano? *Comercio Exterior* 55, no. 7 (July): 561–73.

———. 2007. La globalización de procesos productivos y sus efectos en la economía mexicana. El caso de la industria maquiladora de exportación. In *Co-evolución de empresas, maquiladoras, insitutuciones y regiones: Una nueva interpretación*, ed. Arturo Lara Rivera, 51–96. México, D.F.: M. A. Porrúa.

Cardero García, María, and Lilia Domínguez Villalobos. 2007. ¿Puede México aplicar una política industrial? In *Política industrial manufactura*, ed. José Luís Clava, 23–36. México, D.F.: M. A. Porrúa.

Cardoso, Victor. 2010. Despedidos, 150 mil trabajadores del sector automotriz. *La Jornada* (13 de enero): 20.

Carrillo, Jorge, and Redi Gomis. 2007. ¿La maquila evoluciona?, ¿podrá evolucionar en el contexto? In *Maquiladoras fronterizas: Evolución y heterogeneidad en los sectores electrónico y automotriz*, ed. Jorge Carrillo and María del Rosio Barajas, 17–49. México, D.F.: M. A. Porrúa.

Carrillo, Jorge, and María del Rosio Barajas. 2007. Introducción. In *Maquiladoras fronterizas: Evolución y heterogeneidad en los sectores electrónico y automotriz*, ed. Jorge Carrillo and María del Rosio Barajas, 7–16. México, D.F.: M. A. Porrúa.

Casar, Mará, and Wilson Peres. 1988. *El estado empresario en México*. México, D.F.: Siglo XXI.

Casar Peres, José. 1989. *Transformación en el patrón de especialización y comercio exterior del sector manufacturero Mexicano 1978–1987*. México, D.F.: Nacional Financiera.

Castañeda, Jorge. 1993. Alternativa incómoda. *Proceso*, no. 871 (July 12).

Castañeda, Jorge, and Héctor Aguilar Camín. 2009. Un futuro para México. *Nexos* 21, no. 383 (November): 34–49.

Center for the Continuing Study of the California Economy. 2005. *The impact of immigration on the California economy*, 1–64. Palo Alto: Center for the Continuing Study of the California Economy.

CEPAL (Comisión Económico para América Latina y el Caribe). 2008a. *Balanza preliminar de la economías de América Latina y el Caribe*. Santiago, Chile: CEPAL.

———. 2008b. *Anuario estadístico de América Latina y el Caribe*. Santiago, Chile: CEPAL.

Champlin, Dell, and Eric Hake. 2006. Immigration as industrial strategy in American meatpacking. *Review of Political Economy* 18, no. 1: 49–70.

Chang, Ha-Joon, ed. 2003. *Rethinking development economics*. London: Anthem Press.

Chavez, Gabriela. 2009. Ford duplicará empleos en México. *El Financiero* (October 23): 24.

Chibber, Vivek. 2003. *Locked in place: State building and late industrialization in India*. Princeton, N.J.: Princeton University Press.

Cimoli, Mario. 2000. Conclusions: An appreciative pattern of the Mexican innovation system. In *Developing innovation systems: Mexico in the global context*, ed. M. Cimoli, 278–92. New York: Continuum.

Cimoli, Mario, and Jorge Katz. 2001. *Structural reforms, technological gaps and economic development: A Latin American perspective*. Paper presented at the DRUID-Nelson and Winter Conference, June 12–15, in Aalborg, Denmark.

CNIMME (Consejo Nacional de la Industria Maquiladora y Manufactura de Exportación). 2008. Impacto en el empleo de las empresas exportadoras mexicanas. *Boletín de Comunicación y Difusión Estadística* 1, no. 2 (April): 4.

———. 2009. Estadísticas. *Indicadores básicos de la industria maquiladora y manufacturera de exportación* (September). www.cnimme.org./index.

Cohen, Stephan, and John Zysman. 1987. *Manufacturing matters*. New York: Basic Books.

Colín, Marvella. 2009. Aún remonta, la reactivación del comercio mundial. *El Fianciero* (August 18): 3a.

Concheiro Bórquez, Elvira. 1996. *El gran acuerdo: Gobierno y empresarios en la modernización salinista*. México, D.F.: Instituto de Investigaciones Económicas, UNAM.

CONAPO (Consejo Nacional de Población). 2009. *Migración internacional*. www.conapo.gob.mx.

CONEVAL (Consejo Nacional de Evaluación de la Política de Desarrollo Social). 2008. *Informe de evaluación de la política de desarrollo social en México 2008*. México, D.F.: CONEVAL.

Corro, Salvador. 1993. Se escurre el maquillaje de las cifras oficiales en desempleo, salarial e inflación. *Proceso*, no. 858 (June 21).

Cowie, Jefferson. 1999. *Capital moves: RCA's 70-year quest for cheap labor*. Ithaca, N.Y.: Cornell University Press.

Coy, Peter. 2009. What falling prices tell us. *Business Week* (February 16): 24–26.

Cypher, James. 1990. *State and capital in Mexico: Development policy since 1940*. Boulder, Colo.: Westview.

———. 1991. Promoción de exportaciones: ¿Un nuevo patrón de acumulación? *Revista Mexicana de Sociología* 52, no. 3 (July–September): 81–110.

———. 1993a. The ideology of economic science in the selling of NAFTA: The political economy of elite decision-making. *Review of Radical Political Economics* 25, no. 4: 146–63.

———. 1993b. Estimating the impact of the U.S.-Mexican Free Trade Agreement on industrial labor. In *The North American Free Trade Agreement*, ed. Mario Bognanno and Kathryn Ready, 85–96. Westport, Conn.: Praeger.

——. 2001. NAFTA's lessons: From economic mythology to current realities. *Labor Studies Journal* 26, no. 1 (Spring): 5–21.

——. 2004a. Development diverted: Socioeconomic characteristics and impacts of mature maquilization. In *The social costs of industrial growth in northern Mexico*, ed. Kathryn Kopinak, 343–82. San Diego: Center for U.S.-Mexican Studies, University of California, San Diego.

——. 2004b. Pinochet meets Polanyi? The curious case of the Chilean embrace of the "free" market. *Journal of Economic Issues* 38, no. 2 (June): 527–35.

——. 2005. The political economy of the Chilean state in the neoliberal era. *Canadian Journal of Development Studies* 26, no. 4: 763–80.

——. 2007a. Slicing up at the long barbeque: Who gorges, who serves and who gets roasted? *Dollars & Sense*, no. 269 (January/February): 14–19, 30.

——. 2007b. Shifting developmental paradigms in Latin America: Is neoliberalism history? In *Ideas, policies and economic development in the Americas*, ed. Esteban Pérez and Matías Vernengo, 31–61. London: Routledge.

——. 2009. El auge actual de los commodities y el proceso de primarización en América Latina ¿Al retorno al siglo XIX? *Foro Internacional* 49, no. 1 (January–March): 119–62.

Cypher, James, and James Dietz. 2009. *The process of economic development*. 3rd ed. London: Routledge.

Dávila Flores, Alejandro. 2008. Los clusters industriales del noreste de México (1993–2003). *Región y Sociedad* 20, no. 41: 57–89.

Davis, Diane. 2004. *Discipline and development*. Cambridge: Cambridge University Press.

De la Cruz, Justino, Robert Koopman, Zhi Wang, and Shan-Jin Wei. 2009. Domestic and foreign value-added in Mexico's manufacturing exports. Unpublished paper, U.S. International Trade Commission (May 9): 1–27.

De la Garza Toledo, Enrique. 2004. Modelos de producción en el sector maquilador: Tecnología, organización del trabajo y relaciones laborales. IX Foro de Investigación: Congreso Internacional de Contaduría, Administración e Informática, UNAM.

——. 2005. Modelos de la producción en la maquila de México: La evidencia empírica a partir de la ENESTYC. In *Modelos de producción en la maquila de exportación*, ed. Enrique de la Garza Toledo, 33–72. México, D.F.: Plaza y Valdes Editores.

——. 2007. Los límites de la reestructuración productiva en México. *Trabajo* 3, no. 4 (January–June): 49–79.

Delgado Wise, Raúl. 2004. The hidden agenda of Mexico's Foxista administration. *Latin American Perspectives* 31, no. 5: 146–64.

Delgado Wise, Raúl, and Humberto Márquez Covarrubias. 2007. The theory and practice of the dialectical relationship between development and migration. *Migracion y Desarrollo* no. 9, segundo semestre: 5–24.

Dicken, Peter. 2003. *Global shift*. New York: Guilford.

Duran, José Antonio. 2009. Ford, listo para reiniciar operaciones en Cuatitlán. *El Financiero* (October 7): 13.

———. 2010. Ven autopartes mejor entorno en 2010. *El Financiero* (January 21): 17.

Durán Lima, José, and Vivianne Ventura-Dias. 2003. Comerico intraafirma: Concepto, alcance, y magnitud. *Serie Comericio Internacional* 44. Santiago, Chile: CEPAL.

Durand, Jorge. 2005. De traidores a heroes. Políticas emigratorias en un contexto de asimetrías de poder. In *Contribuciones al análisis de la migración internacional y el desarrollo regional en México*, ed. Raúl Delgado Wise and Beatrice Knerr. México: M. A. Porrúa.

Durand, Jorge, and Douglas Massey. 2003. *Clandestinos. Migración México-Estados Unidos en los albores del siglo XXI*. México, D.F.: M. A. Porrúa.

Dussel Peters, Enrique. 2006. Hacia una política de competitividad en Mexico. *Economía UNAM* 3, no. 9: 65–82.

———. 2009. La manufactura mexicana. *Economía Informa* no. 257 (March–April): 41–52.

———. 2010. Foreign investment: The polarization of the Mexican economy. In *Rethinking foreign investment of sustainable development*, ed. Kevin Gallagher and Daniel Chudnovsky, 51–76. London: Anthem Press.

Dutrénit, Gabriela, and Alexandre O. Vera-Cruz. 2005. Acumulación de capacidades tecnológicas en la industria maquiladora. *Comercio Exterior* 55, no. 7: 574–76.

Economic Policy Institute. 2008. Unions and the economy. www.stateofworking america.org/swa-unionpdf (accessed May 10, 2009).

Economist. 2009. Manufacturing's future: Wanted, new customers. *Economist* 393, no. 8651 (October 3): 36–38.

El Financiero. 1992. Investment flows into commercial building. *El Financiero Internacional* (April 26).

———. 2009. Más credito para la pequeñas empresas proveedores del gobierno Anuncia Calderón. *El Financiero* (August 19): 27.

Faux, Jeff. 2006. *The global class war.* New York: Wiley.

Flores, Abelardo Mariña. 2004. El empleo y las remuneraciones manufactureras en México en el marco del TLCAN. In *México en la región de América del Norte*, ed. Gregorio Vidal, 105–30. México, D.F.: Universidad Autónoma Metropolitana.

Fajnzylber, Fernando. 1983. *La industrialización trunca de América Latina.* México, D.F.: Nueva Imagen.

Galbraith, James. 2009. No habrá regreso a la normalidad. *Ola Financiero* no. 3: 22–40. www.olafinanciera.unam.mx.

Gallagher, Kevin, and Lyuba Zarsky. 2007. *The enclave economy.* Cambridge, Mass.: MIT Press.

Gambrill, Mónica. 2008. Transformación de la industria de la transformación: ¿La 'maquiladorización' de la manufactura? In *La maquila en México*, ed. Alicia Puyana, 59–78. México: FLACSO.

García y Griego, Miguel. 1988. Hacia una nueva visión de la problemática de los indocumentados en Estados Unidos. In *México y Estados Unidos. Frente a la migración de los indocumentados*, ed. M. García y Griego and M. Verea, México: M. A. Porrúa.

Garrido, Celso, and Ricardo Padilla. 2007. Evolución estratégica de la manufactura y nueva organización económica nacional. Problemas y desafíos para el desarrollo manufacturero en México. In *Política industrial manufacturera*, ed. José Luis Calva, 85–103. México, D.F.: M. A. Porrúa.

Garrido, Celso, and Enrique Quintana. 1988. Crisis de patrón de acumulación y modernización conservadora. In *Empresarios y estado en América Latina*, ed. Celso Garrido, 39–60. México, D.F.: CIDE.

Gazcón, Felipe. 2002. Para fusiones y adquisición de empresas, 71% de la IED. *El Financiero* (May 8): 15.

Gereffi, Gary. 1992. Mexico's maquiladora industries. In *North America without border?*, ed. Stephen Randall, 135–51. Calgary, Canada: University of Calgary Press.

———. 2001. Las cadenas productivas como marco analítico para la globalización. *Problemas del Desarrollo* 32, no. 125 (April–June): 9–37.

Glade, William, and Cassio Luiselli, eds. 1989. *The economics of interdependence: Mexico and the US*. San Diego: Center for U.S.-Mexican Studies, University of California, San Diego.

González Amador, Roberto. 2007. Los grupos de poder no quieren pagar impuestos. *La Jornada* (August 9): 23.

———. 2009. Aprobó préstamo por 47 mil mdd. *La Jornada* (April 17): 1.

González G., Susana. 2009. Sólo 403 empresas concentran tres cuartas partes del comercio exterior. *La Jornada* (November 1): 24.

González Pérez, Lourdes. 1993. En contra del TLC la Tercera Parte del Congreso de EU. *El Financiero* (July 17).

Gosh, Bimal. 2006. *Migrants' remittances and development: Myths, rhetoric and realities*. Geneva: International Organization for Migration.

Guadarrama, José, and Noé Cruz. 1988. Estudia el gobierno ceder rubros estratégicos a la iniciativa privada. *El Financiero* (October 3): 24.

Guarnizo, Luis. 2003. The economics of transnational living. *International Migration Review* 37, no. 3: 666–99.

Guerrero, Isabel, Luis Felipe López-Calva, and Michael Walton. 2006. *The inequality trap and its links to low growth in Mexico*. Washington, D.C.: World Bank, 1–49. http://siteresources.worldbank.org/INTMEXICOINSPANISH/Resources/walton -ingles-24-11.pdf.

Guillén Romo, Arturo. 2004. Flujos de inversión extranjera directa en América del Norte bajo el TCLAN. In *México en la región de América del Norte*, ed. Gregorio Vidal, 159–200. México, D.F.: Universidad Autónoma Metropolitana.

Harrison, Bennett. 1994. *Lean and mean*. New York: Basic Books.

Harvey, David. 2003. *The new imperialism*. Oxford: Oxford University Press.

———. 2007. Neoliberalism as creative destruction. *Annals of the American Academy of Political and Social Science* 610 (March): 22–44.

Heilbroner, Robert, and William Milberg. 1995. *The crisis of vision in modern economic thought*. Cambridge: University of Cambridge Press.

Hernández Morón, Leticia. 2009. Reporta alfa buenos resultados. *El Financiero* (September14): 5A.

Hernández Romo, Marcela. 2004. *La cultura empresarial en México*. México, D.F.: M. Á. Porrúa.

Howard, Georgina. 2004. El papel del trabajo: México, empleos, pocos y malos. *La Jornada* (August 9): 2. www.jornada.unam.mx/2004/08/09/004n1sec.html.

Huerta Moreno, Guadalupe, Luis Kato Maldonado, and Abelardo Mariña Flores. 2007. Lineamientos para una política de generación de empleos de calidad para la industria manufacturera. In *Política industrial manufacturera*, ed. José Luis Calva, 104–29. México, D.F.: M. A. Porrúa.

Hunt, E. K. 1979. *History of economic thought: A critical perspective*. Belmont, Calif.: Wadsworth.

IDB (Interamerican Development Bank). 1992. *Economic and social progress report*. Washington, D.C.: Interamerican Development Bank.

IMSS (Instituto Mexicano del Seguro Social). 2009. *Estadísticas*. www.imss.gob .mx.

INA (Industria Nacional de Autopartes). 2008. The automotive parts industry in Mexico. Paper presented at Mexico's Auto Industry Conference, San Luís Potosí, México.

INEE (Instituto Nacional para la Evaluación de la Educación). 2008. Panorama educativo de México. In *Indicadores del sistema educativo nacional*. México, D.F.: INEE.

———. 2009. Panorama educativo de México. In *Indicadores del sistema educativo nacional*. México, D.F.: INEE.

INEGI (Instituto Nacional de Estadística Geografía e Informatica). 1985. *Estadísticas históricas de México, tomo II*. México, D.F.: INEGI.

———. 2006. *II conteo de población y vivienda 2005*. Aguascalientes, México: INEGI.

———. 2009a. Maquiladoras. *Sistema nacional de estadística geografía e informatica*. htpp://www.inegi.gob.mx.

———. 2009b. Banco de Información Económica. *Indicadores económicos de coyuntura: Indicadores estratégicas de ocupación y empleo*. www.inegi.gob.mx.

———. Various years. *La industria automotriz en México*. México, D.F.: INEGI.

Ivarsson, Ing, and Claes Göran Alvstam. 2005. Technology transfers from TNCs to local suppliers in developing countries. *World Development* 33, no. 8 (August): 1325–44.

Jelter, Jim. 2009. Whirlpool to shut Indiana plant, cut 1,100 jobs. *Market Watch* (August 29). www2.marketwatch.com/story/whirlpool-to-shut-indiana-plant-cut -1100-jobs-2009-08-28.

Jones, A. 1986. The hollow corporations. *Business Week* (March 3): 56–59.

Juárez, Humberto. 1999. La productividad y el trabajo en el contexto de la producción esbelta en VW de México. In *Enfrentado cambio/Confronting change*, ed. Humberto Juárez and Steve Babson, 173–205. Puebla, México: Universidad Autónoma de Puebla.

Juárez, Humberto, and Steve Babson, eds. 1999. *Enfrentado cambio/Confronting change*. Puebla, México: Universidad Autónoma de Puebla.

Kapur, Devesh. 2004. Remittances: The new development mantra? G-24 Discussion Paper, Series no. 29 (April). Geneva: UNCTAD, 1–34.

Kay, Cristóbal. 2002. Why East Asia overtook Latin America. *Third World Quarterly* 23, no. 6: 1073–1102.

Kearney, A. T. 2008. *Reigniting Mexico's automotive industry.* Chicago: A. T. Kearney.

Klein, Naomi. 2007. *The shock doctrine.* New York: Metropolitan Books.

Kleinknecht, William. 2009. *The man who sold the world.* New York: Nation Books.

Kohli, Atul. 2004. *State-directed development.* Cambridge: Cambridge University Press.

Kopinak, Kathryn. 1996. *Desert capitalism: Maquiladoras in North America's western industrial corridor.* Tucson: University of Arizona Press.

——, ed. 2004. *The social costs of industrial growth in northern Mexico.* San Diego: Center for U.S.-Mexican Studies, University of California, San Diego.

Krauze, Enrique. 1998. *Mexico: Biography of power.* New York: HarperPerennial.

Lara, Arturo, Jaime Arellano, and Alejandro García. 2005. Cooevolución tecnológica entre maquiladoras de autopartes y talleres de maquinado. *Comerico Exterior* 55, no. 7: 586–600.

Lara Rivero, Arturo, Alejandro García Garnicia, and Gerardo Trujado. 2004. El cluster automotriz en el Estado de México. Retos y oportunidades. *Región y Sociedad* 16, no. 31 (September–December): 83–117.

Leon González, Alejandra, and Enrique Dussel Peters. 2001. El comercio intraindustrial en México, 1990–1999. *Comericio Exterior* 52, no 7: 652–64.

León Zaragoza, Gabriel. 2009. En 8 años se perdieron 885 mil puestos en las industrias de transformación. *La Jornada* (January 18): 21.

Lederman, D., W. Malloney, and L. Serven. 2004. *Lessons from NAFTA for Latin America and the Caribbean countries.* Washington, D.C.: World Bank.

Levine, Elaine. 2001. *Los nuevos pobres de Estados Unidos: Los hispanos.* México, D.F.: M. A. Porrúa.

López, Jorge Alberto, and Óscar Robil M. 2008. Comercio intra-industrial e intra-firma en México en el contexto del proceso de integración de América del Norte (1993–2006). *Economía UNAM* 5, no. 13: 86–112.

Lustig, Nora. 1992. *Mexico: The remaking of an economy.* Washington, D.C.: Brookings Institution.

Lustig, Nora, Barry Bosworth, and Robert Lawrence, eds. 1992. *North American free trade.* Washington, D.C.: Brookings Institution.

MacArthur, John. 2000. *The selling of "free trade."* New York: Hill and Wang.

MacLeod, Dag. 2005. *Downsizing the state: Privatization and the limits of neoliberal reform in Mexico.* University Park: Pennsylvania State University Press.

Made In Mexico. 2009. Frequently asked questions. www.madeinmexicoinc.com/FAQs.htm.

Malkin, Elisebeth. 2006. Detroit, far south. *New York Times* (July 21): C1, C4.

Mallorquín, Carlos. 2007. The unfamiliar Raúl Prebisch. In *Ideas, policies and economic development in the Americas*, ed. Esteban Pérez and Matías Vernengo, 98–122. London: Routledge.

Maria y Campos, Mauricio. 2009. Llegó la hora de cambiar el rumbo industrial. *El Financiero* (August 11), http://impreso.elfinanciero.com.mx/pages/NotaPrint.aspx?IdNota=26084.

Maria y Campos, Mauricio, Lilia Domínguez Villalobos, Flor Brown Grossman, and Armando Sanchez. 2009. *El desarrollo de la industria mexicana en su encrucijada*. México, D.F.: Universidad Iberoamericana.

Márquez, Humberto. 2007. Controversias en el desarrollo económico local basado en las remesas de los migrantes. *Análisis económico* 21, no. 47: 307–30.

Massey, Douglas S., Jorge Durand, and Nolan J. Malone. 2002. *Beyond smoke and mirrors: Mexican immigration in an era of economic integration*. New York: Russell Sage Foundation.

McKelvey, Maureen. 1994. Innovation, national system of. In *Institutional and evolutionary economics*, ed. Geoffrey Hodgson et al., 366–69. Aldershot, England: Edgar Elgar.

Miller, John. 2009. Recession, depression, repression: What's in a name? *Dollars and Sense*, no. 283 (July/August): 13–18.

Miranda, Arturo Vicenio. 2007. La industria automotriz en México, antecedentes, situación actual y perspectivas. *Contabilidad y Administración*, no. 221 (January–April): 211–48.

Mischel, Lawrence, et al. 2007. *The state of working America*. Ithaca, N.Y.: Cornell University Press.

Montesinos, Rafael. 1992. Empresarios en el nuevo orden estatal. *El Cotidano*, no. 50 (September–October): 108–15.

Moreno, Alejandro. 2002. Mexican public opinion toward NAFTA and FTAA. In *Nafta in the new millennium*, ed. Edward Chambers and Peter Smith, 167–212. San Diego: Center for U.S.-Mexican Studies, University of California, San Diego.

Moreno-Brid, Juan Carlos, and Jaime Ros. 2009. *Development and growth in the Mexican economy*. Oxford: Oxford University Press.

Morera Camacho, Carlos. 2005. La gran empresa mexicana en la globalización. *Revista Herramienta*, no. 28 (March): 25–41.

Mortimore, Michael, and Faustino Barron. 2005. *Informe sobre la industria automotriz mexicana*. Santiago, Chile: CEPAL (August), Serie Desarrollo Productivo no. 162, 1–50.

Munck, Ronaldo. 2000. Dependency and imperialism in Latin America. In *The political economy of imperialism*, ed. Ronald Chilcote, 141–56. Lanham, Md.: Rowman & Littlefield.

MUND Group. 2009. A primal fear in Mexico: The social eruption. *Opinion and Policy Report*, Series 9, no. 25 (September 1): 1–3, www.mundgroup.com.

Nacional Financiera. 1995. *La economía mexicana en cifras*. México, D.F.: Nafinsa.

Nadal, Alejandro. 2003. Macroeconomic challenges for Mexico's development strategy. In *Confronting development: Assessing Mexico's economic and social policy challenges*, ed. Kevin Middlebrook and Eduardo Zepeda, 55–88. Stanford, Calif.: Stanford University Press.

Norandi, Mariana. 2008. Ineficaz, el programa de estímulos fiscales para la investigación tecnológica. *La Jornada* (December 6): 42.

OCDE. 2005. La emigración de mexicanos a Estados Unidos. *Comercio Exterior* 55, no. 2: 472–90.

OECD (Organization for Economic Cooperation and Development). 1992. *OECD Economic Surveys: Mexico*. Paris: OECD.

———. 1997. *National innovation systems*. Paris: OECD.

Pages, Eric. 1996. *Responding to defense dependence*. Westport, Conn.: Praeger.

Passel, Jeffrey S. 2005. Unauthorized migrants: Numbers and characteristics. Washington, D.C.: Pew Hispanic Center.

Pérez Aceves, Luis Alberto, and Ignacio Echavarría Valenzuela. 1988. *El fomento a la competitividad industrial mexicana*. México, D.F.: Nacional Financiera.

Phillips-Fein, Kim. 2009. *Invisible hands: The making of the conservative movement from the New Deal to Reagan*. New York: W. W. Norton.

PNUD (Programa de las Naciones Unidas para el Desarrollo). 2004. *Análisis del Sector Automotriz en la Región Centro Oriente*. Guadalajara: PNUD.

Posada, Miriam, and Julio Reyna Quiroz. 2009. Replantear la estrategia industrial para los próximos 30 años, exige Canacintra. *La Jornada* (August 17): 27.

Posada, Miriam, and Juan Antonio Zuñiga. 2009. Busca hacienda que más empresas cumplan. *La Jornada* (October 16): 32.

Puga, Cristina. 2004. *Los empresarios organizados y el tratado de libre comercio de América del Norte*. Mexico, D.F.: M. A. Porrúa.

Puyana, Alicia. 2008. Introdución. In *La maquila en México*, ed. Alicia Puyana, 9–32. México, D. F.: FLACSO.

Rasmussen Reports. 2008. *56% want NAFTA renegotiated, Americans divide on free trade* (June 20): 1–3. www.rassmussenreports.com/publiccontent/general politics/56.

Riding, Alan. 1984. *Distant neighbors*. New York: Knopf.

Robinson, William. 2008. *Latin America and global capitalism*. Baltimore: Johns Hopkins University Press.

Rocha, Alma, and Roberto López. 2003. Política en ciencia y tecnología en México. In *Innovación, aprendizaje y creación de capacidades tecnológicas*, ed. Jaime Aboites and Gabriela Dutrénit, 103–34. México, D. F.: M. A. Porrúa.

Rocha, Lourdes. 2006. Across the board reduction of 53% in tariff rates. *Review of the Economic Situation in Mexico* 82 (October): 382–86.

Rodrik, Dani. 2004. *Industrial policy for the 21st century*. UNIDO/Harvard University, 1–57. http://ksghome.harvard.edu/~drodrik/unidosep.pdf.

Rosio Barajas, María del, Carmen Rodríguez, and Araceli Almaraz. 2007. Complejidad tecnoproductiva y su relación con la formación de capacidades tecnológicas. In *Maquiladoras fronterizas: Evolución y heterogeneidad en los sectores electrónico y Automotriz*, ed. Jorge Carrillo and María del Rosio Barajas, 147–201. México, D.F.: M. A. Porrúa.

Ross Schneider, Ben. 2002. Why is Mexican business so organized? *Latin American Research Review* 37, no. 1: 77–118.

Ruiz Durán, Clemente. 2003. NAFTA: Lessons from an uneven integration. *International Journal of Political Economy* 33, no. 3 (Fall): 50–71.

Salas-Porras, Alejandra. 2007. Los grupos mexicanos y coreanos ante la crisis del estado. *Foro Internacional* 41, no. 2 (April–June): 300–339.

Saldaña, Ivette. 2006. Maquiladoras rompen récord en exportaciones. *El Financiero* (December 1): 19.

———. 2007. Crean alianza para articular la producción automotriz. *La Jornada* (May 7): 18.

Saldaña, Ivette, and Isabel Becerril. 2009. Recesión, oportunidad para reformas. *El Financiero* (August 20): 8.

Sánchez Ugarte, Fernando, Manuel Fernández Pérez, and Eduardo Pérez Motta. 1994. *La política industrial ante la apertura*. México, D.F.: Fondo de Cultura Económica.

Schamis, Hector. 2002. *Reforming the state*. Ann Arbor: University of Michigan Press.

SECOFI (Secretaría de Comercio y Fomento Industrial). 1988. *Apertura comercial y modernización industrial. [Serie cuadernos de renovación nacional X.]* México, D.F.: Fondo de Cultura Económica.

Secretaría de Economía. 2009. *Estadísticas inversión extranjera.* www.economia.gob.mx.

Secretaría del Trabajo y Previsión Social. 2009. Estadísticas del sector. www.stps.gob.mx/DGIET/web/menuinfsector.htm.

Shaiken, Harley. 1990. *Mexico in the global economy*. San Diego: Center for U.S.-Mexican Studies, University of California, San Diego.

Sievers Fernández, Silvia. 2008. Estudio sobre el sector de autopartes en México. PromoMadrid. www.promomadrid.com/tie/files/documents/notasectorialautopartesfinal.pdf.

Soria Hernández, Francisco. 2009. Se carece de una política industrial en el país: Urge impulsar medidas. *La Jornada, Zacatecas* (August 22): 8.

Sosa Barajas, Sergio. 2005. *La substitución de importaciones en el crecimiento económico de México*. México, D.F.: Editorial Tlaxcallan.

Stanford, James. 1993. Continental economic integration: Modeling the impact on labor. *Annals of the American Academy of Political and Social Science* 526, no. 1 (March): 92–110.

Storm, Servaas, and C. W. M. Naastepad. 2005. Strategic factors in economic development: East Asian industrialization 1950–2003. *Development and Change* 36, no. 6: 1059–94.

Székely, M. 2005. Pobreza y desigualdad en México entre 1950 y 2004. *El Trimestre Económico* 72, no. 288: 913–31.

Taboada Ibarra, Eunice, Josefina Robles Rodríguez, and Leticia Velásquez García. 2006. Producción y venta de vehículos automotores en México. *El Cotidiano* 21, no. 137 (May–June): 102–10.

Teichman, Judith. 1995. *Privatization and political change in Mexico*. Pittsburgh, Pa.: University of Pittsburgh Press.

Tello, Carlos. 1996. La economía mexicana: Hacia el tercer milenio. *Nexos* 19, no. 223 (July): 47–55.

Thacker, Strom. 1999. NAFTA coalitions and the political viability of neoliberalism in Mexico. *Journal of Interamerican Studies and World Affairs* 42, no. 2 (Summer): 57–90.

———. 2000. *Big business, the state and free trade.* Cambridge: Cambridge University Press.

United Nations. 2006. *International migration report 2006.* Geneva: United Nations.

U.S. Census Bureau. Various years. *Current population survey.* United States Census Bureau. www.census.gov/cps.

U.S. Council of Economic Advisers. *Economic report of the president, 2009.* Washington, D.C.: U.S. Government Printing Office.

USITC (U.S. International Trade Commission). 1992. *Economy-wide modeling of the economic implications of a FTA.* Washington, D.C. : U.S. International Trade Commission.

———. 1993. *Potential impact on the U.S. economy of the NAFTA.* Washington, D.C.: U.S. International Trade Commission.

Valdés Ugalde, Francisco. 1997. *Autonomía y legitimidad. Los empresarios, la política y el estado en México.* México, D.F.: Siglo XXI.

Van Horn, Robert, and Philip Mirowski. 2009. *The rise of the Chicago school of economics and the birth of neoliberalism.* Cambridge, Mass.: Harvard University Press.

Vera-Cruz, Alexandre, and Gabriela Dutrénit. 2007. Derramas de conocimiento de la industria maquiladora de exportación hacia PYME e instituciones. In *Co-evolución de empresas, maquiladoras, insitutuciones y regiones: Una nueva interpretación,* ed. Arturo Lara Rivera, 215–51. México, D.F.: M. A. Porrúa.

Vieyra Medrano, José Antonio. 2000. Innovación y nuevas estrategias espaciales en el sector automotriz. El caso de la nissan mexicana. *Scripta Nova. Revista Electrónica de Geografía y Ciencias Sociales* 4, no. 69: 121–46.

Vidal, Gregorio. 2004. El crecimiento por medio de la exportación de manufacturas, el avance de la reforma económica y las grandes empresas. In *México en la región de América del Norte,* ed. Gregorio Vidal, 53–78. México, D.F.: Universidad Autónoma Metropolitana.

Villavicencio, Daniel, and Mónica Casalet. 2005. La construcción de un entorno institucional de apoyoa la industria maquiladora. *Comercio Exterior* 55, no. 7: 600–611.

Vita, Matthew. 1993. Mexico spending to sway U.S. on trade pact. *Atlanta Journal* (March 21).

Vlasic, Bill. 2009. Ford looks to the future. *New York Times* (October 22): F1, F14.

Wade, Robert. 1990. *Governing the market: Economic theory and the role of government in East Asian industrialization.* Princeton, N.J.: Princeton University Press.

Wagenheim, Kal, ed. 1993. *Mexico Business Monthly* 3, no. 6 (July).

Woods, Ngaire. 2005. The Bretton Woods institutions and the transmission of neo-liberal ideas in Mexico. In *Economic doctrines in Latin America,* ed. Valpy

FitzGerald and Rosemary Thorp, 217–45. Houndmills, England: Palgrave Macmillan.

World Bank. 2003. *Report on the observance of standards and codes: Corporate governance country assessment, Mexico,* 1–88. Washington, D.C.: World Bank. www.worldbank.org/ifa/rosccgmex.pdf.

——. 2006. *Global economic prospects 2006: Economic implications of remittances and migration.* Washington, D.C.: World Bank.

——. 2008. *World development indicators.* http://databank.worldbank.org/ddp/ home.do.

——. 2009. *World development indicators.* http://databank.worldbank.org/ddp/ home.do.

Zúñiga, Elena, and Paula Leite. 2004. Los procesos contemporáneos de la migración México-Estados Unidos: Una perspectiva regional y municipal. Paper presented at the seminar "Migración México-Estados Unidos: Implicaciones y retos para ambos países." México, D. F.: CONAPO.

Zúñiga, Victor, and Rúben Hernández León, eds. 2005. *New directions: Mexican immigration in the United States.* New York: Russell Sage Foundation.

Index

206 *Index*

production capabilities, 134, 135
productivity, 5, 9, 45, 58, 59, 60, 71,
   84, 88, 89, 90, 93, 94, 103, 110, 120,
   129, 130, 132, 133, 142–144, 150,
   154, 159, 173n1, 179n10, 180n4,
   180n7, 181n9–10, 183n8, 184n12,
   185 n4
profit rate, 88, 89, 170
Program for Productive Integration,
   125, 129
Program for the Temporary Importation
   of Export Items, 107, 108, 178n7,
   180n2
PRONAFICE. *See* National Program to
   Develop Industry and Trade
Puga, Cristina, 70, 72–77, 167, 177–
   178n7

RCA, 89, 91, 179n9
R&D. *See* research and development
Reagan, Ronald, 32, 40, 55, 86, 87, 89
remittances, 51, 138, 143, 145, 147,
   156–158, 161, 164, 166, 170,
research and development, 41, 42, 96,
   103–105, 120, 130, 134, 170
restructuring in Mexico, 11, 19, 41, 43,
   47, 49, 62, 69, 77, 78, 84, 85, 98,
   105, 118, 123, 131, 142, 149, 159,
   168, 171
restructuring in the United States. *See*
   United States
Ricardo, David, 7
Riding, Alan, 4, 6
Rocha, Alma, 135
Rodrik, Dani, 18
Ros, Jaime, 71, 98, 100
Rosio Barajas, María 103

Salas-Porras, Alejandra, 120
Salinas, Carlos, 8, 42, 46–50, 56, 61,
   63, 64, 70, 73–75, 87, 96, 97, 100,
   177n4
Schumpeter, J. A., 101, 132
SECOFI. *See* secretariat of trade and
   industrial development

secretariat of trade and industrial
   development, 19, 20, 60, 77
secretariats of economic development,
   xiii, xiv, 12, 18, 19, 129
Seguro Popular. *See* Comisión Nacional
   de Protección Social
Sematech, 88
Serra Puche, Jaime, 60
Shaiken, Harley, 180n4, 185n4
SIMDE. *See* Sistema de Información
   sobre Migración y Desarrollo
Sistema de Información sobre
   Migración y Desarrollo, 155, 156,
   183n12, 184nn13–14
SLI. *See* state-led industrialization
   policies
social structure of accumulation, 28, 150
Sosa Barajas, Sergio, 37, 122
Spicer, 120, 123
Stanford, James, 68, 69
state capacity, 16, 33
state-led development. *See* state-led
   industrialization policies
state-led industrialization. *See* state-led
   industrialization policies
state-led industrialization policies, 15,
   19, 20, 34, 35, 72, 78,79, 96, 109,
   122, 123, 133, 135, 139, 145, 162,
   167, 176n1
structural adjustment programs, 31, 32,
   160–162
subordinated integration, vii, 11, 52,
   101, 157, 160, 164, 167, 170, 171
System for the Strategic Development
   of the Auto and Auto Parts Industry,
   128

Taiwan, 35, 35
technology, 16, 42, 54, 55, 73, 96–98,
   101, 102, 104, 120, 135, 164, 170,
   178n4; technological applications,
   11; technological autonomy, 133;
   technological capacities/capabilities,
   33, 34, 35, 88, 121, 122, 124, 126,
   130, 131, 133, 135; technological

About the Authors

James M. Cypher is a research professor in the Doctoral Program in Development Studies at the Universidad Autónoma de Zacatecas, Mexico. He is the author of *State and Capital in Mexico* (Westview Press, 1990) and co-author of *The Process of Economic Development* (Routledge, Taylor and Francis, 2009). He received his Ph.D. in economics from the University of California, Riverside. A member of the editorial board of *The International Journal of Development Issues* and *Latin American Perspectives*, he has authored more than one hundred book chapters and articles—several focused on NAFTA's impact on the United States and contemporary economic policies in Mexico.

Raúl Delgado Wise is a specialist on migration, including themes of Mexico-U.S. migration. He is the director of the Doctoral Program in Development Studies at the Universidad Autónoma de Zacatecas, Mexico. He is author or editor of several books and more than one hundred essays, including book chapters and refereed articles. A member of the Mexican Academy of Sciences and the National System of Researchers, he is the editor of both *Migración y Desarrollo* and a book series, "Development and Migration," published by Miguel Angel Porrúa (Mexico City).